KIERKEGAARD'S ATTACK UPON "CHRISTENDOM"

From the Journal, 1853

Something quite definite I have to say

. . . I have something upon my conscience as a writer. Let me indicate precisely how I feel about it. There is something quite definite I have to say, and I have it so much upon my conscience that (as I feel) I dare not die without having uttered it. For the instant I die and so leave this world (so I understand it) I shall in the very same second (so frightfully fast it goes!), in the very same second I shall be infinitely far away, in a different place, where, still within the same second (frightful speed!), the question will be put to me: "Hast thou uttered the definite message *quite definitely?*" And if I have not done so, what then? . . .

There is something quite definite I have to say. But verily I am not eager to say it. On the contrary, I would so infinitely prefer that another should say it—which, however, would not help me, since (as I understand it) it was and remains my task. But eager to say it I am not; on the contrary, I have wished and craved, and sometimes almost hoped that I might be dispensed from saying it. For it is not a cheerful message, this definite thing, and I cannot but think that there are several persons dear to me to whom it would be unwelcome to hear it said. Above all there is among us a right reverend old man, a consideration which has constantly held me back, laid restraint upon my tongue and upon my pen, a consideration for the highest dignitary of the Church, a man to whom by the memory of a deceased father I felt myself drawn with an almost melancholy affection—and I must think that to him especially it will be very unwelcome that this is said.

X[6] B 371

Kierkegaard's Attack Upon "Christendom"

1854-1855

TRANSLATED, WITH AN INTRODUCTION, BY

WALTER LOWRIE

PRINCETON UNIVERSITY PRESS

PRINCETON, NEW JERSEY

ISBN 0-691-01950-9 (paperback edn.)
ISBN 0-691-07102-0 (hardcover edn.)

Second Paperback Printing, 1972
Fifth Hardcover Printing, 1972

Printed in the United States of America by
Princeton University Press
Princeton, New Jersey

PREFACE BY THE TRANSLATOR

STRANGE that it has been left to me to translate this *Attack upon "Christendom,"* to me who as a "priest" am here attacked with the utmost scorn! Strange (and perhaps significant), as I have remarked in the Introduction, that no one else has shown any zeal to make this trenchant attack known to the English-speaking world! I was not eager to do it. I neither commend nor decry this attack. But perhaps it is well that, since it was written from within the Church, it should now be translated by a priest. In Germany it was translated a long while ago by two ex-pastors, and everywhere it has been hailed in an anticlerical, if not in an anti-Christian interest.

As this is Kierkegaard's last work, and almost the last to be translated into English, it is appropriate here to cast a glance backward upon the haphazard production of the past eight years. Many think it astonishing that the whole Kierkegaardian literature (twenty-four volumes in English) has been translated and published in so short a time as eight years. But there have been ten translators collaborating to this end—and S. K. alone produced all this literature in fourteen years! I can appreciate how great a labor that was, for I have translated half of it. It makes no difference now that these books were published in English without much regard either to the original order or to the order of importance, for I have good reason to believe that what S. K. called "my literature" will be available in English by the end of this year. This present work lies outside the limits of that literature, as does also *The Concept of Irony* at the other end, and that too is being translated. Mr. Dru's *Selections from the Journals* belongs to still another category. That book is invaluable to anyone who would understand the life of S. K. or the development of his thought. But there is more light yet to shine from the twenty big volumes of the Journals, and perhaps more than one scholar will feel prompted to develop this rich mine further. Not now, however, in a biographical interest (for Dru has adequately provided for that), but rather in a topical way. It is now very difficult to get a comprehensive view of S. K.'s reflections upon the subjects which chiefly concerned him, for there is as yet no index to the Journals as a whole. It is therefore all the more important that collections should be made of his more important utterances. I am delighted to hear from Mr. Dru that he has undertaken this agreeable and important task.

In itself this is a big book, and therefore I would not make it bigger by including the replies which were made to this attack. It is significant that there were few rejoinders made in print, and almost all are included in the German edition of Dorner and Schrempf—which can therefore be read by those who know no Danish.

I have included, however, fifteen passages from the Journals which illustrate the spirit in which S. K. carried on his attack. It happens that this book contains a prodigious number of title pages (perhaps more than any other book in the world), and that implies as many blank pages. This thought was distressing—until it occurred to me to use them (as S. K. often did) for these passages which the reader ought to know, and which otherwise I should have felt obliged to quote in the Introduction.

I take occasion to remark that, although as a translator of S. K. I have been scrupulous to conform to his style so far as I could, never yielding to the temptation of bettering it, and seldom resorting to the easy path of paraphrase, yet I have not felt bound to follow slavishly his punctuation, which in fact was in his own time regarded as peculiar and was not always consistent. Here I remark particularly upon his use of the dash, which he employed more frequently than any other author I can think of—for the most part appropriately, but sometimes where I have preferred to use a parenthesis, and more often where I have taken the liberty of introducing three closely printed dots (...), which are commonly seen in French, Italian and Spanish books, to indicate an unexpected conclusion. I was encouraged to use it by Henry James, who first made his discovery of it on a visit to Rome and expressed to me his regret that he had not discovered it early enough to make use of it in his books. If I had not used it till now, or if it had never before been used in the world, I should have felt compelled to invent something of the sort when I was translating the *Instant*. But indeed this device is so often appropriate that Northern Europe and North America might well borrow from Southern Europe and South America a custom which is so common that no patent protects it.

I owe it perhaps to Kierkegaard to admit that my use of the diagonal stroke / to indicate a marked disjunction (as in writing "either/or") was not his use. In this case he used a dash or a hyphen, just as he did for such conjunctive phrases as both-and; but I feel sure he would have liked to make this distinction, if it had been suggested to him. This is not my invention, for it is used significantly by the Jena publisher Diederichs, who happens to be the publisher of S. K.'s *Complete Works* in German; and it can appeal to a more remote tradition, namely, to the fact that it was used, though not significantly, in many of the earliest printed books...in place of every other mark of punctuation.

As usual, by the kind permission of Dr. Lange, the last surviving editor (who perhaps no longer survives), I have made use of the notes to the last Danish edition of the *Complete Works*. Not all of them will interest every reader, but they must be held in respect as the cumulative labor of many zealous students. I conceive, however, that I have done a service to the English reader by omitting more than half of them, and the notes which I have added are perhaps more important for the understanding of Kierkegaard.

WALTER LOWRIE

Princeton
April 26, 1943

CONTENTS

From the Journal

THE OBEDIENT HOUND

Imagine a big, well-trained hunting dog. He accompanies his master on a visit to a family where, as all too often in our time, there is a whole assembly of ill-behaved youths. Their eyes hardly light upon the hound before they begin to maltreat it in every kind of way. The hound, which was well trained, as these youths were not, fixes his eye at once upon his master to ascertain from his expression what he expects him to do. And he understands the glance to mean that he is to put up with all the ill-treatment, accept it indeed as though it were sheer kindness conferred upon him. Thereupon the youths of course became still more rough, and finally they agreed that it must be a prodigiously stupid dog which puts up with everything.

The dog meanwhile is concerned only about one thing, what the master's glance commands him to do. And, lo, that glance is suddenly altered; it signifies—and the hound understands it at once—use your strength. That instant with a single leap he has seized the biggest lout and thrown him to the ground—and now no one stops him, except the master's glance, and the same instant he is as he was a moment before.—Just so with me.

XI^2 A 423

INTRODUCTION BY THE TRANSLATOR

I REMARK in the Preface that this last work of Kierkegaard aptly comes *last*, or almost last, in the English edition. I dwell here rather upon the significance of the fact that it was not published *first* in English, as it was in German, and, so far as I know, in every other language into which Kierkegaard has been translated. The *Instant* was published at Hamburg in 1861, and the whole of the *Agitatorische Schriften u. Aufsätze*, translated admirably by Dorner and Schrempf, was published in Stuttgart in 1896. (I say "admirably" to make amends for the reproaches I have leveled against Schrempf's later translations—but it may be significant that Dorner's name appears first on the title page.) It was obviously an anticlerical if not an anti-Christian interest which prompted the early publication of these works. And of course they were misapprehended in lands where S. K.'s works were unknown and little or nothing was known about the man. Very few were aware that this fierce attack upon "Christendom" was written from within the Church. I dwell here upon the fact that nothing of the sort has occurred in England or America, where S. K.'s last work is properly published almost last—and that not as a result of wise planning, but simply because no one has felt an urge to make it known...to the discomfiture of the Church.

This observation, however, is not perhaps unequivocally cheerful; for may it not be that in our time, still more than in the days of Kierkegaard, "there is nothing to persecute"? The world does not persecute world when it discovers it in the Church. And even if it be not true, as S. K. affirms, that Christianity no longer exists, yet surely the fond belief in "Christendom" has been shattered by this present war. Apart from the war, and viewing my country as it was in the period preceding it, I did not need the satire of Kierkegaard to suggest to my mind the doubt whether it can rightly be called a "Christian land." I note that in our last census 48 per cent of the population preferred to say that they were Christians; but it is sure that many, nobody knows how many, made this answer only because they could think of no other religion to name; and the leaders of all the Christian groups reckon that, alas, hardly half that number have any connection whatever with any Church. It is well understood, too, that in intellectual circles the percentage of professing Christians is far smaller. It is a curious coincidence that in "atheistic" Russia exactly 48 per cent reported themselves in the last census as "believers." But we must understand that this figure is a minimum, seeing that in Russia it is inconvenient if not perilous to call oneself a Christian. Having just now returned from Mexico I am impressed by the fact that in this state which is politically non-Christian 98 per cent would profess themselves Christians. I do not need Kierkegaard to tell me that it is a muddled world in which we live. Certainly the notion of "Christendom," "a Christian world," "Christian lands," under "Christian rulers," is now far more problematical than it was a century ago when S. K. wrote. For me, unlike many of my more distinguished contemporaries, it was not only within the last ten years *my* world has been profoundly shaken and has proved to be simply "the world."

There is, however, some consolation in the fact that both in England and America S. K.'s devotional discourses have lately received a degree of attention they have been accorded nowhere else. S. K. complained that while he held out the *Edifying Discourses* with his right hand and the pseudonymous works in his left, everyone grasped with his right hand what he held in the left. The *Discourses* have not been translated in France, where a good beginning has been made with the pseudonymous works. They were translated very tardily in Germany, in spite of the vogue which Kierkegaard enjoyed, and it is likely that they would not all be available even now, were it not that the enterprising publisher of the *Complete Works* felt obliged to make his edition *complete*. Their fate in English has been very different; for whereas only five translators and two publishers have had a hand in the publication of the aesthetic and philosophical works, eight persons have worked on the Discourses, and five publishers have undertaken to disseminate them.

In the Scandinavian countries the *Instant* made, of course, a prodigious impression, although it effected no immediate change in the established order. S. K., instead of being persecuted as he expected, attained again a high degree of popularity. This little brochure was printed in the Swedish newspapers as soon as each copy was issued. It did not need to be translated for Norway. But in both these lands it was of course misunderstood, for no one had apprehended the implications of S. K.'s previous works. It was misunderstood by the zealous young Norwegian priest who furnished the theme for Ibsen's *Brand*. S. K.'s motto was "Either/or"; it never was "All or nothing." Neither was it understood by many people in Denmark, for of course the Journals were not yet made public; and this attack upon the established order, made by a man who had always been known as a conservative in Church and State, and as a devoted supporter of the late Bishop

Mynster, produced the utmost amazement. Inasmuch as S. K. died in the midst of the strife, of an ailment which was very vaguely diagnosed, people were disposed to believe that the whole thing was morbid, that disease accounted for this sudden change. Now when we know his works and can read his Journals such a notion cannot honestly be maintained, the *Attack* cannot be discounted in this way, unless one would claim that his works as a whole can be discarded because (as he was the first to assert) there was something morbid about his life as a whole. At all events, it is clear to us now that the *Attack* was the consistent conclusion of his life and thought.

There is nothing in the *Attack* which cannot be matched by many entries in the Journals which were written after 1850. It has often been said that S. K. during these last years accumulated in his Journals the material for the open attack. This is true in a sense. He stored up ten times as much material as he needed to use—but, strangely enough, he did not use it, except in the very few cases which are indicated here in the notes. This is the more surprising to us because many of the entries in the Journal were written so perfectly that they compare favorably with anything that appeared in the *Instant*. A considerable number can be read in Dru's *Selections*; I have quoted fifteen of them here on the backs of the title pages, and several more are to be found in my *Kierkegaard* (which from p. 495 to the end may serve as an introduction to the *Attack*): I call attention especially to "Endeavour, or a North Pole Expedition," "Star-gazing," "The Tame Geese," "The Professor," which has Martensen in view, and the twin parables, "The Captain of the Ship" and "The Fieldmarshal," which illuminate S. K.'s relation to Bishop Mynster. But S. K. had something else in reserve, nothing less than a complete book, *Judge for Yourself*, which he wrote in 1852—and had kept in his desk all this while. We can understand why he did not publish it at once, for it was an undisguised attack upon the established order. But why not when the open attack had commenced? Why not when the second edition of *Training in Christianity* was published? The only answer is that when he was "working in the instant" the weapons must be short as well as sharp. It is true, the appropriate passages we find in the Journals were short; but S. K. was so amazingly copious that he did not need to use the treasures he had accumulated.

The last number of the *Instant* remained unpublished because when it lay upon his desk completely finished he fell paralyzed in the street and was carried to the hospital. That may be regarded as a sufficient reason. And yet we may wonder that during the forty days he was dying he did not give order that it be sent to the printer. The whole character of the *Instant*, No. X, marks it as an appropriate conclusion of the *Attack*. But S. K. seemed to have no interest in it. Undoubtedly he thought that his death was the only appropriate conclusion. In my *Short Life of Kierkegaard* I picked out, rather arbitrarily, what I was pleased to consider S. K.'s "last words." Yet the last words he actually wrote have perhaps a better claim to be thus signalized. Especially his pathetic confession of a lifelong suffering, and his address to the "plain man," deserve to be treasured as the last words of an intellectual tragic hero.

S. K.'s *Attack upon "Christendom"* will be interesting to many who have no interest in Christianity—not even enough to wish to attack it. Historically it is noteworthy as one of the most prominent examples of popular diatribe, not less worthy of attention than any of the most famous political broadsides.

S. K. was well armed for such an undertaking, for during his years in the university he spent a great deal of time preparing to write a treatise on the use of satire by the Greeks and Romans. That book was not written, but there can be no doubt that S. K. learned much from his study of the subject. It is certain, however, that this "thoroughly polemicalized" young man had a natural bent for satire. He knew also that satire necessarily involves exaggeration. For this reason he held completely in check his rare dialectical ability to see both sides. In the *Instant* this very dialectical man was no longer dialectical. That his satire of the "priests" was vigorously one-sided, he recognized in his conversation with Pastor Boesen, which I have quoted on a title page of the first number of the *Instant*, along with a passage about the "corrective" which justifies such exaggeration.

Some men, and perhaps most Christians, will think that satire ought not to be employed against the Church. That is not my opinion. I believe that the Church has need of it, and I conceive that God is above the Church as well as in it. Moreover, S. K.'s criticism was not directed against the Church as such, but against "Christendom," the established order of things in a presumably "Christian land" and "a Christian world."

His diatribes, particularly those against the priests in an established Church, are often outrageous. In some respects they are not strictly applicable to our day, and least of all to the free Churches in America. And yet it is discomfiting to recognize how often they do apply, and how often they apply with greater force to our age. The economic situation of the ministers of the Gospel is by no means so flourishing now as S. K. depicts it. And yet perhaps the question of *money* looms larger and is more distracting from Christianity in the free Churches than where the priests are paid by the State and that's the end of it. At least this question is now pressed more importunately than ever it was before. In my Communion, what is called the "Every Member Canvass" has grown to be a cloud which obscures the sun, amounting often to a total eclipse of the Gospel.

Outrageous as S. K.'s criticism often is, I am sure that where it wounds most deeply the effect is most salutary. To me it has proved to be a wholesome diet, and most wholesome when I might be expected to be allergic to such food—for I too am a "priest."

Apart from the profit one may derive from criticism, that is, from the negative factors in the *Instant*, one surely will not fail to notice how much there is that is positive and positively edifying. This may not be the first impression, but I could not fail to observe it as I was slowly translating these pages. The *Attack* would not be so effective as it is, if it were not written from within the Church, if the criticism were not prompted and supported by a positive faith. S. K.'s central and most ardent beliefs are summarily expressed in the *Instant*, even where they are not definitely expressed they glimmer through the criticism, and the thought of the majesty of God illuminates many a page. S. K. carried on this controversy with the New Testament in his hand, and for that reason the "priests" found it so difficult to reply. Even the stinging charge that the priests are perjurers could not easily be rebutted. One should recognize that this whole attack was essentially directed against the beginnings of what we know as Modern Liberal Theology. Only after a century, when that has finally collapsed, can S. K.'s satire be read with sympathy and comprehension. The priests might have said in their defense that they had taken the oath upon the New Testament in the sense everybody then attached to it, and that everybody was actuated by the laudable motive of making Christianity more acceptable to the people. But that was what no one could say openly.

It is a curious and a rather ironical reflection that many who would condemn the *Attack* as a whole will find parts of it very much to their liking. Free churchmen will find S. K.'s criticism of an established Church more forceful than their spokesmen have produced; the many Baptist sects will welcome his criticism of infant baptism (although in fact S. K. was not disposed to discard it); Quakers will relish the diatribe against a "hireling ministry"; and Catholics (Roman Catholics at least) will sympathize with his outspoken preference for a celibate clergy. But I should think that everybody must now be ready to listen with a chastened spirit to his passionate contention against the idea of "Christendom." And that was his central theme.

We have reason to take seriously S. K.'s oft reiterated formula: "Especially in Protestantism, and more especially in Denmark." S. K. was at pains to make it clear that his criticism was directed only to that part of "Christendom" which he knew at first hand. It was consonant with the practical aim of the *Instant* that he there suggested no comparison between Protestantism and Catholicism. But in the later Journals this comparison was more common than any other theme except "Christendom." If "Christendom," as I reckon roughly, is the theme of one thousand entries in the Journals of the last five years, there are nearly one hundred which deal critically with Luther and Protestantism, and express appreciation (comparatively at least) of Catholicism and monasticism. S. K.'s contemporaries, though of course this source of information was closed to them, were disposed to conjecture that, if S. K. had lived longer, he must have felt compelled to take refuge in the Church of Rome, as some of the readers of the *Instant* did. That was only a guess, but it was at least more plausible that the guess of Georg Brandes, that he would have "leapt over" to free thought. Perhaps, if S. K. had lived to become a Catholic, he might have written another satire, dealing especially with Catholicism, and more especially with Rome. For all that, he may have been *essentially* a Catholic in his way of thinking. That is what Father Przywara makes out in *Das Geheimnis Kierkegaards*, by which he was able to convince Karl Barth that, as he put it, "If I were to follow Kierkegaard, I might as well go over there," pointing, as he wrote these words near his window in the Hotel Hassler on the Pincian Hill, to the Vatican on the other side of the Eternal City.

It is very much more important to remark that the severity of S. K.'s attitude is in part explained, and in some measure mitigated, by the consideration that the Moral and the thrice repeated Preface to *Training in Christianity* (which he retracted, it is true, but did not discard when he published the second edition) suggest plainly enough, though perhaps unwittingly, the Catholic distinction between the universal precepts of Christ and the "counsels of perfection." This distinction the Protestant Reformers expressly and indignantly rejected. And with this rejection went implicitly the Catholic veneration for the heroes of the faith, the "saints," or, as S. K. here calls them, "those glorious ones." To this whole range of ideas Protestantism is still hostile. Everybody resents this as an invidious distinction. The consequence is that, instead of leveling men up, Protestantism has leveled them down, or, as S. K. says, "place No. 1 has dropped out, and No. 2 has become the first place"; in other words, "Protestantism has become nothing but mediocrity from end to end." Hence his plea that "the ideals must be proclaimed," and the comfort he held out to *all*, if only they really try, that, failing through human weakness to live up to the ideals, they may flee to grace. Naturally, grace is not made very prominent in the *Instant*; but it was very prominent in the Journals, and on his deathbed, responding to Pastor Boesen's question, "Do you rely upon grace?" S. K. responded, "Naturally. What else?" Only he would not at any time have allowed that "grace" was an adequate answer to the anxious query, "whether a man can be a Christian without being a disciple."

There is another respect in which S. K. was more evidently and more fundamentally a Catholic—or perhaps it would be better to say, more consciously in revolt against Protestantism. This appears plainly in the *Instant* by his insistence upon *works*, and by the fact that *here* he has nothing to say about *faith*, except that, according to the New Testament (and the Gospels especially), it must not be "faith alone." He was thoroughly aware that when he insisted upon the imitation of Christ he was stressing a medieval aspect of Catholicism. But his dissent from the Protestant position, especially from the *sola fide*, went far deeper than that. It is shown by his marked preference for the Epistle of St. James, which Luther dismissed as "an epistle of straw." It is shown more generally by his definition of faith as obedience, as the opposite of sin rather than of unbelief. It is significant that he chose to entitle his biggest volume of edifying discourses "The Works of Love." It is so obvious that *love* cannot be "with the tongue"! But S.K. was himself so keenly aware that he was controvening a fundamental position of Lutheranism (*sola fide*) that he was fearful of the offense the publication of this book would give—and greatly surprised that no one raised an outcry. We on the other hand are surprised that he could have entertained such a fear; for now hardly anyone remembers that *sola fide* is a distinction of Protestantism, notwithstanding that it has left evident traces upon our thought and life, and perhaps more than anything else will make S. K.'s satire of "Christendom" unacceptable in our day, if not unintelligible.

I remark in the last place that in this book I have uniformly translated the Danish word *Præst* by the cognate English word. This might seem a matter of course. I have to remark upon it because in all my previous translations I have commonly translated it by "parson" instead of "priest." Others prefer to say "clergyman" or "minister." But that obviously will not do in this book; and here I am not ashamed of being inconsistent. I am not sorry that I have to use the word "priest," for neither would I shun its application to me, nor do I wish to spare other priests of the Anglican Communion (or it may be in the Church of Rome) who might profitably be wounded by it. At the same time it does of course apply to the Protestant ministers of any denomination. The fact is, Luther retained the use of the word "priest" (which is merely old presbyter writ small), and the Scandinavian Churches, like the Church of England, have retained it to this day, though of course without any more suggestion of sacerdotal character than the kindred word *prete* has in Rome and throughout Italy.

KIERKEGAARD AND THE CHURCH

A Supplement to the Translator's Introduction

WALTER LOWRIE would do nothing to dull the cutting edge of Kierkegaard's attack. Neither will I.

Nonetheless, I must do what little I can to discharge an obligation Lowrie laid upon me a few days before his death. "When there comes a new edition of *Attack upon 'Christendom,'*" he said in effect, "write a supplementary essay to underscore, document, and amplify some of the points I made in my own introduction. It is vital that the *Attack* be placed in proper historical and theological perspective."

This I endeavor to do, for I remember how Kierkegaard conceived the role in which he felt Providence had cast him. He was to be nothing more than a "corrective." He then issued a stern *caveat emptor*: "The corrective works confusion only when it is not held in the context of that to which it is a corrective."[1] We see him in context—or we don't see him at all.

I

"It is the peculiarity of the human race," wrote Kierkegaard, "that just because the individual is created in the image of God 'the individual' is above the race. This can be wrongly understood and terribly misused: *concedo*. But that is Christianity. And *that* is where the battle must be fought."[2]

One of the ways in which the Kierkegaardian stress on 'the individual' has been misunderstood and misused is in the contention, constantly recurring, that Kierkegaard had no essential place in his thought for the Church. I too maintain that, measured by the New Testament conception of the Church, Kierkegaard's ecclesiology is defective. But to assert that his doctrine of the Church is defective is different from asserting that he had no doctrine at all.

It must be admitted that in his last months Kierkegaard, breaking a lifelong custom, did cease attending public worship and besought others to do likewise. One Danish biographer gives us the picture

[1] *Papirer*, XI^1 A 28; cp. A 198; XI^2 A 305. To simplify matters, let it be understood that whenever a citation begins with a Roman numeral, followed either by the letters A or B, the reference is to the *Papirer*, i.e., the papers of S. K., most of which are still untranslated. Some of them appear here in English for the first time.

[2] Dru, *Selections from the Journals of Kierkegaard*, No. 1050 = X^2 A 426.

(how well authenticated I know not) of Kierkegaard on a Sunday morning, at the hour of High Mass (*Højmesse*), deliberately taking up a position at a sidewalk café opposite a church, and there conspicuously reading a newspaper so that all the pious en route to service might see. Such a picture pains me, for, like Lowrie, I too am a priest. The prophets of Israel stood *with* the people God had commanded them to condemn. They continued to identify themselves with the community under judgment. As Troeltsch said: "The prophets predicted that the lightning was about to fall—and were struck down by the same lightning which felled their people." To the extent that Kierkegaard, at the very last, dissociated himself from the Established Church, he was, in my judgment, something less than the prophets of Israel—though still a prophet.

II

There is little to be gained, however, by discussing Kierkegaard's ecclesiology in terms of his eccentricities. Already too much of Kierkegaardian research has preferred the man's idiosyncrasies to his ideas, his biography to his beliefs—perhaps because the former are easier to handle. Of biographical considerations, it must suffice to mention three. The facts are these:

(1) Except for the final few months, Kierkegaard went regularly to church, preached in churches on occasion, and on the occasions prescribed received the Sacrament of the Altar. One has only to read his "Discourses for the Communion on Fridays" to see how exalted a conception he had of the Lord's Supper.[3] Repeatedly and ardently he longed to be ordained. He was hindered in this. Sometimes it was because of the emergence of some new crisis in his life (e.g., the affair of "The Corsair" at which time he conceived that God was calling him to remain on the front lines of the battle and not to retreat to a country parish). Other times it was because of the lack of encouragement from the Primate, who was growingly displeased with Kierkegaard's literary output and who accused him of playing a profane game with holy things. Kierkegaard long delayed the publication of some of his later decisively Christian writings because of an agonizing apprehen-

[3] Although many of his discourses were not actually spoken from a pulpit, where are they imagined as being delivered? Precisely *in* church, *in* the context of public worship. One should read—and pray, too—S.K.'s touching Prayer for the Whole State of Christ's Church in the seventh discourse in *Training in Christianity*.

sion that they, being offensive to his bishop, might preclude forever the possibility of his ordination.

When commentators point to the fact that the Kierkegaardian literature does not often and explicitly deal with the doctrine of the Church, and deduce from that that he was not interested in the Church and found little meaning in it, we must reply: *On the contrary!* Here was a loyal son of the Church, longing to serve it as a priest, who—far from deprecating it—was so immersed in its life that he simply *assumed* it. He assumed as a matter of course the existence of the Church with its liturgies, orders, buildings, ceremonies, vestments, sacraments. Like St. Thomas Aquinas (or any other theologian until recent times), he was so living *in* the sacramental, ecclesiological reality that it rarely became a topic for special study. All of the "equipment," the whole of the "Christian inventory," he could safely presuppose—bell, book, and candle. In Kierkegaard, as in Danish Lutheranism, there was no disposition to topple altars, break stained glass windows, strip the sanctuary bare, decapitate sculptures of saints. He reiterated a hundred times: "I have no proposal with respect to a change in externals."[4] The *doctrine* is all right.[5] The hymnal doesn't need revision.[6] Above all, the man who is called to be the critic of the Establishment (*det Bestaaende*, literally, that which stands) must himself stand within it and love it.[7] In short, the State Church of Denmark was part of S.K.'s culture, part of the standard, necessary

[4] Cf., e.g., X^3 A 187, X^5 B 40 (p. 259), X^5 B 107 (p. 293), X^5 B 144. In the *Papirer*, at X^1 A 537, we read: "What in our time needs reforming is not the system of Church government and such—but the concept: Christendom."

[5] Cf. X^4 A 204 and *Journals*, 1185, 1187.

[6] *Concluding Unscientific Postscript* (Princeton, 1941), p. 428: "Possibly no new hymnal is needed. Why does no one hit upon the idea which lies so close at hand, closer perhaps than many will believe: the idea of experimenting with the plan of having the old hymnal furnished with a new binding, to see if a different binding might not do the trick, especially if the bookbinder were to print on the cover, The New Hymnal. The objection may be made that it would be too bad to sacrifice the old binding, since strangely enough the copies of the old hymnal in the hands of the congregation are said to be in very good condition, presumably because the book is so little used, so that the binding would be a useless expense. But this objection must be met with a deep-voiced reply, a deep voice, please note: 'Every serious man in our seriously troubled age readily perceives that something must be done.' "

[7] Cf. VII B 235, p. 64: "The one chosen [to recall the Church to its vocation] must love the Establishment." In X^1 A 598, the theme is repeated. No external changes are wanted. The sole necessity is to draw attention to the fact that "every individual must seek a primitive [i.e., original, firsthand] relationship to God." Cf. also X^4 A 26, 30, 33, 204. One of S.K.'s most trenchant defenses of the Establishment as against the "numerical" appears in X^4 A 363, 365.

environment for making life supportable, the element in which he lived and moved and had his being. His attack arose only when he felt the Church was *in a wrong way* a part of the culture, succumbing to a culture, instead of so relating itself to eternity that it would be in possession of a transcendental principle of criticism by which to judge the culture to which God would have it responsibly related. Kierkegaard never attacked the Church *qua* Church. He inveighed against the Church only when he feared that it was in danger of becoming a culture-religion, a too simple identification of Church and State. The center of his dislike was a marriage of convenience wherein the government was more than willing to pay clerical stipends and provide for the maintenance of church fabrics out of the public treasury in return for the modest, reciprocal favor that, on political and social issues, the Church remain irrelevant and confine itself to "Quiet Hours." In the nineteenth century, to have been born on Danish soil made you, as a Dane, automatically a Christian (unless you were so unfortunate as to be an unconverted Jew, Turk, or Mohammedan—or, even uglier, a Baptist).[8] Church and State became virtual equiva-

[8] Johannes Climacus, if not Kierkegaard himself personally, vented his spleen in the *Postscript*, pp. 49 f.: "How strange is the way of the world! Once it was at the risk of his life that a man dared to profess himself a Christian; now it is to make oneself suspect to venture to doubt that one is a Christian. Especially when this doubt does not mean that the individual launches a violent attack against Christianity with a view to abolishing it; for in that case it would perhaps be admitted that there was something in it. But if a man were to say quite simply and unassumingly, that he was concerned for himself, lest perhaps he had no right to call himself a Christian, he would indeed not suffer persecution or be put to death, but he would be smothered in angry glances, and people would say: 'How tiresome to make such a fuss about nothing at all; why can't he behave like the rest of us, who are all Christians? It is just as it is with F. F., who refuses to wear a hat on his head like others, but insists on dressing differently.' And if he happened to be married, his wife would say to him: 'Dear husband of mine, how can you get such notions into your head? How can you doubt that you are a Christian? Are you not a Dane, and does not the geography say that the Lutheran form of the Christian religion is the ruling religion in Denmark? For you are surely not a Jew, nor are you a Mohammedan; what then can you be if not a Christian? It is a thousand years since paganism was driven out of Denmark, so I know you are not a pagan. Do you not perform your duties at the office like a conscientious civil servant; are you not a good citizen of a Christian nation, a Lutheran Christian state? So then of course you must be a Christian.'

"We have become so objective, it seems, that even the wife of a civil servant argues to the particular individual from the totality, from the state, from the community-idea, from the scientific standpoint of geography. It is so much a matter of course that the individual is a Christian, a believer and so forth, that it is frivolous to make a fuss about it, or to be such a crotcheteer. Since it is always unpleasant to have to admit the lack of something that everyone has as a matter of course, and which therefore properly gets a sort of special significance only when someone is stupid enough to

lents. People, whatever their profession of religious belief or lack thereof, constituted the parish. Resorting to an old cliché, Christianity in Kierkegaard's Denmark (with notable exceptions of deep spirituality) was reduced to the three experiences of being "hatched, matched, dispatched." It was religion at which three things were thrown at you. Water at baptism, rice at marriage, earth at burial. For the rest, most people felt free to go about their business, not feeling much pressure upon their conscience. Even if one deigned to take a pew on the principal feast days, the pulpit seldom pummeled you. The consolations of religion were admirably set forth. Of its possible perturbations, little was to be heard. An ominous silence reigned. *This* is the kind of setup Kierkegaard was attacking. He took his stand not against Christianity but against "the blinding illusion of Christendom," the "geographical Christianity" he so witheringly described in *The Book on Adler*. He opposed the equation: *Mængden* = *Menigheden* (the crowd is identical with the congregation, the Church the same as the State, Christianity coterminous with the world.[9]

(2) In intention, at least, Kierkegaard was not a sectarian, although many splinter groups have sought to claim him as such.[10] It would be no arduous task to collect from his works a bundle of utterances exhibiting the "Godfearing satire" he poured upon "pietistic severity," "party-movements," and "bungling efforts at reforming" the Church, whether from within or without. The evils of the Established Church seemed less dangerous to Kierkegaard than "this evil lust, this flirting with the will to reform."[11] When Kierkegaard, towards the last,

---

betray his defect, what wonder then that no one admits it? In the case of what amounts to something, presupposing skill or aptitude or the like, it is easier to make an admission. But the more insignificant the matter, insignificant, namely, because we are all in possession of it, the more it is stupid and in bad taste to make the admission. And this is the modern category for any sign of concern lest one should not be a Christian: it is in bad taste. *Ergo*, we are all Christians."

9 Cf., e.g., X³ A 574, X¹ A 533, X¹ A 552, X⁵ B 111 (p. 306) and X⁵ B 208 (p. 392), XI² A 264, 410, IX A 264.

10 *Kierkegaard and Radical Discipleship: A New Perspective* (Princeton, 1968), a fascinating and responsible book by an able scholar, Vernard Eller, shows the many affinities between S.K. and the convictions held dear by the Brethren. Yet there is another side to Kierkegaard in which the Brethren would find little comfort or support. S.K. was not friendly toward sects, though he often defended their rights to worship in accordance with their conscience.

11 Cf. "The Moral" in *Judge for Yourselves!* Other references: X³ A 647, 658, 799, 800; X⁴ A 26, 345; *Journals*, 1184. These all demonstrate S. K.'s detestation of the "reforming zeal" of his period. Kierkegaard believed that he had provided an ideal defense of the Establishment. If only the State Church would make the humble ad-

launched his attack, he who had been largely ignored suddenly found himself the darling not only of sectarians but of some politicians as well. Their champion had arisen at last! But with consummate polemical skill this "damned explosive Dane" rose up to smite down those who wanted to uphold him. Although himself fighting the Establishment, he *would* not lend his name or prestige to an anti-Church campaign motivated by political or sectarian hostility. He wanted the *Bestaaende*—the Standing Church—to *stand*, but only on the terms he thought the New Testament would legitimatize.[12]

While not blind to practical questions of reform nor oblivious to the desirability of certain eventual alterations in the Church's structure and praxis, Kierkegaard knew that this is not the place to start. This is wrong end to. Kierkegaard desired essentially not the remodelling of the Church but its revival. "For Revival and Increase of Inwardness" is the subtitle of *Training in Christianity*.[13] This phrase might well serve as the motto for Kierkegaard's whole endeavor in relation to the Established Church. His position is clearly stated in the following Journal entry from 1850 (X^3 A 415):

> From the Christian standpoint, in the highest sense there is no established Church, only a militant one.

---

mission that somehow it was something less than what the New Testament requires, then all right. Let it stand. He put his foot flat down against "wrecking the Establishment in favor of parties and sects." (Cf. X^5 B 117.) He often said that he would sponsor no movement in the direction of "pietistic severity." (Cf. X^3 A 519; cp. 571, 658.) A by now familiar theme recurs in X^3 A 527: "A corrective has not the assignment to push the Establishment out and make himself a new kind of establishment, but, if possible, to make the Establishment more spirited, more inward." Of many references, I cite X^3 A 647, where he averred that one way he supports the Establishment with his insistence on "the individual" is his opposition to parties and sects. One more point: in X^6 B 218 (p. 346), S. K. said straight out that if the Establishment will but make the confession that it falls short of what the New Testament expects of Christ's Church, it is to be preferred to all other alternatives. (Cp. X^5 A 125.)

12 Cf., e.g., X^2 A 193, in which S. K. remarked that his task was not to blow up the Establishment but rather to try to blow into it some spirited inwardness. He also said in X^1 A 92: "I am in the service of the Establishment. I have not collided with *it* but with the universal human. The extraordinary feature is that, so far from my having introduced something new I am, quite to the contrary, designed to help preserve the Establishment." (Cp. X^1 A 74, X^4 A 204 [points 3 and 4], and X^4 A 218.) But S. K. lamented that "the corrective" has a hard time of it. He did *not* want to found a party or a sect; yet this so easily happens. On this point, cf. X^3 A 798. In a score of passages he disclaimed being a *Sværmer*, i.e., an "enthusiast" or near fanatic. No, he said, "I am only a corrective. I have nothing new to bring." (Cp. X^3 A 647; X^3 A 527.) No nonconformist he. He did not even recommend a separation of Church and State. (Cf. X^6 B 261 [p. 434].)

13 Cp. X^1 A 162.

> That is the first consideration.
>
> Yet the second consideration is that there is, empirically and in fact, an established Church. By no means should anyone want to bowl that over or knock it out cold. No. Yet over the Establishment must hang the higher ideality as a quickening possibility: that in strongest Christian terms there is, essentially, no established Church.
>
> This has happened with me by the help of a pseudonym [Anti-Climacus, author of *Training in Christianity, For Self-Examination*, and *Judge for Yourselves!*]: that everything might be purely a movement of the spirit. There is not a shred of proposal with respect to changing churchly externals.
>
> And as the pseudonym lifts his hand to strike this tremendous blow, I step in as a buffer, so that the whole force of it falls on me, that I am such a poor Christian—I who nevertheless remain in the established Church. In this way, everything is movement of the spirit.

In the margin to this entry Kierkegaard added:

> Even in the case of an established Church made up of *earnest* Christians, it would need to be reminded that, from an ideal Christian point of view, there is no such thing as an established Church but only a militant one. Yet this must not be said except from the vantage point of ideality in its distance from the establishment. If ever it should happen that an established Church would not tolerate that this be said even under the stated condition, then it is a sign that such a Church is in error and that a direct attack is called for. (X^3 A 416)

Here, forcefully announced in 1850, is the principle on which Kierkegaard in 1855 justified to himself his direct attack.

(3) When the time came, the attack came. No one who knows Kierkegaard's papers can suppose that the bombardment of incendiary pamphlets was the haste-work of a hot-head. It cost him the agony of endless soul-searching, for he was attacking something to which he was devoted. The point to be secured is this: in attacking the Establishment, S. K. was well aware of the one-sided character of the attack. For the sake of emphasis, I repeat here the first of two Journal entries which Dr. Lowrie has placed on p. 90.

> He who must apply a "corrective" must study accurately and profoundly the weak side of the Establishment, and then vigorously

> and one-sidedly present the opposite. Precisely in this consists the corrective, and in this too the resignation of him who has to apply it. The corrective will in a sense be sacrificed to the established order.
>
> If this is true, a presumably clever pate can reprove the corrective for being one-sided. Ye gods! Nothing is easier for him who applies the corrective than to supply the other side; but then it ceases to be the corrective and becomes the established order. (X^1 A 640)

What could be clearer? Deliberately S. K. suppressed all that he could have said in favor of the Establishment, with conscious exaggeration, to hammer on its weaknesses. Over the years he had been writing books with stronger and ever more stringent criticism of the Church—often hesitating to publish them for fear of the consequences. But what happened? Nothing. Not a ripple. He once said, "It is as if my books had never been written." It was then that he conceived that he must teach by "the irritational method." His formulation of a new program was: "Henceforth I will write in such wise as to *irritate* people into facing the issues. I can compel no man to agree with my opinions, but at least I can compel him to have an opinion."[14] Kierkegaard did not abandon the pen for the sword, but we might say that, towards the last, he laid aside the rapier in favor of a less subtle instrument, the sledgehammer.

III

Entirely apart from all biographical considerations, and abstracting from the special circumstances of his particular historical situation, let us ask how Kierkegaard *in principle* conceived the Church.

A Church there will be, of course. When God touches an individual, that touch always brings him into touch with all other individuals similarly touched. The Church is a congregation composed of such individuals. By "individual" (*den Enkelte*) Kierkegaard meant the

[14] VIII^2 B 193 (p. 301) gives us an insight into S. K.'s conception of how the "irritational method" might work. In this place he reflected on his recurrent stress on the importance of the individual: "I willingly admit that I sometimes . . . have pushed the case as far out in peculiarity as possible—veritably not out of peculiarity. On the contrary, I have in high degree been conscious of what I did, that I acted responsibly, conscious of my responsibility, that not to do so would have been irresponsible. I did it . . . because it was important to me to irritate men into fixing their attention on this point—something one can accomplish neither with ten volumes which develop the doctrine of the individual nor with ten lectures thereon, but in these times exclusively by getting people to laugh at you."

man who, standing before God as he is revealed in Christ, knows himself judged, forgiven, restored to fellowship, taken out of "the world," and sent back into the world as witness for service.

The Christian congregation, a religious concept, "lies on the other side of 'the individual'" and is "by no means to be confounded with what may have *political* validity: the public, the crowd, the numerical, etc."[15] *Menigheden* and *Mængden*, as noted before, are qualitatively different. What constitutes this difference? The congregation, said Kierkegaard, "is a society which lies on the hinter side of human society, a little society which has an inward bond of cohesion—viz., that of being believers; i.e., by accepting and having dedicated their whole life to the Absurd, they have said goodbye to the world and broken with the world. . . . The Christian congregation is a society which consists of qualitative individuals; the inwardness of the society is conditioned (1) by its faith in the Absurd and (2) by its polemical position in relation to the great human society."[16] But the whole difficulty, as Kierkegaard saw it, was that, in the course of time this thing of being a Christian became identical with being a man. "Thus it came about that the Christian congregation was supposedly one and the same thing as the human race. Good night, nurse! Nowadays the Christian congregation equals *Publikum*."[17] Again: "Religiously (in contradistinction to the 'public,' the 'masses,' etc., which politically may have their validity) there are only individuals. And still less from the point of view of the Christian Religion can there be such a thing as the 'masses,' . . . because 'the possibility of offense,' which Christianly is encountered in becoming a Christian, unconditionally makes men first, qualitatively, 'individuals,' whereby this concept secures the 'Christian congregation' as something qualitatively different from the 'public,' the 'masses,' etc., while naturally unconditionally every man can be the individual."[18] In the same entry we read: "'The individual' must in a decisively ethical way have gone between as an intermediate determinant in order to secure that the 'congregation' is not taken in vain as synonymous with the 'public,' the 'masses'; while yet it must be remembered, as is well known, that it is not the individual's relationship to the congregation which determines his relationship to God but his relationship to God which determines his relationship to the congregation."

The same note was struck again and again. One more instance will

[15] *The Point of View*, p. 153. (Cp. X^5 B 215, 216.)
[16] X^2 A 478. [17] *Ibid.* [18] X^5 A 208, p. 392.

suffice: "In the highest religious form, the individual relates himself first to God and then to the congregation; but this first relationship is the highest, though the individual does not neglect the latter."[19] In this connection Kierkegaard called attention to a passage in the *Concluding Unscientific Postscript*,[20] where he contended that "the task is not to begin with the individual and arrive at the race, but to begin with the individual and through the race (the universal) arrive at the individual again." If here we read "Church" for "race," I doubt if Kierkegaard would have objected. The task, accordingly, is: through the instrumentality of the Church to arrest the individual, incorporate him into the fellowship, set him up as a person responsibly related to both Church and State in obedience to God. For of course S. K. knew that the Church, under divine appointment, is the chief agency by which individuals are rescued either from isolated subjectivity or else from faceless anonymity in the public, and through the ministrations of the Church are made individuals, qualitatively understood. However poorly the Church may historically have fulfilled her vocation, she is nonetheless *ecclesia docens*, the principal bearer of revelation, the Mother of Christians. Kierkegaard had no fault to find with the definition of the Church contained in the Augsburg Confession: the Church is the communion of saints, in which the pure Word of God is preached, and the Sacraments are duly ministered.[21] *The Book on Adler*, among other writings, makes evident how clear it was to Kierkegaard that Christianity, though it is far more than doctrine (being, in fact, a way of life), is nonetheless a definite doctrine which must first be taught and accepted passionately before there can be any question of embarking on that life.[22] When an historical Church fails in the task assigned, the Deity is not helpless, not thrown for a loss. He of course finds other ways of getting through to men. Yet normatively (and even in practice, despite all her faults) the Church, with her ordained ministry, common worship, etc., is the *way* God seeks to establish contact with men to win them out from isolated subjectivity or out from engulfment in the masses and into a "primitive God-relationship."[23]

[19] VII A 20.

[20] Page 383 = S.V. VII, p. 418.

[21] X^4 A 246.

[22] Cf., e.g., VII B 235, pp. 198-210; cp. VIII B 82, 13 and B 83 to B 89.

[23] II A 172. S. K.'s respect for the authority of ordination is well known. It found expression repeatedly in his unwillingness to call his discourses "sermons." For him, the sermon implied ordination and authority. His category was "without authority."

"The individual," Kierkegaard insisted, "is *in* the congregation," not a hermit or a recluse.[24] Naturally he goes to church—three times every Sunday! The reason for that Kierkegaard gave with deep human understanding and delightful humor: "The infinitely reflective religious man does the same as the immediately religious man, goes to church three times every Sunday, but conceives it humoristically and with a willingness to repent it at once: humoristically, that he can't help going to church, that he can never tire of hearing God's Word and being in God's House; half repentantly, that it should still be true of him that he needs again and again new incitement in his

---

He was a layman. *The Book on Adler* is in English called *On Authority and Revelation*. Much of that is germane to the present discussion. Cf. also X^3 A 267. As late as 1850 he defended the necessity of the clerical order, a position he never retracted. It is not easy to keep all the skeins here involved from getting hopelessly ensnarled. Yet now it is of importance to weave in a few quotations from *The Present Age* and *The Point of View*. In *The Present Age* Kierkegaard gave us good reasons for his distrust of "the collective idea" and "the principle of association," the logic of which is: "Individually we are nothing, but by the strength of united effort we shall attain the goal." By reverting to this topic almost to the point of monotony, S. K. was telling us that this principle may well have its validity in connection with material and political interests, but that the principle extended to ethical and religious concerns is disastrous. How disastrous it is he made clear in this statement: "It does away with God and eternity and with man's kinship with Deity." (Cf. the entire passage in *The Point of View*, p. 113; cp. *Journals*, 1050.) This is why he said: "It is quite impossible for the community or the idea of association to save our age. . . . Dialectically the position is this: the principle of association by strengthening the individual, enervates him; it strengthens numerically, but ethically that is a weakening. It is only after the individual has acquired an ethical outlook, in the face of the whole world, that there can be any suggestion of really joining together. Otherwise the association of individuals who are in themselves weak, is just as disgusting and as harmful as the marriage of children." (*The Present Age*, pp. 61f.) Thus the Christian Association, the Church, lies *beyond* all human associations *through* individuals. Individuals, each of whom has a God-relationship, may perfectly well exist in the association called the Church. On page 112 of *The Point of View* S. K. remarked: "Perhaps it may be well to note here, although it seems to me almost superfluous, that it naturally could not occur to me to object to the fact, for example, that preaching is done or that the truth is proclaimed, even though it were to an assemblage of hundreds of thousands. Not at all." Finally, this passage from the *Samlede Værker*, VIII, p. 68: "Where the individuals (each one severally) in essential passion relate themselves to an idea, and thereupon in association essentially relate themselves to the same idea, there the relationship is perfect and normal. The relationship is individually distinguishing (each has himself for himself) and ideally uniting. . . . In this way the individuals never come too close to one another, bestially understood, precisely because they are united on the basis of ideal distance. This unity of differences is the well instrumented, rich orchestration of fully sonorous music."

24 X^2 A 390. How absurd it is to find that some translators have rendered *den Enkelte* or *hiin Enkelte* as "that solitary individual," as if S. K.'s ideal were a Simon Styletes!

God-relationship."[25] In this connection Kierkegaard had the humanity to call the Church an "accommodation," an "indulgence." In his goodness God gives the Church to us because we need it. And in church the individual receives, to his great and endless comfort, Absolution and the Sacrament of the Altar.[26] The Church is the powerhouse which generates our zeal, impels us out into the world. There we suffer defeats. This drives us back to the Church. Within its walls we confess our shortcomings, experience the miracle of forgiveness, get up from our knees, and having been stood on our feet again, we go out to tackle the world once more. The dialectic between Christ the Redeemer, whom we adore, and Christ the Pattern, whom out of love and gratitude we would imitate, is exhaustively and beautifully explored in many of Kierkegaard's books, particularly those of his last period. Adoration and imitation—an *in* to the church and an *out* to the world, then back again and out again: this is the permanent rhythm of the Christian life.

Now that we have seen something of what S. K.'s "individualism" imports—that it was not anti-ecclesiastical—we can begin to draw some conclusions. Once again we must be sure we understand Kierkegaard's distinction between *Mængden* (the crowd, the masses, *das Man* as stigmatized by Heidegger) and *Menigheden* (congregation, the assembled People of God). We can afford to hear out our Danish rebel still another time:

> In "the public" and such like the individual is nothing, there is no individual; the numerical is the constitutive factor, and the law for coming into being, a *generatio aeqvivoca. Apart* from "the public" the individual is nothing and neither is he anything, more deeply understood, *in* "the public."
>
> The [authentic] individual is in the congregation; the individual is dialectically decisive as *prius* for forming the congregation, and in the congregation the individual is qualitatively an essential factor, can consequently become at any moment higher than the "congregation," as soon, that is, as "the others" fall away from the idea. The cohesive power for the congregation is that each is an individual, and so the idea. The "togetherness" of the public or perhaps its dissolution lies in the notion that the numerical is everything.

[25] VI A 52.

[26] The best commentary on this statement is to be found in S. K.'s moving "Discourses at the Communion on Fridays." Cp. X^5 A 101 and 103.

> Every individual in the congregation guarantees the congregation. "The public" is a chimera. The individual in the congregation is a microcosm which qualitatively respects the macrocosm. Here applies, in a good sense, *unum noris omnes*. In "the public" there is no individual, the whole is nothing. Here it is impossible to say *unum noris omnes*, for here is no "one." "The congregation" is indeed more than a sum but in truth it is a sum of ones.[27]

"More than a sum." Did Kierkegaard tell us what this "more" is? Not explicitly. But hints there are. The most important one is tucked away in a footnote in the *Postscript*, p. 492. In the text Kierkegaard has been making his favorite point: "Religiously regarded, the species is a lower category than the individual, and to thrust oneself under the category of the species is evasion." The context here is a discussion of an individual's eternal recollection (i.e., consciousness of) his total guilt. But now, what if he retreats in cowardly fashion from this consciousness? What if, to exonerate himself, he takes refuge in a doctrine of Original Sin, as popularly misunderstood? Or what if he flees to a Greek tragic position to complain whimperingly: I couldn't help myself. I'm just a dead-end kid. Born on the wrong side of the tracks. Never had enough Vitamin C., etc. I am only a member of an ill-starred race, eventually an animal race.[28] This, thought Kierkegaard, is an evasion, a craven flight to the temple of aesthetics, a hunt for cover against the relentless scrutiny of ethics. No, ethically and religiously, he and he alone must assume full responsibility. For ethically and religiously the individual is higher than the race.

In this setting comes the footnote (*Postscript*, p. 492) so important for a doctrine of the Church:

> Only in the final definition of the religious as the paradox-religious does the race become higher, but then it is only in virtue of the paradox, and one must have had the intermediate definition of the religious which makes the individual higher than the species, if the spherical differences are not to coagulate and people to prate aesthetically about the paradox-religious.

This being interpreted means: In the paradox-religious sphere (= Christianity), the Church is higher than the individual—yet in such

[27] X^2 A 390.

[28] Painstakingly S. K. went over all this ground in Volume I of *Either/Or*. Cf. the essay on "The Ancient Tragical Motif as Reflected in the Modern."

a way that the absolute importance of each individual severally is not cancelled, and that Christian ethical responsibility is laid more heavily on each and every one—but always with the help of grace.[29] Each person must stand up on his own two feet and take his own medicine—the bitter dosage of ethics. This done, he may then discover in church the sweet medicine, the Elixir of Immortality, qualified exoneration and total absolution. Only those who acknowledge their guilt can go free.

The point is clear. The mystery of the Church is this: it is a fellowship which, far from suppressing individuality, nurtures it, nourishes it, brings it to full flower. It produces an individuality in *anden Potens*, in second potentiality, as Kierkegaard liked to put it. The Church may be compared to the mystery of marriage: bride and bridegroom, the two of them, become one flesh, and yet this is a oneness which does not annul the twoness. The man and the wife are individuals still, each with separate duties, yet the duties become more supportable in the situation of comradeship.[30]

I have had to leave out a hundred relevant quotations, but I submit a little catena of three in conclusion:

> Rightly used, the category "the individual" can never be harmful to the Establishment. Used in peacetime, its function will be: without changing any externals, to awaken inwardness to increased life in the Establishment; and in an unsettled time its function will be more that of supporting the Establishment by leading the individuals to indifference to proposed alterations in externals and thus to supporting the Establishment.[31]

> A remark of Kofoed-Hansen in a sermon on Monday in Whitsun Week struck me today. "One might ask why God, who disrupted the proceedings at Babel (consequently desired to split people up), nevertheless willed to create the Church (consequently unity)." This struck me with reference to my small-scale religious operation: that I want to do away with the public, and yet, if possible, to have *everyone* become the "individual"—*in unity*. The hallmark of the religious is always, to begin with, a negative determinant. The first is always something hit upon by men or worldliness

29 Cf. X^2 A 489.

30 Judge William has something to say about all this in *Either/Or* and *Stages on Life's Way*.

31 IX B 66. Cp. IX B 63, p. 362: "When the 'Missionary' comes he will not seek to overthrow the Establishment but will use the category 'the individual' to strengthen the Establishment."

(Babel, the public, etc.); the religious negates this, and then brings forward in its truth that which men wanted in untruth.[32]

Christianity is also designed for *et Folk*—a people, a land. [And Kierkegaard hesitates not at all in adding]: Twelve men united on being Christians have recreated the face of the world. In actuality there is, therefore, only one danger for a people in Christendom—that the individuals no longer are Christians.[33]

IV

In the light of his attack upon Christendom, people often ask, "What would Kierkegaard have become had he lived longer?" A Roman Catholic? More than a few have suggested that. A sectarian? There are those prepared to make a place for him in their hagiographic calendar. An agnostic or an atheist? This I doubt, but it is open to debate. Perhaps something like the so-called "Non-Church Christians" to be found in Japan? Could be. Interesting questions! And speculation is not to be forbidden. But yet, how un-Kierkegaardian, how non-existentialist these speculations are! The question posed by Kierkegaard is not what *he* would have become. The rude, actual question is: what are *you* to become?

Perhaps it was providential that he died when he did. By prodigious industry he had said at the age of forty-two all that he had to say. He said it powerfully. He challenged the whole lot of us with a stringency that none but the obtuse can evade. The proud Søren Kierkegaard was capable of humility. Refusing the titles of prophet, apostle, or reformer, he claimed nothing more for himself than that he was a "corrective"—and he repeated a thousand times that the corrective, no matter how needed, must never become the normative. The corrective is only "the necessary pinch of spice." No stew can be made of spice alone. With even more humility, he added the prediction that "the next generation will need the opposite of 'the corrective.' "[34]

Valdemar Ammundsen, a great professor of the University of Copenhagen, put the matter right when in 1913 he said succinctly of the enigmatic Dane: "Where Kierkegaard was wrong, that goes on his account. Where Kierkegaard was right, the bill comes to us."

HOWARD A. JOHNSON

Riverside, California
August 12, 1967

[32] X^3 A 63. [33] VIII^2 B 122. [34] X^5 A 106.

ARTICLES IN THE *FATHERLAND*

From the Journal

WHY I MAKE USE OF THIS NEWSPAPER

Luther says somewhere in one of his sermons that properly sermons should not be preached in churches. This he said in a sermon, which surely was delivered in a church, so that he did not say it seriously. But it is true that sermons should not be preached in churches. It harms Christianity in a high degree and alters its very nature, that it is brought into an artistic remoteness from reality, instead of being heard in the midst of real life, and that precisely for the sake of the conflict (the collision). For all this talk about quiet, about quiet places and quiet hours, as the right element for Christianity, is absurd.

So then sermons should not be preached in churches but in the street, in the midst of life, of the reality of daily life, weekday life. Nevertheless, even if it is not too early for us to do it and might perhaps require preparation, in any case I cannot do it, for the simple reason that I lack physical strength. To me it is allotted to speak with the individual, to converse, and then to use the pen.

Nevertheless I desired to attain an approximation to preaching in the street, or to bring Christianity, the thought of Christianity, into the midst of life's reality and into conflict with its various interests. And to that end I resolved to use this journal [the *Fatherland*]. It is a political journal, it has entirely different interests, it is concerned moreover with very many different interests, but Christianity is not its affair.

EP ('54-'55), p. 469

TWENTY-ONE ARTICLES

IN THE *FATHERLAND* 1854-1855

and

THIS HAS TO BE SAID

CONTENTS TO *FATHERLAND* ARTICLES
AND *THIS HAS TO BE SAID*

I. The *Fatherland*, Monday, December 18, 1854

Was Bishop Mynster a "witness to the truth," one of "the genuine witnesses to the truth"—is this the truth?

February 1854. S. Kierkegaard.

In the address which Professor Martensen "delivered on the Fifth Sunday after Epiphany, the Sunday preceding the burial of Bishop Mynster,"[1] a speech of remembrance it might be called for the reason that it brought to Professor *Martensen's* remembrance the vacant episcopal see—in this address Bishop Mynster is represented as one of the genuine witnesses to the truth,[2] this being affirmed in the strongest and most decisive terms it would be possible to use. With the figure of the deceased bishop, his life and the manner of it and the issue of it, before our eyes, we are exhorted "to imitate the faith of the true guide, the genuine witness to the truth" (p. 5), to imitate his faith, for that, as was said expressly of Bishop Mynster, was shown, "not merely by word and profession, but in deed and in truth" (p. 9). The deceased bishop is by Professor Martensen introduced (p. 6) "into the holy chain of witnesses to the truth which stretches through the ages from the days of the Apostles," etc.

Against this I must protest—and now that Bishop Mynster is dead, I can speak willingly, but in this place very briefly, and not at all about what determined me to assume the relationship to him which I assumed.

If the word "preaching" suggests more particularly what is said, written, printed, the word, the sermon, then the fact that in this respect (to allude to only one thing) Bishop Mynster's preaching soft-pedals, slurs over, suppresses, omits something decisively Christian, something which appears to us men inopportune, which would make our life strenuous, hinder us from enjoying life, that part of Christianity which has to do with dying from the world, by voluntary renunciation, by hating oneself, by suffering for the doctrine, etc.—to see this one does not have to be particularly sharp-sighted, if one puts the New Testament alongside of Mynster's sermons.

If on the other hand the word "preaching," proclaiming the Gospel, leads one to think more particularly how far the preacher's life expresses what he says (and note that Christianly this is the decisive thing, whereby Christianity has wished to secure itself against getting docents without definite character, instead of witnesses), the fact that Bishop Mynster's preaching of Christianity was not in character, that outside the quiet hours he was not in character, not even in the role of his own sermons, which nevertheless, as has been said, have in comparison with the New Testament mitigated the Christian conceptions considerably—one does not need to be particularly sharp-sighted to see this, in case one who hears and reads him is duly acquainted with his sermons. In 1848 and thereafter this was visible even to blind admirers, if they were sufficiently acquainted with his sermons to know what they and the quiet hours would prompt one to expect.

So when alongside of it one lays the New Testament, Bishop Mynster's proclamation of Christianity was a very questionable sort of preaching, especially on the part of one who was a witness to the truth. But then to my mind the genuine thing about him was that, as I am firmly convinced, he was willing to admit before God and to himself that by no manner of means was he a witness to the truth—to my mind this admission was the genuine thing about him.

But if from the pulpit Bishop Mynster is to be depicted and canonized as a witness to the truth, one of the genuine witnesses to the truth, then a protest must be made. I see that the *Berlin News* [a Copenhagen paper], which is the official newspaper, just as Professor Martensen is the official preacher, expresses the opinion that Professor Martensen (who with notable haste forestalls the interment and the monument too [which was to be erected to the deceased bishop]) has by this address erected a beautiful and worthy monument to the deceased—I would prefer to say a worthy monument to Professor Martensen himself. But in any case, the monument cannot be ignored, therefore a protest must be made, which perhaps might contribute to make the monument (to Professor Martensen) more enduring.

Bishop Mynster a witness to the truth! You who read this must surely know what is to be understood by a witness to the truth*; but let me

* But perhaps this has been cast into oblivion by Bishop Mynster's preaching in the course of so many years. For this too is one of the defects, and one of the principal defects of his preaching—not the fact that he himself was a government official (from the Christian point of view that is a detraction from his preaching), not the consideration of his own glittering career, rich in enjoyment, no, not this, but the fact that he would authorize that way of proclaiming the Gospel as the true Christian way, and thereby implicitly condemn as an exaggeration the true Christian preaching (by a suffering witness to the truth), instead of making to Christianity the admission that the preaching he represented is something which may be conceded to us men as a dispensation and indulgence, something which we ordinary men have recourse to because we are too selfish, too worldly, too sensual, to be capable of anything more, something which we

remind you that for this it is absolutely necessary for one to suffer for the doctrine, and when it is said emphatically, one of the "genuine" witnesses to the truth, the word must be understood in the strictest sense. Let me then try to indicate by a few strokes what is to be understood by it, in order to make it vivid to you.

A witness to the truth is a man whose life from first to last is unacquainted with everything which is called enjoyment—and, ah, whether to you has been granted little or much, you know how pleasant is that which is called enjoyment! But his life from first to last was unacquainted with what is called enjoyment; on the other hand, from first to last it was initiated into what is called suffering—and, alas, even you who have been exempted from the protracted, the more agonizing sufferings, you know nevertheless from your own experience how one winces at what is called suffering! But to that his life was initiated from first to last, by experiences which are even more rarely talked about among men, because they are more rarely encountered in the world, by inward conflicts, by fear and trembling, by trepidation, by anguish of soul, by agony of spirit, being tried besides that by all the sufferings which are more commonly talked of in the world. A witness to the truth is a man who in poverty witnesses to the truth—in poverty, in lowliness, in abasement, and so is unappreciated, hated, abhorred, and then derided, insulted, mocked—his daily bread perhaps he did not always have, so poor was he, but the daily bread of persecution he was richly provided with every day. For him there was never promotion, except in an inverse sense, downward, step by step. A witness to the truth, one of the genuine witnesses to the truth, is a man who is scourged, maltreated, dragged from one prison to the other, and then at last—the last promotion, whereby he is admitted into the first class as defined by the Christian protocol, among the genuine witnesses to the truth—then at last--for this is indeed one of those genuine witnesses to the truth of whom Professor Martensen speaks—then at last crucified, or beheaded, or burnt, or roasted on a gridiron, his lifeless body thrown by the executioner in an out-of-the-way place (thus a witness to the truth is buried), or burnt to ashes and cast to the four winds, so that every trace of the "filth" (which the Apostle says *he* was) might be obliterated.

This is a witness to the truth, his life and career, his death and burial—

ordinary men have recourse to, and which so understood, in spite of all false reformers, is by no means to be conceitedly and presumptuously repudiated, but is on the contrary to be respected.

and Bishop Mynster, says Professor Martensen, was one of the genuine witnesses to the truth.

Is this truth? To speak thus, is this perhaps also a way of witnessing to the truth? and by that address did Professor Martensen himself appear in the character of a witness to the truth, one of the genuine witnesses to the truth? Verily there is that which is more contrary to Christianity, and to the very nature of Christianity, than any heresy, any schism, more contrary than all heresies and all schisms combined, and that is, to *play* Christianity. But precisely in the very same sense that the child plays soldier, it is playing Christianity to take away the danger (Christianly, "witness" and "danger" correspond), and in place of this to introduce power (to be a danger for others), worldly goods, advantages, luxurious enjoyment of the most exquisite refinements—and then to play the game that Bishop Mynster was a witness to the truth, one of the genuine witnesses to the truth, to play it with such frightful earnestness that one cannot bring the game to a stop, but keeps on playing it into heaven itself, plays Bishop Mynster on into the holy chain of witnesses to the truth which stretches from the days of the Apostles to our times.

Postscript

This article, as one can see from the date, has lain [unpublished] for a considerable time.

So long as there was question of appointment to the episcopal see of Seeland,[3] I thought that I ought to say nothing publically concerning Professor Martensen; for whether he were to become bishop or not, in any case he was a candidate for this office, and presumably desired that so long as this situation lasted as little as possible should happen concerning him.

With Professor Martensen's nomination as bishop this consideration lapsed. But then again the article could not be published and therefore was not. My thought was that there was no reason for haste. Moreover, the nomination of Bishop Martensen called forth an attack upon him from another side and of an entirely different sort: it would have been more than superfluous for me to coincide with this attack; so I waited. My thought was, as I have said, that there was no reason for haste, and that nothing is lost by waiting. Someone may even find that something is gained, may find a deeper significance in the fact that the protest comes so tardily.

Autumn of 1854.

But a protest must be made against this representation of Bishop Mynster as a witness to the truth.

It may be said pretty nearly of Bishop Mynster that he carried a whole generation—it is therefore a difficulty bordering closely upon the impossible to introduce clarity in our confused religious conduct and concepts, so long as a truer illumination is not shed upon the truth of Bishop Mynster's preaching of Christianity, which after all it is my duty to shed, because Bishop Mynster, precisely Bishop Mynster, was, if one would so put it, my life's misfortune—not for the fact that he was not a witness to the truth (that circumstance would not be so dangerous), but for the fact that in addition to all the other advantages which he derived in the most ample measure from preaching Christianity, he had also the enjoyment of declaiming in quiet hours on Sundays and making up for it with worldly shrewdness on Mondays, giving the impression of being a man of character, a man of principle, who stands firm when everything vacillates, who does not fail when all are failing, etc., etc., whereas the truth is that he was worldly shrewd in a high degree, but weak, self-indulgent, and only great as a declaimer—and was my life's misfortune, if one would put it so (though in a very high sense, through the love of divine governance, it turned out to my profit, became my good fortune)—my misfortune was that, being brought up by a father now deceased, upon Mynster's sermons, and prompted by filial piety towards the deceased father, I honored this false draft instead of protesting it.

Now he is dead. God be praised that it could be put off as long as he lived. That was attained which toward the end I was about to despair of,[4] but nevertheless that was attained which was my thought, my wish, which also I can remember to have said once a long while ago to the aged Grundtvig: "Bishop Mynster must first live out his days and be buried with full music"—that was attained, he was indeed, if I may venture to say so, buried with full music. For the monument to him there has surely by this time been received pretty much all that will be received.

So I cannot keep silent longer, the protest must come, all the more serious for its tardiness, the protest against representing from the pulpit, that is, before God, Bishop Mynster as a witness to the truth; for that is false, and proclaimed in this way it is a falsehood which cries to heaven.

December 1854.

II. The *Fatherland*, Thursday, December 30, 1854

There the matter rests!

December 28, 1854.* S. Kierkegaard.

To represent from the pulpit Bishop *Mynster* as a witness to the truth, one of the genuine witnesses to the truth, to assign him a place in the holy chain, etc.—against this a protest must be raised. There the matter rests.

To represent him in this fashion is essentially to make him ridiculous. For I can easily put the thing in another way, attacking from another side. To represent a man who by preaching Christianity has attained

* This article, as one will see, is of December 28, delivered to the *Fatherland* when I saw that same evening, to my surprise, in the *Berlin News*, No. 302,[5] that after all Bishop Martensen has not, as I was prepared to expect, the same idiosyncrasy in relation to short articles of mine as at one time he avowed he had in relation to "the prolix Kierkegaardian literature,"[6] an idiosyncrasy which prevented him from making himself acquainted with it. This is what I saw, but what I neither saw nor see is what his article can accomplish, an article which properly does not require an explicit reply, since it does not alter the case in the least. Bishop Martensen maintains that I have identified the witness to the truth with the blood-witness, and that only thereby am I justified in denying that Bishop Mynster was a witness to the truth. That is not so. Neither in the *article*, where only at the last I point to the blood-witness (but surely the blood-witness too belongs to the witnesses to the truth, especially to the "genuine" witnesses to the truth, or what I have called "the first class according to the Christian protocol," which implies that I must have in mind many more witnesses to the truth than merely the blood-witnesses); so then, neither in the article nor in the *notes* appended to it—one can refer to them both—have I made the witness to the truth and the blood-witness identical, and in the notes I have quite distinctly pointed out the difference between preaching Christianity in such a way that the preacher is "a government official, a man of rank, and his preaching his own glittering career, rich in enjoyment," and on the other hand a "suffering witness to the truth," without maintaining in any way whatsoever that suffering must signify suffering unto death. And this difference is quite sufficient to prove that Bishop Mynster cannot be called a witness to the truth, one of the genuine witnesses to the truth, a link in the holy chain, etc.—On the other hand, as for the various matters about which Dr. Martensen speaks in defense of public morals, speaking presumably in his capacity as the duly elected Bishop of Seeland, but speaking also in the tone of a brawler and pugilist, bewailing the scandal occasioned by the step I have taken, talking about Jesuitism and the like, I may say that this makes absolutely no impression upon me. Partly (and this is the decisive point) because it rests upon a misunderstanding, and partly because Dr. Martensen is too subaltern a person to overawe me, especially since he has begun to wear velvet. Certainly a domestic cannot overawe anybody by his livery, but in the clothes of his master, the noble lord, he is still less awe-inspiring. Besides I am so accustomed to stand a blow, and to stand it until several years later the majority have come over to my opinion (only they forget that I had to stand the blow); so I may as well stand this blow, too—for the sake of elucidating the Christian concepts. And the judgment expressed about Bishop Mynster, one of the genuine witnesses to the truth, a link in the holy chain, must be protested. There the matter rests!

and enjoyed in the greatest measure all possible worldly goods and enjoyments, to represent him as a witness to the truth is as ridiculous as to talk about a maiden who is surrounded by her numerous troop of children. But the fact is, as Luther would say, "Everything that has to do with lechery people in this sinful world know all about, you are promptly understood if you talk about it; but about the Christian concepts they are not so well informed." Hence it is that people do not understand, and therefore censor it, when a protest is raised against a witness to the truth who from a Christian point of view is just as ridiculous as that maiden.

There are lots of things which one can be "at the same time," and it is true particularly of all insignificant things that one can be a number of them "at the same time." One can be both this and that, and at the same time a dilettante violinist, member of a lodge, *Schützenkönig,* etc. The significant thing has precisely this characteristic, that just in proportion as it is significant it is less possible for a man to be that *and* at the same time something else. And the definition "witness to the truth" is a very domineering definition; strictly speaking, it can be combined only with being, apart from that, nothing at all. The term "witness to the truth" stands in relation to the fact that Christianity is heterogeneous to the world, wherefore the "witness" must always be recognizable by heterogeneity to this world, by renunciation, by suffering, and this is the reason why such a mode of being is so little capable of being something else at the same time. But to want to have all worldly goods and advantages (the witness to the truth being what he is precisely by renunciation and suffering), and then at the same time to be a witness to the truth—one might Christianly say, "The deuce of a witness that is! Such a witness to the truth is not merely a monster but an impossibility, like a bird which is at the same time a fish, or like an iron tool which has the remarkable peculiarity of being made of wood."

Such is the situation. But remember it was not I who began the thing of measuring Bishop Mynster's life by the scale of a witness to the truth. No, it is a friend, Professor Martensen, who has done the deceased this scurvy service and furnished the occasion for me to say that, viewed under the illumination provided by Professor Martensen, Bishop Mynster was "in a high degree a worldly shrewd man, but weak, self-indulgent, and great only as a declaimer"—this scurvy service which yet cannot perhaps be called entirely disinterested, for the possible successor to the see of Seeland, who at present is the successor, was indeed well served by the suggestion of such an easy way of being himself promoted up to the rank of a witness to the truth.

If there actually is in this land so little sense of what Christianity is that a man might be unable to understand with what justification I must protest against this forgery in the strongest terms, and by drawing the most glaring contrasts, I can put the protest in another form. I maintain that by depicting from the pulpit Bishop Mynster as a witness to the truth, one of the holy chain of witnesses, a wrong is done in the highest degree to every other distinguished and well-deserving man in the land. A jurist like Privy Counselor Ørsted, a poet like Heiberg, a scholar like Madvig, a physician like Bang, theatrical artists like Nielsen, Rosenkilde, Physter, and so on in so many professions—all such men, although it cannot by any means be said that in their lifetime they are more agreeably situated and get more of the earthly goods and enjoyments than Bishop Mynster got, but on the contrary may be said to be situated less agreeably, all such men have exactly the same claim as Bishop Mynster to be buried as witnesses to the truth.

But the Protestant clergy still continue to have a curious crotchet in their heads. Although they have become in their "existence" entirely like men of every other class, who, without exceeding the limits prescribed by civil law, seek to develop what gifts they may have, and thereby strive to attain earthly rewards and pleasures like all the rest, nevertheless *at the same time* they want to be something more, to be witnesses to the truth. And this came very clearly to evidence in the memorial address made by Professor Martensen. Therefore a protest should be made as emphatically as possible, people's blood must be stirred, passions set in motion—and that of course can be done only when a man is not afraid of the immediate consequence, that many will become furious at him, which he ought not to fear but to understand, as a surgeon understands that the patient will shriek and kick. A protest must be made, and the blow for the provocation given should fall upon the head—and when the article came out Professor Martensen had long been the head.

So it ought to be; so it was; there the matter rests!

. . ."also out of filial piety towards a deceased father I honored the false draft (the semblance of being a man of character which Bishop Mynster presented) instead of protesting it." There the matter rests.

If the *friends* of the deceased, his adherents and admirers, when they are a bit more composed, will not understand that at least I have not had any advantage from my relationship to Bishop Mynster—I pray them to examine the account—that in my relationship to him I have shown a resignation which very rarely is shown by a younger man to an elder, that I have done and borne what very seldom a younger man does and bears in relation to an elder—if they will not understand this, and understand also what is implied in it, that they owe me a debt of gratitude for the many years I have borne with the deceased—if they will not understand this, well, in God's name, it's their affair.

To the *enemies* of the deceased I would say, not to exult and rejoice as though they had gained something, which, as I see it, they have not gained. Their position, as I view it, is entirely unchanged; and, if the occasion were to present itself, it would not be impossible that I might still come forward in the usual way (precious memories—how gladly I did it!) to fight against his enemies in behalf of Bishop Mynster, the pastor of my deceased father.

In Denmark Bishop Mynster was unique in his kind; there is only one person who is in the right against him, and that is I. I have not condemned Bishop Mynster; no, but in the hand of divine governance I was the occasion for Bishop Mynster to pass judgment upon himself. His sermon on Sunday either he did not know on Monday, or he dared not or would not acknowledge it as his—for, ironically enough, I simple-mindedly was his own sermon on Monday; and if on Mondays Bishop Mynster had not with worldly shrewdness shirked the duty of assuming the logical consequence of his Sunday sermon, if he had put into effect a mode of existence and action which corresponded with the tenor of his Sunday address, instead of helping himself out with worldly shrewdness of various patterns, his life would then have taken on an entirely different aspect.

But such a judgment only an enemy can be in haste to pronounce as long as the man lives. He who is devoted to him says, "The judgment must be postponed until the very last; he might indeed even at the last moment avert the judgment and do an immense amount of good by a little word; and everything ought to be done that resignation is able to do in order to move him to utter this word."

So then, there the matter rests: also out of filial piety towards a deceased father I honored this false draft instead of protesting it.

"I was his own sermon on Monday," that I was; for by enduring year after year this provocation, and enduring it moreover with unaltered resignation as I did, I have become something different from what I was, or it became clearer and clearer to me what I was, "my life's misfortune by the love of divine governance turned out to my profit, became my good fortune." My relationship to Bishop Mynster during many years was a unity of a deeply laid purpose on my part which I pursued with the greatest solicitude, and of my own development by the cooperation of divine governance. It will be understood then that I cannot take account of what every anonymous writer, every "Aesculapius" [the signature in the *Copenhagen Post*] brings out in a newspaper, or what a serious-minded man from Nørrebro with all the seriousness of the *Flying Post* says to explain to people that I lack seriousness.

And as for the cry which is heard, this cry about attacking a dead man who cannot answer, etc., it may be said of this that it is a misunderstanding, also that it is chiefly a hubbub of women. I have told how the case stands: "God be praised that it could be postponed as long as the old man lived; at the end I was on the point of despairing of it."

Yes, God be praised that I was spared from being obliged to embitter in the most frightful measure the last years of an old man's life by showing that compared with the Christianity of the New Testament the Mynsterish preaching and ecclesiastical rule (if it would not make the admission, and make it as solemnly as possible, that it was not the Christianity of the New Testament) was an illusion of the senses, that all his "earnestness and wisdom" was, Christianly considered, *lèse-majesté* against Christianity, which scorns in its divine majesty to be served (as if it were politics, a kingdom of this world) by worldly shrewdness. Moreover, viewing the case from another side, I have neglected nothing which might be incumbent upon me as a duty towards the cause I have the honor to serve. Toward the end of his life I pressed upon the old man as closely as I could (but in an indirect way, by *Training in Christianity*) the question whether he would give battle. By what he did[7] I was to my sorrow convinced how weak he was. Out of consideration for him I concealed this from the contemporaries, and said it only to him personally, as emphatically as possible. However, since this fact of his weakness was a fact, I had to employ a little precautionary measure in view of the extremest eventuality. That was done in *Self-Examination*, in which, as one can see, I dissected him, but did it to be sure so hiddenly that not even his enemies have seen it, so hiddenly that newspaper articles have quoted this passage to my discredit, regarding it as a eulogy of him, whereas just there I had employed my precautionary measure in view of the ultimate which might occur, and said in effect: "Your Reverence is absolutely not in the character of your sermons." But I hid that. And why? Naturally because I always wished, if it were possible, to carry out my first thought, which was so dear to me: Mynster shall live out his days and be buried with full music. Privately I have talked emphatically enough to Bishop Mynster; in my writings I have carried out my task, and by my existence, my activity as an author, I am a constant attack upon the Mynsterish preaching of Christianity, yet in such a way that at any instant it was possible for Bishop Mynster by making an admission to come to an agreement with me, so that I would have been his defense. But I know very well how most people read, how thoughtlessly, and that therefore, if I wanted to do so (and that I did for several reasons, "also out of filial piety towards a deceased father"), by inserting a little compliment to him there was the *charmant* possibility of making most people believe that we were in agreement, so that my activity consequently had the effect of enhancing his prestige in the eyes of most people, and every sort of disturbance, scene, catastrophe, situations which were so distasteful to the old man, were happily avoided. About our unity the old man knew better, both because he read my works rather carefully, and because I talked to him in private, although he certainly never doubted my sincere devotion to him, even when it appeared to me most imperiled.

So then, God be praised that this was attained which was my first thought, my wish which was so dear to me, which toward the end I was so near despairing of, that Mynster shall live out his days and be buried with full music; the monument will also be erected in his honor—but then no further, and least of all must he go down in history as a witness to the truth, one of the genuine witnesses to the truth, one of the holy chain of witnesses. There the matter rests!

III. The *Fatherland*, Friday, January 12, 1855

A challenge to me by Pastor Paludan-Möller

January 11. S. Kierkegaard.

Pastor Peludan-Möller has published a brochure against me which a reviewer in the *Berlin News* has of course extolled as exceedingly fine—a situation which recalls the scene in *Figaro*[8] where Bartolo and Basil thank one another in sign-language for having espoused the cause of Signorina Marcellina. Honestly, I find it quite reasonable that, seeing that I, even if I would, cannot possibly manage to answer or thank all of the many who oppose me—I find it quite reasonable in them that they contrive to answer and thank one another reciprocally.

So then a brochure against me by Pastor P. M., and in it a feature to which the *Berlin News* has promptly given the greatest possible publicity, namely, a challenge to me which assumes perhaps (who knows?) that as usual I will preserve silence. In my article in the *Fatherland* I said of Mynster's preaching that "it soft-pedals, slurs over, suppresses, omits, something decisively Christian." That gives occasion for challenging me to prove this with the New Testament for reference, so that somehow it might be worth noticing. For that is the way Pastor P. M. would confute it.

"So that somehow it might be worth noticing"—what can this mean? If I now were to enter into this plan, I might find in the end that I was an April fool, because I had not made sure of an authentic interpretation of the phrase "so that somehow it might be worth noticing."

This, however, I shall overlook; but the reason why I do not propose to enter into this plan is that I am fearful it might be a trap, so that, if I went into it, it would come about that the whole question and the statement of it would in a short time become quite different from what it is. The question is: "Was Bishop Mynster a witness to the truth, one of the genuine witnesses to the truth, one link in the holy chain of witnesses? Is this the truth?" The question is about an energetic protest from my side against representing from the pulpit Bishop Mynster as a witness to the truth, one of the genuine witnesses to the truth, one link in the holy chain of witnesses. And this would now perhaps be consigned to oblivion, the whole thing being transformed into a prolix, learned, theological investigation, with citations and citations, etc., about Bishop Mynster's preaching, an investigation in which by reason of the great number and learning of the participants we would soon find ourselves buried up to our ears. No, I thank you!*

* I beg of everyone who may be willing to follow my advice that, if he is minded to make a public utterance, he would observe the strictest diet with respect to not entering into general, broad, learned, prolix, academic discussions with lexicon and grammar and the immense mass of scholarly apparatus and the multitude of citations, enough to obscure even what is as clear as the sun; for thereby he will only be of service to my opponent, who precisely by this device (just as one quenches fire with featherbeds, and as one produces oblivion by prolixity) may manage to elude the short, clear factual point, the point which perhaps for the Established Church is definitive, namely, this thing of representing from the pulpit Bishop Mynster as a witness to the truth, one of the genuine

What I have said is short and to the point. Bishop Mynster's preaching soft-pedals, slurs over, suppresses, omits something of the most decisively Christian. When that is said, everyone can see it, especially the plain man. To the man who, being better educated, knows all about this sort of thing I can say: Bishop Mynster's preaching is related to the Christianity of the New Testament as Epicureanism is to Stoicism, or as cultivation, refinement, education, is related to a fundamental change of character, to a radical cure. In no instance does his preaching bring Christianity up to what it is everywhere in the New Testament, namely, a breach, the very deepest and most incurable breach with this world—any more than did Bishop Mynster's life (as is easily explained by his infinite dread of everything radical) resemble even in the remotest way a breach with this world—unless we are satisfied with the explanation: One is *tout-à-fait* a man of the world, a man entirely of this world, and "at the same time" one has broken with this world—which corresponds with attaining and enjoying all worldly goods and advantages by the preaching of Christianity, and being "at the same time" a witness to the truth; and that, as I showed (alluding also to maidenhood, virginity, as a beautiful symbol of heterogeneity to this world) corresponds to a virgin with her numerous flock of children.

Here I might end. Let me, however, add a few words prompted by an utterance made as I recall by one of his defenders,[9] the justice of which even the most zealous admirers of Mynster will surely admit. "Bishop Mynster was not really a preacher of repentance." But this, especially in the case of a witness to the truth, is a dubious recommendation; for all true Christian preaching is first and foremost a preaching of repentance. "Bishop Mynster was rather a preacher of peace." But this, especially in the case of a witness to the truth, is a dubious recommendation: in the character of a preacher of peace to proclaim the doctrine of Him Who Himself said (these are known to be His own words), "I came not to bring peace but dissension"—He came indeed into the world not to enjoy but to suffer. And therefore it is that I have said of Bishop Mynster, that viewed in the light of a witness to the truth and Christianly appraised, he was self-indulgent: self-indulgently he loved "peace," the first requisite for enjoying life, according to the

witnesses to the truth, one in the holy chain of witnesses, a statement which was not improved but aggravated, to the detriment of the Church, by the ill-advised impudence of this same man—the chief pastor of the Church, the Honorable and Right Reverend Bishop *Martensen*—in the face of a protest which Christianly was justified in the very highest degree.

old saying of Epicurus,[10] *nihil beatum nisi quietum*, i.e. the first requisite for the enjoyment of life is peace.

Let then so much suffice for this time. It is an exception I have made. In the main I must leave it to the many who oppose me to answer and thank one another reciprocally.

IV. The *Fatherland*, January 29, 1855

The point at issue with Bishop Martensen,

as conclusive, Christianly, for the hitherto dubious state of the Established Church, Christianly considered.

January 26, 1855. S. Kierkegaard.

The point at issue is this: about representing from the pulpit Bishop Mynster as a witness to the truth, one of the genuine witnesses to the truth, one in the holy chain of witnesses.

This it is which must constantly be held fast, this it is which everyone who takes the matter seriously must every day have stamped upon his mind, in order to be able to hold it fast in spite of the mass of confusion which in the past days has been poured out through the press.

This is the issue—and it will be evident that the new Bishop, by thus canonizing Bishop Mynster, makes the Established Church, from the Christian point of view, an impudent indecency.

For if Bishop Mynster is a witness to the truth, then, as even the blindest can see, every priest in the land is a witness to the truth. For what was distinguished and extraordinary in Bishop Mynster has nothing whatever to do with this question whether he was a witness to the truth or was not a witness to the truth, a question which has to do with character, life, existence; and in that respect Bishop Mynster was perfectly homogeneous with every other priest in the land who does not offend against civil justice. So every priest in the land is at the same time a witness to the truth.

But when the ordinary preaching of Christianity here in this land, the official preaching of Christianity, performed by royal functionaries, men of consequence, whose preaching is their worldly career—when this preaching of Christianity is put alongside of the New Testament, alongside of what Jesus Christ (the poor, humiliated man, mocked and spat upon) requires of "a disciple of Jesus Christ" (and such surely the priest should be, if he is to be accounted a witness to the truth), alongside of what Jesus Christ requires, that the doctrine be preached "for naught," that the doctrine be preached in poverty, in abasement, with renunciation of everything, in the most unconditional heterogeneity to this world, at the furthest remove from all use or application of worldly power, etc.—then it is seen only too easily that the official preaching of Christianity, compared with the New Testament, can only be defended (if it can be) in the way I one time indicated by the pseudonym Anti-Climacus. With respect to this, however, it is to be noted, that the Established Church has hitherto let nothing be heard from it, has not in the remotest way showed a disposition to make known how remotely it is related to New Testament Christianity, and it is not even possible to say of it with truth that it is an effort in the direction of coming closer to the Christianity of the New Testament.

On the contrary, so soon as it is said that a priest is at the same time a witness to the truth, that very instant the Established Church is, Christianly considered, an impudent indecency. With this assertion the Established Church can no longer be regarded as an extreme instance of leniency which nevertheless is related to the Christianity of the New Testament, but it is openly an apostasy from the Christianity of the New Testament; with this assertion it is, Christianly, an impudent indecency, an effort in the direction of making a fool of God, making a fool of Him, as though we did not understand what He is talking about in His Word; for when in His Word He talks about preaching the doctrine for naught, we understand it to mean that preaching is of course a livelihood, the surest way to bread and steady promotion; when in His Word He talks about preaching the Word in poverty, we understand thereby some thousands yearly in stipend; when in His Word He talks about preaching the Word in lowliness, we understand it as making a career, becoming Your Excellency; and by heterogeneity to this world we understand a royal functionary, a man of consequence; by abhorrence for the use and employment of worldly power we understand using and being secured by worldly power; by suffering for the doctrine we understand using the police against others; and by renunciation of everything we understand getting everything, the most exquisite refinements, for which the heathen has in vain licked his fingers—and at the same time we are witnesses to the truth.

The Honorable and Right Reverend Bishop Martenson, Privy Counselor (whoever it may be he counsels)[11] transforms the whole Church

Establishment, Christianly understood, into an impudent indecency by representing from the pulpit Bishop Mynster as a witness to the truth, one in the holy chain of witnesses. No man who bears in mind what Christianity teaches, that he is going to confront an eternal responsibility, a judgment (where the Judge is the humbled man, mocked, spat upon, crucified, Who said, "Follow me," "my kingdom is not of this world"), an accounting in which acts of *lèse-majesté* against Christianity are the crimes last forgiven—no one who bears this in mind can hold his peace with regard to Bishop Martensen's new doctrine defining what is to be understood by a witness to the truth, one in the holy chain of witnesses—no one can hold his peace, even though (which to me is neither here nor there), even though I should be the only one who does not keep silent; it is enough for me that in eternity it will be noted that I did not hold my peace.

I here repeat my protest, not softened but sharpened: I would rather gamble, carouse, fornicate, steal, murder, than take part in making a fool of God; rather pass my days in bowling alleys and billiard halls, my nights in gaming and at masquerades, than take part in that kind of seriousness which Bishop Martensen calls Christian seriousness; yea, I would rather make a fool of God bluntly, climb up to a high place or go out into the open where I am alone with Him, and say, "Thou art a wretched God, worth no more than to be made a fool of"—rather than make a fool of Him by solemnly representing that I am holy, that my life is sheer zeal and ardor for Christianity, yet—O cursed ambiguity!—in such a way, be it noted, that "at the same time" this is constantly my temporal and earthly profit; representing that my life's first and last interest is enthusiasm for preaching the Gospel, yet in such a way, be it noted, that there are certain things I prefer both first and last to ignore, and when they are talked about I act as if I didn't understand them, as if I didn't understand what God is talking about, that what He talks about is suffering for the doctrine, suffering hunger and thirst and cold and nakedness and imprisonment and scourging, that this is what He understands by being a witness to the truth, and that if I shrink back from these terms and would prefer a merrier path, prefer that the preaching of Christianity might be like every other human labor, or rather even richer in pleasure than the others, so that if it is practicable, if in this way I can become blessed like the witness to the truth, I shall thank my God for it and restrain my cursed mouth from twaddling about being at the same time a witness to the truth, and finally, if I cannot control my tongue, I shall at least confine myself to talking about this in the parlor, over a cup of tea with my wife and some prating friends, but keep a watch upon myself in the pulpit.

But from the pulpit—therefore before God—to represent Bishop Mynster as a witness to the truth, one of the genuine witnesses to the truth, one in the holy chain of witnesses—before God, whose presence was assured by calling upon Him to be present in the prayer before the sermon—to represent him (for this too was done), to represent this man—God in heaven!—before the congregation as a pattern, before a Christian congregation, and therefore as a Christian pattern! So the "way" has now become a different one, not that of the New Testament: in humiliation, hated, forsaken, persecuted, condemned to suffer in this world—no, the way is: admired, acclaimed, crowned with garlands, accorded the accolade of knighthood as the reward of a brilliant career! And as the "way" has become a different one, indeed the very opposite, so too has the interpretation of Biblical passages become different. When we read in the New Testament the passage which Bishop Martensen used in the memorial address, Hebrews 13:7, "Remember those who had the rule over you . . . and considering the issue of their life, imitate their faith," this is not any longer to be understood to mean, consider the issue of their life, i.e. see that their life was sheer renunciation and sheer suffering for the doctrine; remain true to yourselves until the last, do not regret having sacrificed everything, but also in death, perhaps a martyr's death, preserve the boldness of faith—in this way it is now no longer to be understood; no, you shall now understand it thus, as Bishop Martensen teaches: Consider Bishop Mynster, see the issue of his life, consider that he attained the rank of Excellency; consider the issue of his life, you yourselves know what preparations were made for the most pompous funeral: consider this, and follow him, he is the way, not Christ, who says warningly, "What is exalted among men is an abomination in the sight of God" (Luke 16:15).

If my memory is not at fault, a complaint has just now been made somewhere in our land by the Bishop that a church was improperly used for a political meeting. Suppose that somewhere else people had the idea of using the church for a ball—what is that in comparison with using the church under the name of Christian worship to make a fool of God! But of course when the bishop himself does that, no one can complain of it...to the Bishop.

For my part I have no mind to make complaint to anybody, I merely repeat my protest. Maybe I shall not be understood—well, I am understood by God, and I understand myself. Maybe it will go ill with me—well, that is what the New Testament presupposes. Maybe I shall not succeed—well, in a Christian sense, victory is only won by defeat!

But when scandal has been given, a scandal must be raised against it, and one must not complain that the step I have taken has unfortunately[12] aroused so much scandal. No, it has not yet aroused scandal enough in proportion to the scandal of representing from the pulpit Bishop Mynster as a witness to the truth, one of the genuine witnesses to the truth, one link in the holy chain. "The blood must be stirred, passion set in motion"—if it is visited upon the operator, that is just a part of the operation. After more than forty years of conjuring tricks performed with great worldly shrewdness, when the conjurer moreover was made a witness of the truth, one cannot come off easily, unless one would contrive to be transformed, together with one's protest, into a little conjuring act as a continuation of the old enchantment.

V. The *Fatherland*, January 29, 1855

Two new witnesses to the Truth

January 26. S. Kierkegaard.

"There is a diversity of gifts," Bishop Martensen says so justly in the *Berlin News*, No. 302. The late Bishop had an extraordinary gift for covering over the weak side of the Established Church and its frailties; the new Bishop Martensen, also a gifted man, has a rare gift for laying bare, by every least thing he undertakes to do, one or another weak side of the Established Church. The late Bishop had an unusual gift for yielding shrewdly, for giving way, for accommodating himself; Bishop Martensen (for there is a diversity of gifts) has the gift, at this time especially perilous to the Church, of wanting to brave it out. Yet it might be, possibly it is the thought of divine governance, that the Establishment should survive as long as the old man lived, who also was gifted to that effect, and that after his death the Establishment shall fall, and to that effect we have Bishop Martensen in the episcopal chair, a man who is gifted precisely in that direction. Surely nothing more than Bishop Martensen is needed to bring that about, I perhaps shall be quite superfluous, or what I can manage to do will be something entirely subordinate, and yet even in this regard I am not wholly without gifts, inasmuch as I have the gift to see...what Bishop Martensen lays bare.

Now what I protested against was the linguistic solecism of calling what we mean by priests, deans, bishops, "witnesses" or "witnesses to the truth"; it was against this linguistic usage I protested, because it is blasphemous, sacrilegious—but Bishop Martensen is resolved to brave it out, as one may see from his ordination[13] address,* where he spouts incessantly about witnessing, being a witness, a witness to the truth, etc.

In the New Testament Christ calls the Apostles and the disciples "witnesses," requires them to witness to Him. Let us see now what is to be understood by this. These are men who by the renunciation of all things, in poverty, in lowliness, and thus ready for every suffering, were to go out into the world which expresses mortal hostility to the Christian way of life. This is what Christ calls "witnesses" and "witnessing."

What we call "priest," "dean," "bishop," indicates a livelihood, like every other employment in the community, and in a community, be it noted, where, since all call themselves "Christians," no danger is in the remotest degree connected with teaching Christianity, where on the contrary this profession may be considered one of the most agreeable and the most highly honored.

Now I ask, is there the least resemblance between these priests, deans, bishops, and what Christ calls "witnesses"? Or is it not just as ridiculous to call such priests, deans, bishops, "witnesses," just as ridiculous as to call a maneuver on the town common a "battle"? No, if the clergy want to be called "witnesses," "witnesses to the truth," they must also resemble what the New Testament calls witnesses, witnesses to the truth; if they have no mind at all to resemble what the New Testament understands by witnesses, witnesses to the truth, neither must they be called that; they may be called "teachers," "civil functionaries," "professors," "councilors," in short, what you will, only not "witnesses to the truth."

But Dr. Martensen remains indefatigable in affirming that they are witnesses, witnesses to the truth. If the clergy understand their own interests, they will not hesitate to beg the Bishop to go easy with this linguistic usage which makes their whole order ridiculous. For it is true that I know several men who are highly respectable, competent,

* The speeches made on that occasion have now come out in print. The presentation address by Dean Tryde, a thing of naught, is distinguished by the fact that, as if it were something, a footnote remarks, "The author feels called upon to declare that naught has been omitted, naught has been changed."

eminently competent clergyman; but I venture to assert that in the whole realm there is not a single one who viewed in the light of a witness to the truth is not comical.

And, to put it mildly, it is not seemly for a bishop to make the whole clerical order ridiculous, neither is it seemly for a bishop to transform a solemn action like an episcopal consecration into something one does not know whether to laugh or cry over, all for the sake of braving out the linguistic use of "witnesses" and of "witnesses to the truth." The ordination occurred the day after Christmas, the feast of the martyr Stephen. How satirical! The Bishop takes occasion to say, among other things, that the word "witness to the truth" "rings on this day with a peculiar sound." That is undeniable—only that peculiar sound is a dissonance, for the fact that either Stephen becomes ridiculous by the help of "various witnesses to the truth" whom Dr. Martensen has ready to hand, or all of them become ridiculous in the character of witnesses under the light shed upon them by Stephen.

VI. The *Fatherland*, March 20, 1855

With regard to Bishop Mynster's death

Mark 13:2. Seest thou these great buildings?
There shall not . . .

March 31, 1854.* S. Kierkegaard.

Certainly it would have been most desirable if it had ended with Bishop Mynster saying to the nation straightforwardly and as solemnly as possible that what he represented was not the New Testament Christianity but, if one would put it so, a pious tempering and mitigation of it, which in manifold ways was enveloped in illusion.

This did not come to pass!

For my part I maintain inalterably my assertion, only that now I utter aloud and publicly that concerning which I dealt secretly with the deceased Bishop, hidden from his enemies (for against them I fought for him), hidden from the many, who surely had no presentiment of it: my assertion that official Christianity, the official preaching of Christianity, is in no sense the Christianity of the New Testament.

* Notice the year and the date. [Bishop Mynster died at the beginning of February; so this was written not quite two months later.]

In any case this then must be admitted as loudly and openly as possible, so that divine governance, if it might be pleased to do so, could take a hand, and then we would have opportunity to see whether it is willing to permit such a preaching of Christianity. But without such an admission the official preaching of Christianity, by giving itself out to be the Christianity of the New Testament, is—unconsciously or well-meaningly—an illusion. Christianity cannot be well served by calling this sort of thing Christianity, with the implication that it is the Christianity of the New Testament; and Christianly the congregation cannot be well served thereby, for it fails to observe what Christianity according to the New Testament is.

Feast of the Annunciation

O thou, whosoever thou art under whose eye this falls—when I read in the New Testament the life of our Lord Jesus Christ here on earth, and see what he meant by being a Christian—and when I reflect that now we are Christians by the millions, just as many Christians as we are men, that from generation to generation Christians by the millions are handed over for inspection by eternity—frightful! For that there is something wrong with this, nothing can be more certain. Say for thyself what good it does—even if it were ever so pious and well-meant!—what good it does to wish (lovingly?) to confirm thee in the vain conceit that thou art a Christian, or to wish to alter the definition of what it is to be a Christian, in order presumably that thou mayest more securely enjoy this life; what good it does thee, or rather is not this precisely to do thee harm, since it is to help thee to let the temporal life go by unused in a Christian sense—until thou art standing in eternity where thou art not a Christian, in case thou wast not one, and where it is impossible to become a Christian? Thou who readest this, say to thyself: Was I not in the right, and am I not, in saying that first and foremost everything must be done to make it perfectly definite what is required in the New Testament for being a Christian; that first and foremost everything must be done in order that at least we might become attentive?

VII. The *Fatherland*, Wednesday, March 21, 1855

Is this Christian worship, or is it treating God as a fool?

[A question of conscience (to ease my conscience)]

May 1854. S. Kierkegaard.

When at a given time the state of the case is this, that, being privately aware, one makes as if nothing were the matter, whereas as a matter of fact everything is changed:

when the *teacher* (the priest) is bound by an oath upon the New Testament, is ordained, whereas as a matter of fact he not only has no portrait-resemblance to a disciple of Jesus Christ, but not even a caricature resemblance; no, is precisely the direct opposite of it, the trivial contrary;

when the *doctrine* which is preached as God's Word is different from God's Word for the fact that it is not the same, nor the opposite, but neither one thing nor the other, which is precisely what is most contrary to Christianity and to God's Word;

when the *situation* in which we speak (and the situation is what really defines how we are to understand what is said), when the situation no more resembles that in the New Testament than a bourgeois parlor or the child's playroom resembles the most frightful conflict we are confronted with in the most appalling reality, or resembles it even less, in so far as people spiritlessly pretend that the two situations resemble one another;

when the state of the case is this—and then, privately aware of it, people make as if nothing were the matter: is this then Christian worship, or is it treating God as a fool, treating Him as a fool by such an official worship, perhaps with the notion that, if only we call this Christianity, we can get away with it, by preachifying this at Him every Sunday we can make Him believe that this is Christianity?

By way of explanation

Ascension Day.

1. *As to what I have said of the teacher (the priest), that he is the trivial contrary.*

The portraitlike description of the priest is this: a half worldly, half Churchly civil servant, a person of rank, who (with the hope of promotion according to seniority, and of becoming in his turn recipient of a knightly order—how thoroughly in the spirit of the New Testament!) makes certain of a living for himself and his family, if necessary by the help of the police (who exact the tithes), (is this, I wonder, in compliance with the word of the Apostle, 1 Corinthians 9:26, "not to run uncertainly"?*), makes certain of a living, supports himself by the fact that Jesus Christ was crucified, maintaining that this profound earnestness (this imitation of Jesus Christ?) is the Christianity of the New Testament, complaining sadly and with sighs that unfortunately there are so few true Christians—a fact which is sure enough—and for all that he walks in long robes, which Christ, however, does not exactly recommend when both in Mark and Luke He says (Mark 12:38; Luke 20:46), "Beware of those who go about in long robes."

2. *As to what I have said about the "situation."*

In the New Testament the situation is this: the speaker, our Lord Jesus Christ, Himself absolutely expressing opposition, stands in a world which in turn absolutely expresses opposition to Him and to His teaching. When of the individual Christ requires faith, then (and with this we have a sharper definition of what He understands by faith), then by reason of the situation this is not feasible without coming into a relationship with the surrounding world which perhaps involves mortal danger; when Christ says, "Confess me before the world," "Follow me," or when He says, "Come unto me," etc., etc., then, by reason of the situation which furnishes the more express understanding, the consequences will always be exposure to danger, perhaps to mortal danger. On the other hand, where all are Christians, the situation is this: to call oneself a Christian is the means whereby one secures oneself against all sorts of inconveniences and discomforts, and the means whereby one secures worldly goods, comforts, profit, etc., etc. But we make as if nothing had happened, we declaim about believing ("He who

* The Apostle understands it thus: "I buffet my body" in order not to run uncertainly.

knows best, that is our priest"[14]), about confessing Christ before the world, about following Him, etc., etc.; and orthodoxy flourishes in the land, no heresy, no schism, orthodoxy everywhere, the orthodoxy which consists in playing the game of Christianity.

VIII. The *Fatherland*, Thursday, March 22, 1855

What must be done

—whether by me or by another

Monday in Whitsun Week. S. Kierkegaard.

First and foremost, and on the greatest possible scale, an end must be put to the whole official—well-meaning—falsehood which well-meaningly—conjures up and maintains the illusion that what is preached is Christianity, the Christianity of the New Testament. Here is a case where no quarter must be given. If the Freethinkers have already dealt this falsehood a pretty shrewd blow, it can be only more forcible (if one does not wish otherwise) when he who fights has not Satan on his side but God.

Then when that is done, the question must be put in this form: After all, is not this really the true situation, that from generation to generation things have so gone from bad to worse with us men, that we men from generation to generation are so degenerate, so demoralized, have to such a degree become hardly more than beasts, that unfortunately the situation is such that—instead of the impudent fudge about Christianity being perfectible,[15] and we advancing, to such a point indeed that Christianity no longer satisfies us—that we wretched, pitiable men, who are priced by the dozen or the score, when it comes to the point are not really able to bear this divine thing which is the Christianity of the New Testament, and that therefore we must be content with the sort of religiousness which is now the official thing—when already it has been made known, you are to note, that it is not the Christianity of the New Testament? In this way the case must now be stated, and the question must be put, whether perhaps it is with the human race as it is with the individual, who the older he grows the more good-for-nothing he becomes—something he cannot alter and therefore must humbly put up with—whether it is perhaps the same with the race, so that it cannot be altered, and it is not God's requirement of us that we should alter it, but we must put up with it, humbly acknowledging our wretchedness; whether the human race has not now reached the age when it is literally true that no longer is there to be found or to be born an individual who is capable of being a Christian in the New Testament sense. In this way the case must be stated: away then, away with all optical illusions! Out with the truth! Out with the declaration that we no longer are capable of being Christians in the New Testament sense!—and, for all that, we feel the need of daring to hope in an eternal blessedness, which we also might get on very different terms than those proposed by the New Testament.

When the case is stated thus, it will become apparent whether there is anything true in this expectation, whether it has the consent of divine governance—if not, then everything must fall to pieces, in order that in this horror the individual might again come into existence who could bear the Christianity of the New Testament. But an end must be put to the official—well-meaning—falsehood.

IX. The *Fatherland*, Monday, March 26, 1855

The religious situation

January 1855. S. Kierkegaard.

The religious situation in our country is: Christianity (that is, the Christianity of the New Testament—and everything else is not Christianity, least of all by calling itself such), Christianity does not exist—as almost anyone must be able to see as well as I.

We have, if you will, a complete crew of bishops, deans, and priests; learned men, eminently learned, talented, gifted, humanly well-meaning; they all declaim—doing it well, very well, eminently well, or tolerably well, or badly—but not one of them is in the character of the Christianity of the New Testament. But if such is the case, the existence of this Christian crew is so far from being, Christianly considered, advantageous to Christianity that it is far rather a peril, because it is so infinitely likely to give rise to a false impression and the false inference that when we have such a complete crew we must of course have Christianity, too. A geographer, for example, when he has assured himself of the existence of this crew, would think that he was thoroughly justified in putting into his geography the statement that the Christian religion prevails in the land.

We have what one might call a complete inventory of churches, bells, organs, benches, alms-boxes, foot-warmers, tables, hearses, etc. But when Christianity does not exist, the existence of this inventory, so far from being, Christianly considered, an advantage, is far rather a peril, because it is so infinitely likely to give rise to a false impression and the false inference that when we have such a complete Christian inventory we must of course have Christianity, too. A statistician, for example, when he had assured himself of the existence of this Christian inventory, would think that he was thoroughly justified in putting into his statistics the statement that the Christian religion is the prevailing one in the land.

We are what is called a "Christian" nation—but in such a sense that not a single one of us is in the character of the Christianity of the New Testament, any more than I am, who again and again have repeated, and do now repeat, that I am only a poet. The illusion of a Christian nation is due doubtless to the power which number exercises over the imagination. I have not the least doubt that every single individual in the nation will be honest enough with God and with himself to say in solitary conversation, "If I must be candid, I do not deny that I am not a Christian in the New Testament sense; if I must be honest, I do not deny that my life cannot be called an effort in the direction of what the New Testament calls Christianity, in the direction of denying myself, renouncing the world, dying from it, etc.; rather the earthly and the temporal become more and more important to me with every year I live." I have not the least doubt that everyone will, with respect to ten of his acquaintances, let us say, be able to hold fast to the view that they are not Christians in the New Testament sense, and that their lives are not even an effort in the direction of becoming such. But when there are 100,000, one becomes confused—They tell a ludicrous story about an inkeeper, a story moreover which is related incidentally by one of my pseudonyms,[16] but I would use it again because it has always seemed to me to have a profound meaning. It is said that he sold his beer by the bottle for a cent less than he paid for it; and when a certain man said to him, "How does that balance the account? That means to spend money," he replied, "No, my friend, it's the big number that does it"—big number, that also in our time is the almighty power. When one has laughed at this story, one would do well to take to heart the lesson which warns against the power which number exercises over the imagination. For there can be no doubt that this innkeeper knew very well that one bottle of beer which he sold for 3 cents meant a loss of 1 cent when it cost him 4 cents. Also with regard to ten bottles the innkeeper will be able to hold fast that it is a loss. But 100,000 bottles! Here the big number stirs the imagination, the round number runs away with it, and the innkeeper becomes dazed—it's a profit, says he, for the big number does it. So also with the calculation which arrives at a Christian nation by adding up units which are not Christian, getting the result by means of the notion that the big number does it. For true Christianity this is the most dangerous of all illusions, and at the same time it is of all illusions precisely the one to which every man is prone; for number (the high number, when it gets up to 100,000, into the millions) tallies precisely with the imagination. But Christianly of course the calculation is wrong, and a Christian nation composed of units which honestly admit that they are not Christians, *item* honestly admit that their life cannot in any sense be called an effort in the direction of what the New Testament understands by Christianity—such a Christian nation is an impossibility. On the other hand, a knave could not wish to find a better hiding-place than behind such phrases as "the nation is Christian," "the people are making a Christian endeavor," since it is almost as difficult to come to close quarters with such phrases as it would be if one were to say, "N. N. is a Christian, N. N. is engaged in Christian endeavor."

But inasmuch as Christianity is spirit, the sobriety of spirit, the honesty of eternity, there is of course nothing which to its detective eye is so suspicious as are all fantastic entities: Christian states, Christian lands, a Christian people, and (how marvelous!) a Christian world. And even if there were something true in this talk about Christian peoples and states—but, mind you, only when all mediating definitions, all divergencies from the Christianity of the New Testament, are honestly and honorably pointed out and kept in evidence—yet it is certain that at this point a monstrous criminal offense has been perpetrated, yea, everything this world has hitherto seen in the way of criminal affairs is a mere bagatelle in comparison with this crime, which has been carried on from generation to generation throughout long ages, eluding human justice, but has not yet got beyond the arm of divine justice.

This is the religious situation. And to obviate if possible a waste of time I will at once anticipate a turn which one will perhaps give the matter. Let me explain by means of another case. If there were living in the land a poet who in view of the ideal of what it is to love talked in this fashion: "Alas, I must myself admit that I cannot truly be said to be in love; neither will I play the hypocrite and say that I am endeavoring more and more in this direction, for the truth unfortunately is that things are rather going backward with me. Moreover, my observation convinces me that in the whole land there is not a single person who can be said to be truly in love"—then the inhabitants of the land could reply to him, and in a certain degree with justice: "Yes, my good poet, that may be true enough with your ideals; but we are content, we find ourselves happy with what we call being in love, and that settles it." But such can never be the case with Christianity. The New Testament indeed settles what Christianity is, leaving it to eternity to pass judgment upon us. In fact the priest is bound by an oath upon the New Testament—so it is not possible to regard that as Christianity which men like best and prefer to call Christianity. As soon as we assume that we may venture to give the matter this turn, Christianity is *eo ipso* done away with, and the priest's oath...but here I break off, I do not wish to draw the inference before they constrain me further to do so, and even then I do not wish to do it. But if we do not dare to give the matter this turn, there are only two ways open to us: either (as I propose) honestly and honorably to make an admission as to how we are related to the Christianity of the New Testament; or to perform artful tricks to conceal the true situation, tricks to conjure up the vain semblance that Christianity is the prevailing religion in the land.

X. The *Fatherland*, Thursday, March 28, 1855

A thesis

—only a single one

January 26, 1855. S. Kierkegaard.

O Luther, thou hadst 95 theses—terrible! And yet, in a deeper sense, the more theses, the less terrible. This case is far more terrible: there is only one thesis.

The Christianity of the New Testament simply does not exist. Here there is nothing to reform; what has to be done is to throw light upon a criminal offense against Christianity, prolonged through centuries, perpetrated by millions (more or less guiltily), whereby they have cunningly, under the guise of perfecting Christianity, sought little by little to cheat God out of Christianity, and have succeeded in making Christianity exactly the opposite of what it is in the New Testament.

In order that the common Christianity here in our country, the official Christianity, may be said truly to be even so much as related to the Christianity of the New Testament, we must make it known, as honestly, as openly, as solemnly as possible, how remote it is from the Christianity of the New Testament, and how little it can truly be called an endeavor in the direction of coming nearer to the Christianity of the New Testament.

So long as this is not done, so long as we either make as if nothing were the matter, as if everything were all right, and what we call "Christianity" is the Christianity of the New Testament, or we perform artful tricks to conceal the difference, tricks to support the appearance that it is the Christianity of the New Testament—so long as this Christian criminal offense continues, there can be no question of reforming, but only of throwing light upon this Christian criminal offense.

And to say a word about myself: I am not what the age perhaps demands, a reformer—that by no means, nor a profound speculative spirit, a seer, a prophet; no (pardon me for saying it), I am in a rare degree an accomplished detective talent. What a marvelous coincidence that I am contemporary precisely with that period of Church history which, in a modern sense, is the period of "witnesses to the truth," when all are "holy witnesses to the truth."

XI. The *Fatherland*, Friday, March 30, 1855

"Salt"[17];

for "Christendom" is...the betrayal of Christianity;
a "Christian world" is...apostasy from Christianity.

February 1855. S. Kierkegaard.

Before a man can be made use of as I am here, governance must coerce him dreadfully—this too is the case with me.

Protestantism, Christianly considered, is quite simply an untruth, a piece of dishonesty, which falsifies the teaching, the word-view, the life-view of Christianity, just as soon as it is regarded as a principle for Christianity, not as a remedy [corrective] at a given time and place.

For this cause to enter the Catholic Church would for all that be a precipitate act which I shall not commit, but which perhaps people will expect, since in these times it is as though it were entirely forgotten what Christianity is, and even those who have the best understanding of Christianity are only tyros.

No, one can well be alone in being a Christian. And if one is not very strong in the spirit, a good maxim of human prudence is, "The fewer the better." And above all in Christendom, the fewer the better! For in the last resort, precisely to the concept "Church" is to be traced the fundamental confusion both of Protestantism and of Catholicism—or is it to the concept "Christendom"?* Christ required "followers" and defined precisely what he meant: that they should be salt, willing to be sacrificed, and that a Christian means to be salt and to be willing to be sacrificed. But to be salt and to be sacrificed is not something to which thousands naturally lend themselves, still less millions, or (still less!) countries, kingdoms, states, and (absolutely not!) the whole world. On the other hand, if it is a question of gain and of mediocrity and of twaddle (which is the opposite of being salt), then the possibility of the thing begins already with the 100,000, increases with every million, reaching its highest point when the whole world has become Christian.

For this reason "man" is interested and employed in winning whole nations of Christians, kingdoms, lands, a whole world of Christians—for thus the thing of being a Christian becomes something different from what it is in the New Testament.

And this end has been attained, has been best attained, indeed completely, in Protestantism, especially in Denmark, in the Danish even-tempered, jovial mediocrity. When one sees what it is to be a Christian in Denmark, how could it occur to anyone that this is what Jesus Christ talks about: cross and agony and suffering, crucifying the flesh,

* Thou who readest this, impress upon thy mind what follows. When Christianity came into the world the task was to spread the teaching. In Christendom, where the evil lies precisely in the false breadth of spread, brought about by a false way of spreading it, what is called upon to counteract this evil (the breadth of spread) must above all things take care not to have itself the form of extension—therefore the fewer the better, preferably in a literal sense a single person, for from the broad spread (extension) comes the evil, and so the counteraction must come from...the intensive.

suffering for the doctrine, being salt, being sacrificed, etc.? No, in Protestantism, especially in Denmark, Christianity marches to a different melody, to the tune of "Merrily we roll along, roll along, roll along"—Christianity is enjoyment of life, tranquillized, as neither the Jew nor the pagan was, by the assurance that the thing about eternity is settled, settled precisely in order that we might find pleasure in enjoying this life, as well as any pagan or Jew.

Christianity simply does not exist. If the human race had risen in rebellion against God and cast Christianity off from it or away from it, it would not have been nearly so dangerous as this knavishness of doing away with Christianity by a false way of spreading it, making Christians of everybody and giving this activity the appearance of zeal for the spreading of the doctrine, scoffing at God by offering Him thanks for bestowing His blessing upon the progress Christianity was thus making.

What is to be understood by being a Christian Christ Himself has declared, we can read in the Gospels.—Then He left the earth, but predicted His coming again. And with regard to His coming again there is one prediction of His which reads: "When the Son of Man cometh, will He find faith on the earth?" If it is all as it should be with the immense battalions of Christians, nations, kingdoms, lands, a whole world of Christians, then the prospect of His coming is remote. Seen conversely, one might well say, Everything is ready for His coming.

Thanks be to you, ye silk and velvet priests, who in ever more numerous troops offered your services when it appeared that profit was on the side of Christianity; thanks be to you for your Christian zeal and fervor in behalf of these millions, of kingdoms and lands, of a whole world of Christians; many thanks, it was Christian zeal and fervor! For if things were to remain as they were, if only a few poor, persecuted, hated men were Christians, where was the silk and velvet to come from, and honor and prestige, and worldly enjoyment more refined than that of any other voluptuary, refined by the appearance of holiness which almost laid claim to worship! Disgusting! Even the most abandoned scum of humanity have, after all, this advantage, that their crimes are not extolled and honored, almost worshiped and adored, as Christian virtues.

And ye mighty ones of the earth, princes and kings and emperors—alas, that even for an instant ye could have let yourselves be beguiled by these crafty men, as though God in heaven were after all only the highest superlative of human majesty, as though in a human sense He had a cause,[18] so that obviously it was infinitely more important to Him that a mighty man, not to say a king, an emperor, was a Christian, than that a beggar was! O my God, my God, my God! No—if there is, Christianly, any difference before God, then the beggar is infinitely more important to Him than the king—infinitely more important, for to the poor the Gospel is preached! But, true enough, to the priest the king is infinitely more important than the beggar. "A beggar, what help will he be to us? We might have to give him money." Impudent scoundrel—yes, Christianity is precisely...to give money. "But a king, a king! That is prodigiously important for Christianity." Thou liar—no, but he is important for thee. For when the king is a Christian, then the group of mighty ones who are his associates follow him at once (and hence in the case of a king who is a Christian it is so ominous that no transition to being a Christian is effected which is much more than a change of costume), and when the king and his mighty ones have become Christians, or are so called, then more and more follow (and hence in the case of a king who is a Christian it is so ominous that the whole thing becomes a change which yet is no change), and then when the whole nation has become Christian, then (behold therefore why it is so important that the king is a Christian!), then come silk and velvet, and stars and ribbons, and all the most exquisite refinements, and the many thousands per year. The many thousands—this is blood-money! For it was blood-money Judas received for Christ's blood—and these thousands and millions were also blood-money, which was procured for Christ's blood and by betraying Christianity and transforming it into worldliness. Only that—is it not true, thou shopkeeper's soul clad in velvet?—only that the case of Judas is almost laughable, so that on internal grounds one is nearly tempted to doubt if it is historically true, that a Jew—and that is what Judas was after all—that a Jew had so little understanding of money that for thirty pieces of silver he was ready (if one would put it so) to dispose of such a prodigious money value as Jesus Christ represented, the greatest source of revenue ever encountered in the world, on which a million quadrillions have been realized, to dispose of it for thirty pieces of silver! But we are going forward, the world is perfectible; Judas after all expresses something less perfect: first because he took only thirty pieces of silver, next because he did not have himself honored and praised, almost worshiped and adored, as a true adherent of Christ.

And thou, thou thoughtless multitude of men—but herewith I have said enough, and to boot, wherefore I say no more! Alas, thou art not merely deceived, but thou desirest to be deceived! What help can it do thee then to have sincere love, what does all disinterestedness help?—thou art not merely deceived—then indeed there might be some help for it—but thou desirest to be deceived![19]

XII. Articles in the *Fatherland*, March 31, 1855

What do I want?

March 1855. S. Kierkegaard.

Quite simply: I want honesty. I am not, as well-intentioned people represent[20] (for I can pay no attention to the interpretations of me that are advanced by exasperation and rage and impotence and twaddle), I am not a Christian severity as opposed to a Christian leniency.

By no means. I am neither leniency nor severity: I am...a human honesty.

The leniency which is the common Christianity in the land I want to place alongside of the New Testament in order to see how these two are related to one another.

Then, if it appears, if I or another can prove, that it can be maintained face to face with the New Testament, then with the greatest joy I will agree to it.

But one thing I will not do, not for anything in the world. I will not by suppression, or by performing tricks, try to produce the impression that the ordinary Christianity in the land and the Christianity of the New Testament are alike.

Behold, this it is I do not want. And why not? Well, because I want honesty. Or, if you wish me to talk in another way—well then, it is because I believe that, if possibly even the very extremest softening down of Christianity may hold good in the judgment of eternity, it is impossible that it should hold good when even artful tricks are employed to gloss over the difference between the Christianity of the New Testament and this softened form. What I mean is this: If a man is known for his graciousness—very well then, let me venture to ask him to forgive me all my debt; but even though his grace were divine grace, this is too much to ask, if I will not even be truthful about how great the debt is.

And this in my opinion is the falsification of which official Christianity is guilty: it does not frankly and unreservedly make known the Christian requirement—perhaps because it is afraid people would shudder to see at what a distance from it we are living, without being able to claim that in the remotest way our life might be called an effort[21] in the direction of fulfilling the requirement. Or (merely to take one example of what is everywhere present in the New Testament): when Christ requires us to save our life eternally (and that surely is what we propose to attain as Christians) and to hate our own life in this world, is there then a single one among us whose life in the remotest degree could be called even the weakest effort in this direction? And perhaps there are thousands of "Christians" in the land who are not so much as aware of this requirement. So then we "Christians" are living, and are loving our life, just in the ordinary human sense. If then by "grace" God will nevertheless regard us as Christians, one thing at least must be required: that we, being precisely aware of the requirement, have a true conception of how infinitely great is the grace that is showed us. "Grace" cannot possibly stretch so far, one thing it must never be used for, it must never be used to suppress or to diminish the requirement; for in that case "grace" would turn Christianity upside down.—Or, to take an example of another kind: A teacher is paid, let us say, several thousand. If then we suppress the Christian standard and apply the ordinary human rule, that it is a matter of course a man should receive a wage for his labor, a wage sufficient to support a family, and a considerable wage to enable him to enjoy the consideration due to a government official—then a few thousand a year is certainly not much. On the other hand, as soon as the Christian requirement of poverty is brought to bear, family is a luxury, and several thousand is very high pay. I do not say this in order to deprive such an official of a single shilling, if I were able to; on the contrary, if he desired it, and I were able, he might well have double as many thousands: but I say that the suppression of the Christian requirement changes the point of view for all his wages. Honesty to Christianity demands that one call to mind the Christian requirement of poverty, which is not a capricious whim of Christianity, but is because only in poverty can it be truly served, and the more thousands a teacher of Christianity has by way of wages, the less he can serve Christianity. On the other hand, it is not honest to suppress the requirement or to perform artful tricks to produce the impression that this sort of business career is simply the Christianity of the New Testament. No—let us take money, but for God's sake not the next thing: let us not wish to gloss over the Christian requirement, so that by suppression or by falsification we may bring about an appearance of decorum which is in the very highest degree demoralizing and is a sly death-blow to Christianity.

Therefore I want honesty; but till now the Established Church has not been willing of its own accord to go in for that sort of honesty, and neither has it been willing to let itself be influenced by me. That does not make me, however, a leniency or a severity; no, I am and remain quite simply a human honesty.

Let me go to the utmost extreme in order, if possible, to make people understand what I want.

I want honesty. If that is what the human race or this generation wants, if it will honorably, honestly, openly, frankly, directly rebel against Christianity, if it will say to God, "We can but we will not subject ourselves to this power"—but note that this must be done honorably, honestly, openly, frankly, directly—very well then, strange as it may seem, I am with them; for honesty is what I want, and wherever there is honesty I can take part. An honest rebellion against Christianity can only be made when a man honestly confesses what Christianity is, and how he himself is related to it.

If this is what they want, if they are honest, open, candid, as it is seemly for a man to be when he talks with his God, which therefore everyone is if he respects himself and does not so deeply despise himself that he would be insincere in the face of God—well then, if we honestly, candidly, frankly, completely admit to God how it really stands with us men, that the human race in the course of time has taken the liberty of softening and softening Christianity until at last we have contrived to make it exactly the opposite of what it is in the New Testament—and that now, if the thing is possible, we should be so much pleased if this might be Christianity. If that is what they want, then I am with them.

But one thing I will not do; no, not for anything in the world: I will not, though it were merely with the last quarter of the last joint of my little finger, I will not take part in what is known as official Christianity, which by suppression and by artifice gives the impression of being the Christianity of the New Testament; and upon my knees

I thank my God that He has compassionately prevented me from becoming too far embroiled in it.[22]

If then official Christianity in this country takes occasion from what is said here to employ power against me, I am ready; for I want honesty.

For this honesty I am ready to take the risk. On the other hand, I do not say that it is for Christianity I take the risk. Just suppose the case, suppose that quite literally I were to become a sacrifice: I would not even in that case be a sacrifice for Christianity, but because I wanted honesty.

But although I dare not say that I make a venture for the sake of Christianity, I am fully and blessedly convinced that this venture of mine is well-pleasing to God, has His consent. Yea, this I know, that it has His consent that in a world of Christians, where millions upon millions call themselves Christians, there is one man who says, "I dare not call myself a Christian, but I want honesty, and I will venture unto the end."

XIII. The *Fatherland*, Saturday, April 7, 1855

With reference to an *anonymous* proposal[23] made to me in No. 47 of this newspaper

April 4, 1855. S. Kierkegaard.

To propose to me that I write a presentation of the teaching of the New Testament, perhaps a big book, a dogmatic treatise, which again perhaps could best be written on a scientific journey in foreign parts, makes upon me (as doubtless it does upon those for whom my articles in the *Fatherland* are a living issue), makes upon me the impression that either it is a piece of foolishness, or that a trap is laid for me, in order that I might let the instant be filched from me, view the task amiss, the consequence of which possibly might be, either that I perish, or else remain away on a prolix scientific investigation. Instead of exhorting me to write a new work, the anonymous writer might rather (for to me it seems preferable that the contemporaries be exhorted to read over and over again my articles in the *Fatherland*) have exhorted the contemporaries to make themselves better acquainted with my earlier works, with the *Concluding Postscript, Sickness unto Death,* and especially with *Training in Christianity,* which last book, it is true, cannot at the instant be had from the booksellers, but that will soon be made good, since it is being printed for a new edition.[24] These books are related precisely to the instant, furnish for the instant the introductory knowledge which is desirable, for they are the introduction to...the instant.[25]

XIV. The *Fatherland*, Thursday, April 11, 1855

Would it be best now to "stop ringing the fire alarm"?

April 7, 1855. S. Kierkegaard.

This proposal has been made to me. However, I cannot in this respect humor anybody (supposing it is I who am ringing the bell); it would be inexcusable to leave off tolling as long as the fire is burning. But strictly speaking it is not I who am ringing the bell, it is I who am starting the fire in order to smoke out illusions and knavish tricks; it is a police raid, and a Christian police raid, for, according to the New Testament, Christianity is incendiarism, Christ Himself says, "I am come to set fire on the earth," and it is already burning, yea, and it is doubtless becoming a consuming conflagration, best likened to a forest fire, for it is "Christendom" that is set on fire. And it is the prolixities which have to go, the prodigiously prolix illusion fostered by the (well-meant or knavish) introduction of scientific learning into the Christian field, the prodigiously prolix conceit about millions of Christians, Christian kingdoms and lands, a whole world of Christians. This doubtless suits the convenience of princes of the Church, for the sake both of pecuniary advantage and of material power, and for the sake of what is the most exquisite and delicate refinement, that of scoffing at God and the New Testament, and being credited with zeal and fervor for spreading the doctrine. It is the prolixities which have to go, and that precisely by means of the burning question (if the fire is not quenched), the burning question of the instant: that official Christianity is not the Christianity of the New Testament.

No, official Christianity is not the Christianity of the New Testament. Anybody can see that merely by casting a fleeting but impartial glance at the Gospels, and then looking at what we call "Christianity." The reason why this is not seen is that by all sorts of tricks of optical illusion the great mass of men are prevented from seeing impartially, and the reason for that is that there have been introduced by the State 1000 officials who have such difficulty about seeing impartially because the question of Christianity is stated for them at the same time in pecuniary terms, and naturally they do not want to have their eyes opened to what has hitherto been regarded as the surest way to bread, the surest of all, though it is a questionable way of livelihood, perhaps in a Christian sense even a "prohibited way"; the reason is that hundreds of men are introduced who instead of following Christ are snugly and comfortably settled, with family and steady promotion, under the guise that their activity is the Christianity of the New Testament, and who live off the fact that others have had to suffer for the truth (which precisely is Christianity), so that the relationship is completely inverted, and Christianity, which came into the world as the truth men die for, has now become the truth upon which they live, with family and steady promotion—"Rejoice then in life while thy springtime lasts."[26]

Otherwise everybody must be able to see that official Christianity is not the Christianity of the New Testament, does not resemble it any more than the square resembles the circle, no more than enjoyment resembles suffering, or loving oneself resembles hating oneself, or desiring the world resembles renouncing the world, being at home in the world resembles being a stranger and a pilgrim in the world, or going to business, to a dance, or a wooing, resembles following Christ—not a bit more; the Christian battalions which "Christendom" places in the field no more resemble what the New Testament understands by Christians than did the recruits which Falstaff enlisted[27] resemble able-bodied, well-trained soldiers eager for battle; they cannot be more truly said to strive in the direction of what the New Testament understands by a Christian than a man who is walking with even pace out through West Gate can be said to be striving out through West Gate; and what we call a teacher in Christianity (a priest) no more resembles what the New Testament understands by a teacher in Christianity, no more resembles it than a chest of drawers resembles a dancer, has no more relation to what the New Testament understands by a teacher's task than a chest of drawers has to dancing—with this I say nothing disparaging of the priest from a civil or human point of view, any more than I deny that a chest of drawers may be an exceedingly useful and serviceable piece of furniture; I only say that it has no relation to dancing.

Postscript

What I write is certainly written without any hostile animus against the clergy. Why should I have such an animus? The clergy are of course to my notion (if only they don't have to be witnesses to the truth) just as capable, respectable, estimable a class in the community as any other class whatsoever. The theological candidate came into the picture *bona fide*—true, there is certainly something very amiss in the fact that he came in, but he came in *bona fide*. The responsibility properly belongs to the State; if then Church and State become separated, it is plainly the duty of the State to take care of the priest with whom it has made a contract. What has the State to do *dans cette galère?* To arrange for 1000 livings *per conto* the suffering truth, and to wish to give the divine its protection—both are equally preposterous.

XV. The *Fatherland*, Thursday, April 11, 1855

Christianity with a government commission
or
Christianity without a government commission

April 8, 1855. S. Kierkegaard.

In a little masterpiece by State Counselor Heiberg called "The Fairies"[28] the schoolmaster Grimmermann had, as everyone knows, the experience of plunging down inadvertently 70,000 fathoms below the surface of the earth, and, still more unexpectedly if possible than his fall was inadvertent, he found himself surrounded by gnomes. "What nonsense," says Grimmermann, "there are no gnomes, and here is my commission [to prove it]." But, alas, to come to the gnomes with a royal commission is labor lost. What the devil do the gnomes care about a royal commission? Their kingdom is not of this world; obviously for them a royal commission = 0, at the very most it has the value of paper.

I was led to think of this scene by Bishop Martensen's authoritative article against me a while ago. It was clear to me that what he was really boasting of against me (who, as he says, have only a "private Christianity") was...his royal commission, the fact that with him is to be found Christianity by royal commission.

But to come, *Christianly*, to me and people of my sort with a royal commission is to come off no more successfully than did Grimmermann with his commission.

A royal commission! But do not misunderstand me. There are few men who—in civil life—have the almost absolute respect for a royal commission that I have. I have often had to hear it said by my acquaintances that politically I was a nincompoop who bows seven times before everything that has a royal commission.

On the other hand, when it is a question of Christianity, I understand the matter differently. By virtue of a royal commission—for surely a royal commission is something which is related to a kingdom of this world—to wish to have any authority whatever in relation to what concerns not merely a kingdom of another world, but a kingdom whose passion precisely is, come life come death, not to want to be a kingdom of this world—yes, this is still more droll than Grimmermann's appeal to his royal commission to impress the gnomes.

Thus it is I understand the matter: precisely this—I repeat it—precisely this fact—note it well, for, Christianly considered, it is decisive for the whole ecclesiastical establishment; what the consequences of saying this possibly may be for me I shall have to put up with—precisely this fact that I have no royal commission is my legitimation, and Christianly, though always negatively, it is an immense advantage over having a royal commission. Grimmermann only makes himself ridiculous; but, Christianly, to appeal to one's royal commission is really to inform upon oneself as one who is unfaithful to the kingdom which would not at any price be a kingdom of this world, or as one whose Christianity is...playing Christianity.

XVI. The *Fatherland*, Friday, April 27, 1855

What a cruel punishment!

April 25, 1855. S. Kierkegaard.

Dean Bloch introduces the article he writes against me in No. 94 of this newspaper by referring to another article written against me earlier in the same paper by an anonymous author, whose article Dean Bloch (an obsequious Basil) recognizes appreciatively in the strongest and most deferential terms as what might be called a "leading article." And there is something in that, for it leads astray, and it is natural therefore that it was anonymous, as a leading article under the present circumstances certainly could not be.

However, Dean Bloch is by no means in complete agreement with the anonymous author; only for a short stretch can he follow the leading article of the anonymous author; the Dean soon has to turn off and strike into another path. His article then becomes what one might call a thunder-leading article (a lightning conductor), if by that one does not think of leading the lightning away but of leading the thunderstorm down upon a man, upon poor me.

If I do not reform, the Dean would have me punished ecclesiastically. And how? Indeed the punishment is cruelly devised; it is so cruel that I counsel the women to have their smelling salts at hand in order not to faint when they hear it. If I do not reform, the church door should be closed to me. Horrible! So then, if I do not reform, I should be shut out, excluded from hearing on Sundays during the quiet hours the eloquence of the witnesses to the truth, which if it is not literally *unbezahlbare*, is yet priceless. And I, silly sheep, who can neither read nor write, and therefore, being thus excluded, must spiritually pine away, die of hunger, by being excluded from what can truly be called nourishing, seeing that it nourishes the priest and his family! And I should be excluded from the other services of divine worship which the royally authorized (but the fact that they are royally authorized is, Christianly, the scandalous part of it), spiritually-worldly entrepreneurs have arranged. Terrific! Terrific punishment, terrific Dean! Alas, where are ye now, my vanished poet-dreams? I dreamed that I was called Victor[29]—and the truth is that it is Dean Bloch who bears this name; what not even Bishop Martensen was capable of doing, Dean Bloch is capable of, he is able to tag me.

However, it turns out so fortunately for me that whereas, for example, the punishment of compelling me several times every Sunday to hear the eloquence (if not *unbezahlbare*, at least priceless) of the witnesses to the truth would create disturbance in my customary mode of life, the application of that other punishment would not in the least alter a way of life which for Christian reasons I have chosen and to which during a considerable time I have already become accustomed. So if this punishment should be inflicted upon me, I shall live on without noticing it any more than I notice here in Copenhagen that in the distant town of Aarhus[30] a man is giving me a thrashing. Only I have one wish. If that is fulfilled, the infliction of this punishment will not cause even the very least change in my customary mode of life upon which I set such great store. The wish is that I may be permitted to continue without any change to pay the tithes (which we call priest's money), lest the altered form of the tax bill might cause me to notice the change.

By way of a postscript

Here I might conclude. But since Dean B. has cut such a great figure (perhaps with the feeling that he too is representative of the whole order), I shall nevertheless seize this opportunity of introducing a doubtful Christian query. Can one be a teacher of Christianity by royal authorization? Can Christianity (the Christianity of the New Testament) be preached by teachers royally authorized? Can the sacraments be administered by them? or does not this imply a self-contradiction? By ordination the priest is properly related to a kingdom which is not of this world, but having also royal authorization—ah, this "also," is it not an exceedingly questionable word, or do also and either /or come perhaps to the same thing? "Also"—does not a teacher of Christianity by being also royally authorized become something just as curious and remarkable as the thing they are making such a complaint about in the newspapers, that a Jewish priest (rabbi), by being also a Knight of Dannebrog, is assumed to be a professor of the Evangelical Christian religion?[31] But if such is the case, might it not end with the pipe playing another tune, so that it would not be a question of shutting the door on me, but it would be the priest who had to shut up the shop, or (recalling the thundering Dean) the firecracker booth?

Allow me moreover—for I see from Dean B.'s article that it is necessary—to quote again a Scripture text which I have quoted before. It is Christ's own word: "When the Son of Man cometh, shall He find faith on the earth?" So then, Christ conceives of a possibility that at His coming again the situation might be such that Christianity does not exist at all. And it is also implied in this word that Christ conceived more particularly of this apostasy from Christianity as due to craftiness and knavery; He does not seem to expect that the situation would be such that there was no one who called himself a Christian; He does not ask whether the Son of Man will find any Christians. What if He had conceived it thus: there will be found millions of Christians, Christian states and countries, a Christian world, thousands of mercantile priests—but faith (what He understands by faith), will that be found on earth? The apostasy from Christianity will not come about openly by everybody renouncing Christianity; no, but slyly, cunningly, knavishly, by everybody assuming the name of being Christian, thinking that in this way all were most securely secured against...Christianity, the Christianity of the New Testament, which people are afraid of, and therefore industrial priests have invented under the name of Christianity a sweetmeat which has a delicious taste, for which men hand out their money with delight.

Finally, a word to thee, O thou who with some interest for thine own sake readest what I write. Let me urge upon thee one thing: read my articles often, and impress upon thy mind especially the Scripture texts, so that thou hast them by heart. What I bring forward is precisely what it is the priest's interest to hide, suppress, tone down, leave out. If then thou hast no other information about what Christianity is than at the very most what thou dost get by hearing the priest, thou canst be pretty sure of living on in complete ignorance of what does not suit the convenience of official Christianity. It is in that state they propose to deliver thee over at death to the accounting of eternity, where doubtless it will serve for thy excuse that others more especially bear the guilt, but where nevertheless it remains thy responsibility whether thou hast not taken the thing too light-mindedly, by believing too light-mindedly the priest, perhaps just for the reason that he has royal authorization.

XVII. The *Fatherland*, Thursday, May 10, 1855

A result

April 23. S. Kierkegaard.

By a series of articles in this newspaper I have now, as they say in military language, opened and maintained a lively fire against the official Christianity, and thereby against the clergy in this land.

And on their side, what have the clergy done? For their part—yea, though I am unwilling to be so courteous, I am compelled to say it, for it is true—they have preserved a significant silence. It is strange: if they had replied, something exceedingly fatuous was sure to come out, perhaps the whole thing would have been fatuous; now on the contrary, how significant the whole thing has become by reason of this significant silence!

What then does this significant silence signify? It signifies that what concerns the clergy is...their livings. In any case it signifies that the clergy are not witnesses to the truth, for in that case it would be inconceivable that the whole clerical order—especially after its chief, the Most Reverend Bishop *Martensen* had made such a luckless attempt at speaking—could want to preserve silence, while it was so openly made known that the official Christianity is aesthetically and intellectually a laughingstock, an indecency, in the Christian sense a scandal.

Assuming on the other hand that the living is what concerns the clergy, the silence is perfectly natural. For I have not taken aim at livings in a finite sense, and well known as I am to the clergy, they can be very sure that such a thing could never occur to me; they know that not only am I no politician, but that I hate politics, that indeed I might be inclined to fight for the clergy, if in a finite sense people want to assail the livings.

Hence this complete silence—my attack has not really concerned the clergy at all, that is, it has no relation to what does concern them. Take an example from—I had almost used the wrong expression and said, "another world"—take an example then from the same world...from the shopkeeper's world. If it were possible to attack a shopkeeper in such a way that people knew that his wares were bad—but this did not result in having the least effect upon his usual turnover: then he would say, "To me such an attack is perfectly indifferent; for the question whether my wares are good or bad does not in and for itself concern me at all, what concerns me is the turnover. Yes, I am to such a degree a shopkeeper that, if one could prove not only that the coffee I sell is mildewed, spoiled, but that what I sell under the name of coffee is not coffee at all—if I am assured that this attack will have no effect whatever upon the turnover, such an attack is to me perfectly indifferent. What does it matter to me what sort of stuff people guzzle under the name of coffee? What concerns me is the turnover."

And in this the shopkeeper, *qua* shopkeeper, is in the right—and so too with their silence are the clergy, if the clergy are regarded as a mercantile class.

What was it I protested against a while ago? Did I protest against regarding the clergy as a mercantile class? No, I have protested against the fact that they want to be regarded as witnesses to the truth. By the assertion that they are witnesses to the truth the clergy are put at the furthest possible remove from being witnesses to the truth, least of all social classes are they witnesses to the truth.

A German author has said that the most honest class in the community are the shopkeepers, because they say plainly that it is profit they are after. I would propose a rather more complete scale of measurement: the most honest are the usurers, for they say plainly: Here you are cheated. Next to them come the shopkeepers, and last would come the fantasy-production by Bishop Martensen, "The Witnesses to the Truth." It was against Bishop Martensen's fantastical imaginations I protested. I did not give the question this turn: The clergy must be obliged to be witnesses to the truth. No, I gave it this turn: This signboard must be taken down. For example, it would occasion great confusion and disorder, nay, in many cases even serious harm, if one person or another were to take a fancy to put over his door the sign: Practicing Physician, or were to hang out a red light. Social order must require all these signboards to be taken away. And so it is with having a signboard out as a Practicing Witness to the truth. This is as though calculated to prevent the introduction of even the least bit of truth into the world; for people will say, "Where there are 1000 witnesses to the truth, it must indeed be a world of truth"—sure enough, if precisely these 1000 signboards were not the most dangerous falsehood in this...world of truth. Let them then take this sign down. That the clergy should have a signboard hanging out is indeed perfectly natural, only not as witnesses to the truth.

And that they are not witnesses to the truth is now, by evidence close at hand, made visible to anyone who is willing to see. Assuming that what I say is true—if the clergy had been witnesses to the truth, they would not have kept silent but declared themselves for the truth. Assuming that what I say is false—if the clergy had been witnesses to the truth, they would not have kept silent but declared themselves against this falsehood. Putting it the other way—if the clergy had been witnesses to the truth, the one thing they would not have done is precisely what they have done: they would not by silence try to slink away from any truth (assuming that what I say is true), or by silence let any falsehood prevail (assuming that what I say is false).

Postscript

May 6.

In order to make the contemporaries take notice, and in order to preclude the clergy from the evasion that this was something nobody read, I have made use of a political journal with a wide circulation.

In covenant with God as I am, disinterested as all my effort was—humbly before God, with a proud feeling of my own integrity, I dare to entertain the greatest conception of the cause I have the honor to serve, of its importance, of its success, though I must to be sure entertain the greatest conception of its difficulty. For what well could be more difficult, more desperate, than to have to introduce the ideals in a generation which is ruined by shrewdness and lack of principle, in which therefore the priests too (it is a pitiful way to earn money!) live off of the vain conceit that all are Christians, or, when one looks more closely, may be said (most pitiful way of all to earn money!) to live off of the fact that most people do not want to have the bother or to expose themselves to the legal inconvenience which might be connected with the admission that they neither are Christians nor imagine that they are.

This has now been attained: that the population is aware of the protest against the assumption that official Christianity is the Christianity of the New Testament, and that the population is aware of the objection raised against accounting the "priest" a "witness to the truth," seeing that what concerns him is the...turnover.

This ought to be brought to public attention in such a form that no one could say, This is something nobody has read—for this reason I made use of a political journal with a wide circulation.

XVIII. The *Fatherland*, Thursday, May 10, 1855

A monologue

. . . After all, Stundenstrup[32] is clearly in the right about the Town Hall, that it is a very handsome building, and that for the song at which these "honest men" are willing to dispose of it, it is the most brilliant transaction that can well be imagined. This must be conceded by his paternal uncle at the town of Thy, by all the kindred in Salling, and by all shrewd men wherever they are.

What Stundenstrup neglected to consider was whether these honest men stood in such a relation to the Town Hall that they were able to dispose of it. If not, then the price, if it were only four shillings and sixpence, would be very dear...for the Town Hall. So then, cheapness is not to be extolled unconditionally, it has its limits: if one does not get the thing one buys for an incredibly low price, the price is not cheap but very dear.

So it is with Christianity. That an eternal blessedness is an inestimable good, far more considerable than the Town Hall, and if it can be bought for the song at which the priests dispose of it, it may be considered a far, far, far more brilliant transaction than that of Stundenstrup's in buying the Town Hall—that I am willing to concede.

The only difficulty I feel is whether the priests stand in such a relation to the blessedness of eternity that they are able to dispose of it. For if not, then, though it were only four shillings sixpence, it is an enormous price.

The New Testament defines the terms for blessedness. Compared with the New Testament price—but I confess that expressions fail me to indicate to what degree, in comparison with the New Testament, the priest's price is cheap, a regular selling-out price. But, as I have said, does the priest stand in such a relation to the blessedness of eternity that he can dispose of it, and you buy it of him?

For if the priest does not stand in such a relation to the blessedness of eternity that he is able to dispose of it, as in fact he does not, since he is not our Lord; and if the priest's Christianity, the official Christianity, is not the Christianity of the New Testament, resembling it no more than a square resembles a circle, what good does it do me that his prices are cheap? As for winning an eternal blessedness by buying from him, I get no nearer to it, not the least bit; so what I attain by buying from him is (if one would put it that way) to perform a good work of a sort, that is, to contribute my mite to the end that 1000 university graduates may be able to live each with a family.

May 6. S. Kierkegaard.

XIX. The *Fatherland*, Friday, May 15, 1855

About a silly assumption of importance over against me and the view of Christianity I stand for

Though I regard this self-importance as so silly that not the least attention ought to be paid to it, yet for the sake of the many it is best perhaps for me to say a word about it once for all.

That I, a laureate in theology like others, and what is more, a pretty old hand at authorship, so that I am at least on a par with the parsons—that I should not know just as well as any priest or professor in the land what is commonly said in defense of the Establishment and its Christianity—that really is a silly asumption.

The fact is that in works under my own name or that of pseudonyms I have treated and described fundamentally, as I always do, the various stages through which I passed before reaching the point where I now am. So in those books more especially which are ascribed to the pseudonym Johannes Climacus[33] one will find pretty much all that can be said in defense of that sort of Christianity which is rather closely akin to that of the Established Church, and will find it described in such a way that I should like to see if there is any contemporary in our land who can do it better.

How silly then to inculcate in a lecturing tone and with great assumption of importance over against me the thing that I have finished and left behind me in order to get further forward in the direction (if I may so speak) of discovering the Christianity of the New Testament! Do not misunderstand me: I do not find it silly for one to hold that view of Christianity which I, after I had made it known, left behind me; but I find it silly for a man to want to inculcate *that* over against me in a lecturing tone and with great assumption of importance, to want to talk of my lack of acumen in not being able to see—to see that very thing which one will find presented in my works, with certainly as much acumen as the person in question who says this to my face is able to do it.

To name one exponent of this silly assumption of importance I will mention *Dr. Zeuthen*.[34] He has, it appears, established himself in the *Evangelical Weekly* and now inculcates from time to time in an instructive manner and with great assumption of importance what he might have read, e.g. in the *Concluding Postscript*. But this is inculcated for *my* instruction by Dr. Z., who thus implies that he is in possession of the acumen which he expressly says is lacking in me. It is a modest kind of pleasure he gets out of this—and yet in another sense it is neither modest nor humble, as Dr. Z. himself must know better than anyone, since in the role of an author, as everybody knows, he has devoted himself principally to the subject of modesty and humility, but of course without being guilty of any one-sidedness, such, for example, as the notion that theory and practice ought to correspond.

This was the word I wanted to say. One can read my works. He who does not want to do so can leave them alone. But really I do not care to go through the lesson over again with everyone who wants to inculcate, and for my instruction at that! what I have fully discussed.

Only one thing more, since I have my pen in hand. The fact that by this sort of Christianity which Bishop Mynster and now Bishop Martensen represent one can readily beguile oneself and thereupon make a brilliant career in this world which is the inventor of it—that I admit, I have never had any doubt of it. If anyone can furnish me with a communication from the other world, and if it is to the effect that this sort of Christianity is recognized there as the Christianity of the New Testament, then I am fighting a phantom and am a fool. But then there still remains One whom I take with me (in my disrepute),[35] God in heaven, whose word indeed is the New Testament; for if the report from the other world is as I have assumed it to be, then God, the God of truth, is the greatest liar of us all.

April 1855.

I wrote these lines towards the end of April. But, thought I, there is no haste about having them printed—perhaps there may come an additional incentive to print them.

It did not fail to come. For as I see now, that the Dr. Bartolo of the *Evangelical Weekly* (i.e. Zeuthen) has found his grateful Basil,[36] an anonymous writer in the *Copenhagen Post* who would disarm me with the scattered remarks of Dr. Zeuthen which are interspersed in various articles, to which I have not replied. In this, as in every untruth, there is some truth. The truth is that I have passed over in silence Dr. Z.'s scattered remarks. This truth, and the circumstance that Dr. Zeuthen's utterances are found in a weekly which surely is read only by theologians, is used to produce a fantastic effect, as though what Dr. Z. expounds were something very important. Perhaps it may be possible to succeed in fooling somebody in this way.

With the anonymous writer in the *Copenhagen Post* I shall deal no further. But let me take this opportunity to recall how the case truly stands with me and my appearance in a daily paper. I am not a completely unknown person who writes a newspaper article and then ought to submit to the necessity of discussing things on perfectly equal terms with every chap who writes. No, the question here is about a matter which in one sense was finished in a whole literature of important works, to which works of mine I refer those who really are interested. It was for religious reasons I decided to use a widely circulated political journal—to make people take notice. This I have religiously understood as my duty, and I do it also with joy, even though it is very distasteful to me. But, humbly before God, with a proud consciousness of my right, which I dare and ought to have, I shall guard myself well against too much chumminess with everyone who writes some sort of a thing in a newspaper.

May 13, '55. S. Kierkegaard.

XX. The *Fatherland*, Thursday, May 16, 1855

With regard to the new edition of *Training in Christianity*[37]

I have let this book come out in a new edition without any alteration because I regard it as a historic document.

If now it were for the first time to come out, now when the consideration of piety towards the old bishop no longer applies, and when I am convinced (partly by letting this book come out the first time) that the Establishment is, Christianly, indefensible, it would have been altered in the following respects:

It would not have been by a pseudonym but by me; and the thrice-repeated Preface would have been omitted, and of course also the Moral to Part I, where the pseudonym gives a turn to the matter such as I had sanctioned in the Preface.

My earlier thought was: if the Establishment can be defended at all, this is the only way, namely, by pronouncing a judgment upon it poetically (therefore by a pseudonym), thus drawing upon "grace" raised to the second power, in the sense that Christianity would not be forgiveness merely for what is past, but by grace would be a sort of dispensation from following Christ in the proper sense and from the effort properly connected with being a Christian. In that way truth would enter into the Establishment after all: it defends itself by condemning itself; it acknowledges the Christian requirement, makes for its own part an admission of its distance from the requirement and that it is not even an effort in the direction of coming closer to it, but has recourse to grace "also with respect to the use one makes of grace."[38]

This to my thinking was the only means of defending, Christianly, the Establishment; and to avoid any sort of hasty action I ventured to give the matter this turn, in order to see what the old Bishop would do about it. If there was power in him, he must do one of two things:

either declare himself decisively for the book, venture to go with it, let it count as the defense which would ward off the accusation against the whole official Christianity which the book implies poetically, affirming that it is an optical illusion, "not worth a sour herring"; *or* attack it as decisively as possible, brand it as a blasphemous and profane attempt, and declare that the official Christianity is the true Christianity. He did neither of the two, he did nothing; and it became clear to me that he was impotent.

Now on the other hand I am clear within myself about two things: that the Establishment is, Christianly, indefensible and every day that it endures is a crime; and that one is not permitted to draw upon grace in that way.

Therefore take away the pseudonymity, take away the thrice-repeated Preface and the Moral; then *Training in Christianity* is, Christianly, an attack upon the Establishment; but for a consideration of piety towards the old bishop, and because of prudential slowness, this remained hidden under the form of...the last defense for the Establishment.

Moreover I know very well that the old bishop saw in the book an attack; but, as I have said, he impotently chose to do nothing, except at the most to condemn it in the drawing-room, but not even in private conversation with me, and that in spite of the fact that I begged him to do so after it was reported to me with his consent what judgment he passed upon it in the drawing-room.

April 1855. S. Kierkegaard.

THIS HAS TO BE SAID; SO BE IT NOW SAID

BY

S. KIERKEGAARD

Copenhagen
Published by C. A. Reitzel's Estate and Heirs
Bianco Luno's Press
1855

[Issued on May 16]

"But at midnight there is cry."
Matthew 25:6.

THIS HAS TO BE SAID; SO BE IT NOW SAID

December 1854.

THIS has to be said; I oblige no one to act accordingly, I have no authority to do so. But having heard it, thou art made responsible, and now must act upon thine own responsibility, in such a way that thou canst justify thine action before God. Perhaps one will hear it in such a way that he does what I say; another in such a way that he understands it as well-pleasing to God and thinks he does God a service by taking part in raising a cry against me. Which of the two matters not to me, to me it matters only that it has to be said.

This has to be said; so be it now said.

Whoever thou art, whatever in other respects thy life may be, my friend, by ceasing to take part (if ordinarily thou dost) in the public worship of God, as it now is (with the claim that it is the Christianity of the New Testament), thou hast constantly one guilt the less, and that a great one: thou dost not take part in treating God as a fool by calling that the Christianity of the New Testament which is not the Christianity of the New Testament.

Herewith—Yea, O God, let that now come to pass which thy will is, infinite Love!—herewith I have spoken. If an ambiguous shrewdness which in its own mind knows best what the situation really is should think it shrewdest, if possible, to act as if nothing had happened—nevertheless I have spoken...and the Establishment has perhaps lost; for one can also lose by keeping silent, especially when the situation is, as it is, that not a few know more or less clearly what I know, only that no one will say it; for when such is the case, one thing only is needed, a sacrifice, one person to say it—and now it is said.

May 1855.

Yes, such is the fact: the official worship of God (with the claim of being the Christianity of the New Testament) is, Christianly, a counterfeit, a forgery.

But thou, thou plain Christian, on the average thou hast no suspicion, art entirely *bona fide*, confiding in the conviction that everything is all right, that it is the Christianity of the New Testament. This forgery is so deeply ingrained that doubtless there even are priests who continue to live on in the vain conceit that everything is all right, that it is the Christianity of the New Testament. For really this forgery is the counterfeit which came about in the course of centuries, whereby little by little Christianity has become exactly the opposite of what it is in the New Testament.

So I repeat. This has to be said: by ceasing to take part in the official worship of God as it now is (if in fact thou dost take part in it) thou hast one guilt the less, and that a great one: thou dost not take part in treating God as a fool.

It is a path full of dangers along which thou goest towards the reckoning of eternity. The priest says pretty much the same thing; but there is one item he forgets to mention and to warn against: the danger of letting thyself be caught, or that thou art caught, in the monstrous illusion the State and the priest brought about, making men believe that this is Christianity. Therefore wake up, be on thy guard, lest thou mightest think to secure eternity for thyself by taking part in what is only a new sin. Wake up, look out! Whoever thou art, this much thou canst perceive, that he who is here speaking does not speak in order to earn money, for rather he pays money out; nor to win honor and prestige, for he has voluntarily exposed himself to the opposite. But if such is the case, then thou canst also understand that this means that thou shouldst take notice.

This is all true! I don't think this is only applicable to the Danish situation of 130 years ago. It applies every bit as much today, right here in America. And it applies to all churches!

ACCOMPANYING SHEET

From the Journal

WORKING CATASTROPHICALLY

I had reflected that, if a catastrophic effect were to be produced, I must come out, after the most complete silence, unexpectedly with "the Cry" that our public worship is mockery of God and to take part in it is a crime. But before I was yet quite clear about this there was something else I did, namely, bring out the article about Mynster against Martensen. By that the catastrophic effect was already weakened. Besides when I consider that "Cry" I see that, as I have planned it, it needs an accompanying sheet, but this accompanying sheet would again weaken the catastrophic effect. Then I have great misgiving with regard to myself, whether—if the thing should be attained—I am up to going to prison, to being if possible executed, whether all this sort of combat would not upset me so that I should be unable to perform my part. However, in any case this must be left to God.

. . . .

It must be gone about in this way. One must begin by showing that the thing is so serious that all learned strife is a childish prank. One must therefore require of the Establishment, require of it in the name of Christianity, that it employ the means it possesses to protect itself. So one must oneself demand that the case be brought to trial.

XI² A 263, 265

April 9, 1855.

Just as carefully as it has been hidden hitherto what my task might be, just as cautiously as I have remained in impenetrable obscurity with respect to my purpose, just so decisively shall I now, when the instant has arrived, make it known.

The question about what Christianity is, and therewith in turn the question about the State Church, or the National Church, as they now want to call it, the amalgamation or union of Church and State, shall be brought to the most definite decision. It cannot and shall not go on from year to year as it did under the old bishop [who might be supposed to say], "It will last anyway as long as I live," nor as the new one seems to want it to do by understanding our age as a great period of transition, which in plain language comes to the same thing as, "It will last anyway as long as I live."

To be so sorely taxed as I am and must continue to be is certainly not a thing which, humanly speaking, one could call desirable, though in a far deeper sense I must thank divine governance for it as for the greatest benefaction. To be so sorely taxed as the contemporary age must be if the matter is to be taken in hand decisively, is, as I can understand very well, a thing which, humanly speaking, no one can desire, a thing which one would wish at almost any price to avoid, if one does not learn to be uplifted by the thought that the decisive thing is in a far deeper sense the most beneficial. It is my firm conviction that it could have been avoided, that the decision could have been postponed for a generation, if the deceased bishop had not been what he was, if his whole relation to me had not been from year to year a more revolting untruth. It is my opinion that it perhaps might have been avoided if the present bungler (with such a business as I have in hand one employs the true word, like a natural scientist in his descriptions; there is no place here for compliments) had not cut such a dash [literally: struck so hard] that by the necessity of contradiction I must carry the thing to the utmost extreme. In any case, now it has been determined: the case, the question, shall be pressed to the last conclusion.

The only thing I could wish to learn as soon as possible is whether the Government is of the opinion that Christianity (at least what calls itself Christianity—and in parenthesis be it remarked that, if it wishes the help of Government, it betrays the fact that it is not the Christianity of the New Testament) should be defended by the use of judicial power or should not.

Do not misunderstand me, as though it were my thought that, if this was the opinion of the Government, I then would be willing to keep my mouth shut, go around by another street. By no means. Doubtless for a man in my state of health, when by reason of an unfortunate physical weakness one needs exercise in a very special degree, it may be a very serious thing, a thing one must shrink from, the thought of arrest, etc. But I dare not give way; a higher power compels me, one which bestows power, it is true, but also will be unconditionally obeyed, unconditionally, blindly, as a soldier obeys the word of command, if possible with the involuntary precision with which the cavalry horse obeys the signal.

Do not misunderstand me either in another sense, as though in any way it were my intention, if on the part of the Government measures were taken against me, then if possible by the aid of a popular movement to try to make a counter demonstration. By no means. I am so far from this that I understand it as my task to ward off such a thing as well as I can, I who never have had anything to do with popular movements but have been kept pure in the separateness of "the single individual," purer if possible than the purest virgin in Denmark.

I only wished to learn whether my task will be to arm myself with patience and peace of mind in the prospect of trial, arrest, etc., or whether the Government is of the opinion that Christianity must defend itself, and that 1000 priests with family over against literally one single man may be regarded as having sufficient physical power, an almost inhuman disproportion, so that the State ought rather (for I never can forget the joke, even when I am talking of the greatest decision of my life) to give me the aid of several policemen against these 1000 priests, forbid them to act against me en masse, apprehend some of the worst twaddlers and when they are guilty for the third time prosecute them for twaddle, contributing in that way to insure that the question of spirit (and Christianity is surely spirit) would be so far as possible decided by spirit.

It cannot escape the vigilant eye of the Cultus Minister that I do not in the remotest degree infringe upon any civil institution whatsoever, and indeed a man who literally stands alone can never become a physical power. I pay the Church tithes like everybody else, I exhort everyone to whom my words have any weight to behave as I do, and I am firmly resolved to have no dealings with any man of whom I learn that in a civil sense he gives the priests even the very least annoyance. It is, Christianly, a galimatias in which we live; but this is not something the present-day priests have brought about; no, it goes far back in time. We are all of us to blame, and all of us deserve punishment; but really that would after all be a very gracious punishment to be let off with the obligation to support the actual garrison of priests we now have.[39]

April 11, 1855.

In torments such as seldom a man has experienced, in spiritual exertions which in the course of a week would deprive another man of his senses, it is true that I am also a power—undeniably a seductive conviction for a poor man, if the torment and exertion did not predominate to such a degree that often enough my wish is death, my longing the grave, and my request that my wish and my longing might soon be fulfilled. Yea, O God, if Thou wert not omnipotence which is able omnipotently to compel, and if Thou wert not love which is able irresistibly to move, on no other terms, at no other price, could it for one second occur to me to choose that life which is mine, and which is further embittered by what for me is unescapable, the impression I must get of men, and not least of their mistaken admiration. Every creature is at its best in its own element, can properly only live in its element, the fish cannot live on the land, nor the bird in the water—and to require spirit to live in the environment of spiritlessness means death, means to die slowly in agony, so that death is a blessed relief. Yet thy love, O God, moves me, the thought of daring to love Thee prompts me (under the possibility of being almightily compelled) with joy and gratitude to will to be what is the consequence of being loved by Thee and loving Thee: to be a sacrifice, sacrificed on behalf of a generation for which ideals are nonsense, are naught, for which the earthly and the temporal are seriousness, a generation which worldly shrewdness in the form of Christian teachers has shamefully, in a Christian sense, demoralized.

XXI. The *Fatherland*, Saturday, May 26, 1855

That Bishop Martensen's silence is, Christianly, (1) unjustifiable, (2) comical, (3) dumb-clever, (4) in more than one respect contemptible

(1) That, Christianly, it is inexcusable. It is the duty of a Christian, as an Apostle also enjoins, to be always ready to give answer concerning the hope that is in him, that is, concerning his Christianity. And how reasonable that is. A Christian, the lover and votary of the truth, ought he not always to be willing to give a good account of himself and the views which he holds, always ready to witness to truth and against falsehood, abhorring most of all the thought of hiding himself from anything or anybody? And now a Christian bishop, and the chief bishop of the land! The chief bishop of the land—it is to him the community looks, from him it expects guidance, upon him it relies to witness against falsehood and declare himself for the truth.

But how does this chief bishop of the land comport himself? Pretty much like the boys on New Year's Eve, who when they see their chance seize the opportunity to throw a pot at people's doors, and then make off, around by another street, so that the police may not catch them. Thus Bishop Martensen thought he saw his chance in the big rumpus occasioned by my article about Bishop Mynster, and threw over my head a garbage-pail of abuse and coarse words—and then made off. From that instant he preserved the profoundest silence, in spite of the fact that the thing only began to be really serious after that time; for with every subsequent article in the *Fatherland* it has become far more serious than was the question whether I really had been too impertinent to a deceased person.

But Bishop Martensen preserves the profoundest silence. And that in spite of the fact that he had been challenged to express his view.[40] Not only did he not reply to this challenge, but there came out in the *Berlin News* an anonymous article counseling him against answering this challenge.

And this (which recalls Leporello's line: "I answer not, whoever it may be"[41]), this we are asked to regard as justifiable in a witness to the truth, a Christian bishop, the highest in the land, upon whom the community can depend! No, such a silence is, Christianly, unjustifiable; and such a pitiful exhibition is, Christianly, far worse than if the Bishop had taken to drink.

(2) It is comical. Wherever the comical is, there is also, as one of my pseudonyms teaches,[42] a contradiction. So it is now with silence. Silence may have many various qualities in the direction of good or of evil, but silence is comical when it has the confounding quality that it... speaks. This is comical—a silence which speaks, speaks in a loud voice and says what it conceals in a tone which everyone can hear, says precisely what one wants to hide by means of silence, as when the Countess Orsini says to Marinelli,[43] "I want to whisper something to you," and thereupon shouts in a loud voice what she wanted to say, so does this silence shout in a loud voice what it conceals. Like making oneself invisible by putting a white stick in the mouth, whereby nothing more is attained than to make the white stick also visible—so does this silence shout louder than the most solemn declaration of the Bishop: it says clearly, "I am in a fix." It shouts so clearly that it can be heard not only by men of superior understanding, but that the people, the plain man, can understand it; and it shouts so loud that it can be heard in a neighboring kingdom.[44]

(3) It is dumb-clever. It is not simply dumb; no, it is dumb by wanting to be clever, dumb-clever. It is as when there is something a teacher doesn't know—which may perfectly well occur—and he then does not himself say straightforwardly, "I don't know it," but shrewdly wants to make as if he knew it, and the pupils then quietly take it upon themselves to subtract from his reputation the amount they infer from this. Presumably this shrewdness is thought to be so clever, but nevertheless it is dumb, for with every day Bishop Martensen maintains silence people quietly subtract from his reputation. Even if a silence has not the fatal characteristic of betraying what it conceals, yet to be able to hold out requires a reputation acquired and maintained through many years, when it is not an entirely unimportant person who is the opponent. And here it is a beginner in the episcopate, a beginner who began as lucklessly as did Bishop Martensen with his talk in the *Berlin News*; and the opponent is from an intellectual and literary point of view at least equally qualified, except that I have not the, Christianly, comic qualification of being Privy Counselor and earning many thousands in wages.

No, this silence is dumb-clever. This even those can see who have not the true measure of what this silence signifies.

For Bishop Martensen and I are, as they say, not entirely unacquainted. For many years there has been literarily a difference between us.[45] But as long as the old bishop lived, who was definitely such a friend of quietness, I was watchful on my part (*also* out of piety towards a deceased father) that the thing might pass off quietly. It passed off quite quietly in the affair of the System,[46] where Bishop Martensen did not pull the longest straw. I did not want to attack him by name—and Bishop Martensen preserved silence. Even when he who might well be regarded by Bishop Martensen as the most dangerous person to say it, that is, when Professor Nielsen gave him to understand in print[47] that my pseudonym had disposed of him, which then the next most dangerous person to say it, namely, Dr. Stilling, in print[48] gave him to understand again, what subsequently has been said to him in print very straightforwardly[49]—Bishop Martensen preserved silence.

Then he thought I had put my foot in it by talking about Bishop Mynster, that the feeling was hostile to me, and one saw from his article how eager he was to overwhelm me with coarse language, how eager he was to speak, if only he thought he could come out best.

And so again he wants to assume silence! Indeed, as a dumb-clever silence, this silence deserves to be called the Martensian silence, in distinction from the silence of Brutus and of William of Orange.

(4) It is in more than one respect contemptible. I will only stress two points. When one is a man, it is contemptible not to behave like a man, not to face danger manfully, to win or to lose decisively, but to try to slink from it. And this is doubly contemptible when one allows oneself to be paid by the State for assuming a position of rule, and perhaps apart from that has a tendency to play the role of ruler.

And this silence is contemptible because it is as though calculated to mean various things according to the outcome.

Worldly wisdom teaches that one "should never have anything to do with a phenomenon."[50] And I am to be classed under the category of a phenomenon: I am in fact one of those incommensurables who have not standardized their effort for a government post, etc.

So one keeps silent. If it proves that the phenomenon forces his way through—why, good gracious, one has said nothing, one's silence was respect, or perhaps "Christian resignation," which is the word Professor Nielsen unfortunately played into Martensen's hand,[51] without taking the precaution to have Bishop Martensen at least recant his abuse, for otherwise it is a queer sort of Christian resignation which keeps silent after having poured out all the abuse, such a resignation is pretty much like the repentance for theft which retains the stolen property.—If on the contrary it proves that the phenomenon does not force his way through—well, then one's silence was superiority, which so long as the outcome is critical one tries one's best to make it appear, in order to weaken the phenomenon.

How contemptible such a silence is, which instead of acting resolutely wants to await the outcome in order to give a false coloring to one's silence!

S. Kierkegaard.

Postscript

This, religiously, is a case I have to prosecute; therefore I must do what I am doing, whether personally it is agreeable to me or repugnant.

I understand very well that when one at such an early age as Bishop Martensen[52] has (yea, when I think of the New Testament and the oath made upon it, it is highly satirical!) been so fortunate (!) as to make a glittering (!) career (!), I understand very well that one may wish for rest (but the Christianity of the New Testament is precisely unrest) in order to enjoy (but the Christianity of the New Testament means to suffer) these earthly goods: the rich revenues, the consideration in the community, the agreeable feeling of having an influence upon the welfare of many men. I understand also very well (and in *one* sense this is no disparagement of Bishop Martensen) that Bishop Martensen could not wish to be so audacious as to declare publicly in his own name and as Bishop that the official Christianity is the Christianity of the New Testament or even merely an effort in that direction, and that therefore he might come to the conclusion (for indeed he first made what for silence was a very luckless attempt at speaking) that for him silence was the only way out or the only shift. But it does not follow from this that I have to keep silent to this silence, or to what, although impotently, yet perhaps insolently, it aims to bring about, namely, that a man who by divine governance was very early singled out and slowly educated for a particular work (and this is my case), a man who with a disinterestedness, exertion and diligence which in our situation is almost unique has only wished one thing[53]—that such a man (perhaps also as a reward for uprightly renouncing the things which are Christianly questionable, like profit, rank, titles, decorations, etc.) might come to be regarded as a sort of ranter whom the higher clergy did not think it worthwhile to answer, so that the plain man, relying upon the higher clergy might think himself justified in thinking that what this ranter says is twaddle (though what he says is Christianly perhaps the most thoroughly justified protest that ever was made), a notion to which someone already has tried to give currency. This was in the *Daily Sheet*, an anonymous writer[54]—presumably a pastor of souls! True, he was himself kind enough to concede to me "great talents," but for all that he came out with it that to the plain man what I said appeared to be twaddle. O honest, upright, conscientious care for souls! Say that the plain man says this...in order to get him to say it! I however am of a different opinion, I who after all have perhaps some acquaintance too with the plain man. For is it not true, thou plain man, that thou art very well able to understand this? My notion is that precisely thou art able to understand it much more easily and better than demoralized priests and a depraved gentility. It is true I am sure that thou canst perfectly well understand that it is one thing to be persecuted, maltreated, scourged, crucified, beheaded, etc., another thing when comfortably settled, with family, and steadily promoted, to live off the description of how another was scourged, etc. But this also is a difference between the Christianity of the New Testament and the official Christianity.

If now, as by the prompting of Professor Nielsen's article, there should come out here again in the *Berlin News* anonymous articles, perhaps even from Norway, counseling Bishop Martensen against letting himself in for it, surely the populace will gradually understand what such a thing signifies and will be obliged to Bishop Martensen for the contribution he makes to the public entertainment by means of anonymous articles which counsel him against letting himself in for it. Or should Bishop Martensen (as I hear is the case with individual priests here in the city) prefer to say one thing or another in a church—then it is not my fault if it should come to the pass that people laugh aloud in church; for regarded from the comical side this line of action is an exceedingly valuable contribution to the understanding of what "the witnesses to the truth" mean by "witnessing."

Do not misunderstand me, as though it were my notion with this that I am here writing, to wish to provoke Bishop Martensen to a discussion, thinking that we should learn from it something very important and instructive. By no means. In this respect I am essentially through with Bishop Martensen and know well what there is in him. Not that; but Bishop Martensen is in fact the chief bishop, it is owing to him I succeeded in getting in a blow at this thing about "witnesses to the truth"—and, as I have said, religiously regarded, this is a case I have to prosecute, and therefore it is my duty to take advantage of everything that turns up, to make it visible, so that everyone who will see can see: (1) what these witnesses to the truth really are, that what concerns them is not the truth, but to produce or maintain an appearance; (2) what miserable expedients they employ, wherefore it surely will also end in failure; (3) that the question about the Established Church is not a religious but a financial question, that what keeps up the Establishment is the 1000 royally authorized teachers, who standing to the Establishment in the relation of shareholders, quite rightly are silent about what I talk of, for I have no power to take from them their incomes; (4) what good reason and right that man has to be tranquil and unconcerned who in the matter of eternal blessedness relies upon "the witnesses to the truth."

Finally, what was so desirable for the cause (and so desirable that I hardly dared to expect it, and was fully prepared to see that from the very beginning Bishop Martensen would keep silent)—that has been attained. The thing was to get Bishop Martensen to speak, if only for once, in order that whosoever is willing to see might have a measure of what power he has when it comes to a pinch. Then the thing was to force him if possible back into silence. That was done. Let him then go on playing with silence. When one knows what his speech signifies, one knows also what his silence signifies. By his silence he succeeded perhaps, yet hardly, in fooling himself, but not anyone who is willing to see—and that is what he fairly deserves.

THE TEN NUMBERS OF THE *INSTANT*

and

WHAT CHRIST JUDGES

and

THE UNCHANGEABLENESS OF GOD

in the order in which they were published

CONTENTS TO THE *INSTANT*, WHAT CHRIST JUDGES, AND GOD'S UNCHANGEABLENESS

Although the first number of the *Instant* is dated May 24, it was not published until after the last article in the *Fatherland*.

The dates printed in brackets before particular articles in the *Instant* are found only in the rough draft.

THE INSTANT

No. 1

Contents

May 24, 1855. S. Kierkegaard.

Copenhagen

Published by C. A. Reitzel's Estate and Heirs

Bianco Luno's Press

From the Journal

INTRODUCING THE ABSOLUTE

If the absolute is to be introduced—and this age excels to the most dreadful degree in taking up everything characterlessly "to a certain degree" —prudence requires one not to do what commonly one would preferably desire to do, both for one's own sake and for the sake of others, before making the decisive attack, that is, to go to the rulers and say it to them, in order to see if possibly they might not yield a little. No, one cannot do this because—well, the misfortune is precisely this, that one cannot be sure, however strongly one might express oneself, that they would not take it up "to a certain degree," and so one would have bungled one's task of introducing the absolute. No, like the spring of the wild beast, or like the swift blow of the bird of prey, so it is the absolute must be introduced, especially in the face of this characterless "to a certain degree."

XI¹ A 526

Prelude

[April 20.]

PLATO says in a well-known passage in his *Republic*[1] that something good can result only if those men come into positions of rule who have no liking for it. His meaning doubtless is, that ability being assumed, unwillingness to rule is a good guarantee that a man will rule truly and ably, whereas an ambitious man may only too easily become one who abuses his power to tyrannize, or one whom a liking for rule brings into an obscure dependence upon those over whom he is supposed to rule, so that his rule becomes an illusion.

This remark may also be applied to other situations where something really serious has to be done. Ability being assumed, it is best that the person in question should have no liking for the task. For doubtless it is true, as the proverb says, that liking makes the work go swiftly, but real seriousness only appears when a man with ability is compelled by a higher power against his liking to undertake the work—so it stands with ability opposed to liking.

To be a writer—well, yes, that does delight me; if I must be honest, I may say that I have been in love with writing—but, mind you, in the way I like to do it. What I have loved is exactly the opposite of working in the instant, what I have loved is the detachment in which, like a lover, I can dangle after the thoughts, and like an enamoured musician toying with his instrument I can wheedle out the expressions exactly as thought requires them—blissful pastime! in an eternity I could not become tired of this occupation!

To contend with men—well, yes, that does delight me in a certain sense. I am by nature so polemically constituted that I only feel myself really in my element when I am surrounded by human mediocrity and paltriness. Only on *one* condition, however, that I be permitted silently to despise, to satiate the passion which is in my soul, contempt, for which my life as an author has richly provided me with occasions.

So I am a man of whom it may be truly said that I have not the least liking for working in the instant—and presumably it is precisely for this reason I am selected for it.

If I am to work in the instant, I must, alas, bid farewell to thee, beloved detachment, where there was no need to hurry, always plenty of time, where I could wait hours, days, weeks, to find exactly the expression I wanted, whereas now I must break with all such cherished aims of love. And if I am to work in the instant, there will be a great many people to whom I owe it that at least from time to time I make reference to all the trifling things about which mediocrity with great self-importance orates in an instructive tone, all the galimatias it gets out of what I write by first putting it therein, all the lies and slander a man is exposed to against whom the two great powers of society, envy and stupidity, must by a certain necessity be united in conspiracy.

Why then am I willing to work in the instant? I am willing to do it because I should eternally regret having left it undone; and if I were to allow myself to be frightened away from it, I should eternally regret that the generation now living would find the true presentation of Christianity interesting and curious at the very most, so as to remain where they are, in the vain conceit that they are Christians and that the play-Christianity of the priests is Christianity.

About "This has to be said"—or how is a decisive effect to be produced?

The protest I have made against the Established Church is decisive. If now some one would say, as I am prepared to hear even my most kindly critic say, "But the protest is so frightfully decisive!" I might say in reply, "It cannot be otherwise"; or I might answer with a word of one of my pseudonyms[2]: "When the castle door of inwardness has long been shut and finally is opened, it does not move noiselessly like an apartment door which swings on hinges."

However, I can explain myself also more precisely. To produce a decisive effect—and this is the task now—is not a thing that can be done like everything else; and now especially when the misfortune of our age is precisely this motto, "to a certain degree," going in for things to a certain degree, when precisely this is the disease which has to be cured, one must above all take care if possible that it does not come to pass that only to a certain degree one goes into this matter—for with that all is lost. No, a decisive effect is produced in a different way from other things. Like the spring of a wild beast upon its prey, like the blow of the eagle in its swoop—so it is that the decisive effect is produced: suddenly, concentrated upon one point (intensive). And as the beast of prey unites shrewdness and strength: first it remains perfectly quiet, quiet as no tame beast can be, and then collects itself wholly in one spring or blow, as no tame beast can collect itself or can raise itself for a spring—so is the decisive effect produced. First quietness, so quiet as it never is on a still day, quiet as it is only before the thunder—and then the storm breaks loose.

Thus it is the decisive effect is produced. And believe me, I know only too well the defect of this age, that it is characterlessness, everything to a certain degree. But as "a mirrorbright shield of polished steel,"[3] so bright that "when the sun's rays fall upon it they are reflected with a double splendor," as such a shield fears most of all even the very least touch of stain, since even with the least stain it is not itself, so does the decisive purpose fear every contact of or with this thing of "to a certain degree." That I understand. Should not I understand it who am known to all, even to the children in the street, by the name of "Either/Or"?

For what is either/or, if I am to say it, who surely must know? Either/or is the word before which the folding doors fly open and the ideals appear—O blissful sight! Either/or is the token which insures entrance into the unconditional—God be praised! Yea, either/or is the key to heaven! On the other hand, what is, was, and continues to be man's misfortune? It is this "to a certain degree," the invention of Satan or of paltriness or of cowardly shrewdness, which being applied to Christianity (by a preposterous miracle, or with miraculous preposterousness) transforms it into twaddle! No: Either/or! And as it is on the stage, that however tenderly the actor and actress embrace one another and caress one another, this remains nevertheless only a theatrical union, a theater-marriage; so also in relation to the unconditional all this thing of "to a certain degree" is theatrical, it grasps an illusion; only either/or is the embrace which grasps the unconditional. And to speak about something it never could occur to me to talk about except in contrast to what follows, to speak about life's vain pleasantries, I remark that just as every officer who belongs to the King's personal entourage bears a sign (a mark of distinction) whereby he is recognized,[4] so were all those who truly have served Christianity marked by either/or, an impression of majesty, or an expression of the fact that they stand in relation to the Divine Majesty. Everything which is only to a certain degree has not served Christianity, but perhaps itself, and can never honestly demand any other mark of distinction than at the most (as on a letter to frank it) "In the King's Service"[5]; for what is in God's service is either/or.

Is it justifiable on the part of the State—the Christian State!—to make, if possible, Christianity impossible?

The question itself certainly stands in no need of any explanation as a preliminary to answering it. Everyone surely must say for himself that this cannot be justified.

So what needs to be explained is that what the State has done and is doing is, if possible, to make Christianity impossible. For the factual situation in our land is, that Christianity, the Christianity of the New Testament, not merely does not exist, but, if possible, is made impossible.

Suppose that the State employed 1000 officials who with their families lived by opposing and hindering Christianity, and so were pecuniarily interested in doing it—that indeed would be an attempt in the direction of making Christianity, if possible, impossible.

And yet this attempt (which after all has the advantage of openness, that it openly proposed to hinder Christianity) would not be nearly so dangerous as what actually occurs, that the State employs 1000 officials who, under the name of preaching Christianity (here precisely lies the great danger, in comparison with wishing quite openly to hinder Christianity), are pecuniarily interested in: (a) having men call themselves Christians (the bigger the flock of sheep the better), assume the name of being Christians; and (b) in having it stop there, so that they do not learn to know what Christianity truly is.

The existence of these 1000 officials amounts to this, that when you hold up alongside of them the New Testament, it is easily seen that their whole existence is an impropriety. If on the one hand people did not assume the name of Christians, the priests would have nothing to live on; but if on the other hand they were obliged to preach what Christianity truly is, this would be the same thing as to open men's eyes to the fact that the very existence of the priest is an impropriety, that even though the teacher of Christianity gets something to live on, yet to be a priest cannot be...a royal appointment, a career, and steady promotion.

And this, this consequence, does not come about in the name of hindering Christianity, it is not with this in view the 1000 officials with family are paid; no, it comes about under the name of preaching Christianity, spreading Christianity, laboring for Christianity. Between too little and too much, which are said to spoil the broth, between this too little, that men do not assume the name of Christian, and this too much, that they might learn to know what Christianity truly is, and might really become Christians, between these two is balanced, with the seriousness of a tight-rope dancer, the official, state-churchly, or national-churchly Christianity of "Christendom," which does to be sure produce, in comparison with the New Testament, astonishing results...Christians by the millions, all of the same quality.

Is not this then about the most dangerous thing that could be thought of in order, if possible, to make Christianity impossible? The "priest" is pecuniarily interested in having people call themselves Christians, for every such person is in fact (through the State as intermediary) a contributing member, and at the same time contributes to the power of the clerical order—but nothing is more dangerous to true Christianity, nothing more contrary to its nature, than to get men to assume light-mindedly the name of Christian, to teach them to think meanly of what it is to be a Christian, as if it were something one is as a matter of course. And the "priest" is pecuniarily interested in having it stop there, with the assumption of the name of Christian, and that men should not learn to know what Christianity truly is, for with that the whole machinery with the 1000 officials and state power to back them would go up in the air. But nothing is more dangerous to true Christianity, nothing more contrary to its nature, than this criminal abortion which causes the thing to stop there, with the assumption of the name of being a Christian.

And this is supposed to be laboring for Christianity, spreading it abroad, working for it!

There is to me something so abhorrent and shocking even in the thought of such a sort of divine worship, which worships God by taking Him for a fool, that I shall endeavor with all my might, as far as I am able, to ward this off, and to open the eyes of the populace to the true situation, so that they may be prevented from becoming guilty of a crime in which really the State and the priests have implicated them. For however frivolous and sensual the populace may be, there is nevertheless too much good in the people for them to want to worship God in that way.

Therefore let light be cast on the subject, let it be made clear to men what the New Testament understands by being a Christian, so that everyone can choose whether he will be a Christian, or whether, honestly, uprightly, frankly, he will not be one. And let it be said in a loud voice before the whole people that to God in heaven it is infinitely dearer that they honestly admit, as the condition precedent to becoming Christians, that they are not and will not be Christians. This is infinitely dearer to Him than this loathsome notion that to worship God is to take Him for a fool.

Yea, thus it must be done: light must be cast upon the darkness in which the subject is kept by the State or National Church. Instead of having an absolute respect for what the New Testament understands by being a Christian, and then putting to oneself the question how many Christians there may be in the land, people give a different turn to it and say, There are a million men in the land, *ergo* a million Christians—and so they employ 1000 officials to live off of this. And then a step further: they invert the argument and infer that if there are 1000 officials who have to live off of Christianity (and that is what we have now), then there must also be a million Christians; we must stick to it stoutly that there are a million Christians, for otherwise we cannot assure all these officials of a livelihood.

So then there are 1000 officials who live off of it, with a family, *ergo* there must be a million Christians. The preaching of Christianity therefore corresponds to this (to this very peculiar sort of a fix into which men have brought themselves): to work for Christianity becomes, as I have said, to get people to assume the name of Christian, and at the same time to make it stop there, and that is what I call, "if possible, to make Christianity impossible," whereby in turn (to repeat myself) the people become guilty of a crime they otherwise would be free from, that of taking God for a fool under the name of worshiping Him, which I (who to be sure have had little thanks for loving men) will nevertheless strive in every way to avert.

I see very clearly that if the matter is taken up in the way I have indicated, there must emerge a very serious question, in an earthly and temporal sense, about the sustenance of these officials; for just as people talk about castles in the moon, so have these parties a vested interest in a chimera...a million Christians; and when it comes to this I am the most accommodating person in the world, eager to help, and as far as possible from wanting to take part in the annoyances the priests may have from other quarters, from certain politicians. It was just in order to be able to get at the question that I had to get that thing Bishop Martensen began to cook up about being a witness to the truth—I had to get that blown away as it were. Before everything else this disgusting rubbish had to be disposed of. Now—let us be good-tempered about it!—now we can talk rationally about what in a simple human sense is a very serious matter. And that way of talking is, I think, the most advantageous to us all. The sort of priests we have would certainly do best not to strike up the tune of wanting to be witnesses to the truth; for, if they do—well then, the difficult problem is solved with infinite ease: one has only to withdraw their whole stipend and save the expense of pensions. Witnesses to the truth must know how to put up with that sort of thing; and the idea about witnesses to the truth, that the priests are witnesses to the truth, if it had not come from a bishop (and was therefore stupid and offensive), but from a shrewd statesman, from a cultus minister, for example, who wanted to get rid of the clergy in an adroit way, would have been a very clever idea.

"Take an Emetic!"

[April 27.]

Doubtless there are a number of people upon whom my articles in the *Fatherland* have made an impression. Perhaps their situation is pretty much like this: they have become attentive, or at least they have begun to reflect whether the whole matter of religion is not in a pitiable state; but on the other hand there is so much that inclines them not to give themselves up to such thoughts, they love the customary order of things, which they are very loath to let go.

So their situation is pretty much like that of a man who has a bad taste in the mouth, a coated tongue, a little shivering fit, and so the physician tells him to take an emetic.

And so say I too: Take an emetic, come out of this lukewarmness. Think then first for an instant of what Christianity is, what it requires of a man, what sacrifices it demands, and what sacrifices also have been made for it, so that (as one reads in the stories) even "delicate maidens" (who did not, like our maidens, fill up their time by questioning whether they should wear light-blue or coquelicot at the theater) did not shrink back but, commending their souls to God, valiantly surrendered their "tender bodies" to the cruel executioner. Think first for an instant of this. And then make it clear to yourself, perfectly clear and vivid, the thought—gulp down the dose, however disgusting it is—of living in such a way that it is supposed to be *Christian* worship when in a quiet hour a man dramatically costumed steps forward and with dismay depicted by his face, with smothered sobs, proclaims that there is an eternal accounting, an eternal accounting before which we are going to appear—and then that we are living in such a way that outside the quiet hour to disregard even one or another conventional consideration, not to speak of one's advancement, one's earthly advantage, the favor of people of importance, etc., is regarded as something that could not possibly occur to anybody, and of course not to the declaimer; or, if somebody does it, this is punished by being regarded as a sort of madness—think of living in such a way, and that this is supposed to be *Christian* worship. Doesn't the emetic now have effect?

Well, then, take another dose. Make it clear to yourself and perfectly vivid how loathsome it is to live in such a way that *this* is supposed to be *Christian* worship: that when the declaimer dies there steps forth a new declaimer in costume and from the pulpit describes the deceased as a witness to the truth, one of the genuine witnesses to the truth, one of the holy chain of witnesses. Does it not take effect?

Well, then, take still another dose. Make it clear to yourself and perfectly vivid how disgusting it is to live in such a way that when one man says, "No, a witness to the truth one certainly could not call the deceased declaimer," that then it is supposed to be Christian zeal, perpetually repeated, with the greatest possible diffusion, to pronounce upon this man the judgment that he defiles—do you hear that!—defiles a worthy man's memory, violates the peace of the grave—do you hear that!—he violates the peace of the grave, etc., etc.

Surely it has taken effect now; and you'll be all right, the bad taste will disappear, i.e. you will have made up your mind that the whole thing is rotten, nauseating, yet nevertheless it could only begin to have the effect it ought to have when Bishop Martensen introduced the word "witness to the truth."

So let it work, and after God thank Bishop Martensen for such an exceedingly efficacious emetic.

AN EXTRA

From the Journal

THE CORRECTIVE

He who must apply a "corrective" must study accurately and profoundly the weak side of the Establishment, and then vigorously and one-sidedly present the opposite. Precisely in this consists the corrective, and in this too the resignation of him who has to apply it. The corrective will in a sense be sacrificed to the established order.

If this is true, a presumably clever pate can reprove the corrective for being one-sided. Ye gods! Nothing is easier for him who applies the corrective than to supply the other side; but then it ceases to be the corrective and becomes the established order.

BR p. 173

From Pastor Boesen's conversations with S. K. in the hospital

Boesen. Would you have no change made in your utterances? They do not correspond to reality but are more severe.

Kierkegaard. It has to be thus, otherwise it is of no avail. When the bomb explodes, I know well enough, it must be thus! Do you think I should tone it down, first speak to awaken, and then to tranquillize? Why do you want to disturb me in this way?

In my work I have now got so near to the present, the instant, that I cannot do without an organ by means of which I can instantly address myself to the present time; and this I have called:

THE INSTANT

Should anyone who is interested in this matter wish for his own convenience to be well assured of getting what may come out, he can send his subscription to the publisher. But I reserve to myself in *every* respect the *most absolute* freedom—in no other way can I do it.

I call it the *Instant*. Yet it is nothing ephemeral I have in mind, any more than it was anything ephemeral I had in mind before; no, it was and is something eternal: on the side of the ideals against the illusions. But in *one* sense I must say of my whole previous work, that its time has not yet come; I have stood remote, yea, even very remote from the present time, and only near in the sense that this remoteness was thoroughly calculated and purposeful. Now, on the contrary, I must assure myself in every eventuality of being able to take advantage of the instant.

I do not seek to persuade anyone to subscribe, far rather I beg everyone at least to reflect before doing it. Eternally he will not regret having heeded my talk, but it would be possible that he might come to regret it temporally. I who am called "Either/Or" cannot be at the service of anybody with both-and. I have in my possession a book which doubtless is all but unknown in this land, the title of which I will therefore cite in full: *The New Testament of our Lord and Saviour Jesus Christ.* Although I stand in a perfectly free relation to this book, and am not, for example, bound to it by an oath, yet nevertheless this book exercises a great power over me, inspires me with an indescribable horror of both-and.

THE INSTANT

No. 2

Contents

June 4, 1855. S. Kierkegaard.

Copenhagen

Published by C. A. Reitzel's Estate and Heirs

Bianco Luno's Press

From the Journal

SEVERITY / LENIENCY

In my presentation severity is a dialectical "moment" in Christianity; but leniency is just as strongly expressed; the former is represented by the poetical pseudonyms, the latter by me personally. Thus it is the age has need of it, for it has taken Christianity in vain. But it would be an entirely different thing if a desperate man had nothing else to say about Christianity than that it is the cruelest self-torture. To put an end to coquetry I have had to apply severity—and have applied it precisely in order to give impetus to the resort to leniency. If I had only understood its frightful severity, I would have kept silent.

I think I dare say of myself that I undoubtedly have at my disposal a profounder pathos in preaching the lenience of Christianity than anyone else has who preaches in our land.

X^2 A 525, p. 378

To "My Reader!"[6]

[April 27.]

TO THEE whom I have called "my reader" I should like to say a few words.

When a man ventures out so decisively as I have done, and upon a subject moreover which affects so profoundly the whole of life as does religion, it is to be expected of course that everything will be done to counteract his influence, also by misrepresenting, falsifying what he says, and at the same time his character will in every way be at the mercy of men who count that they have no duty towards him but that everything is allowable.

Now, as things commonly go in this world, the person attacked usually gets busy at once to deal with every accusation, every falsification, every unfair statement, and in this way is occupied early and late in counteracting the attack. This I have no intention of doing.

And it for this reason I would say a few words to thee, my reader, in order to put thee seriously in mind of something. That the person attacked is so dreadfully busy in defending himself—just think of it a moment; might not this generally be due to the fact that in a simple egotistic sense of the word he is interested in protecting himself, fearing that the falsification of what he says, and the bad reports about him personally would injure him in an earthly and temporal sense? And—just think of it a moment!—dost thou not believe that precisely in this situation the reason why most people come out publicly is that ultimately they have earthly and temporal ends in view and are therefore so busy about justifying themselves against attack? Dost thou not believe that this disposition to bustle does harm also for the fact that it makes men disinclined to get at the truth of the matter for themselves, to put themselves to any inconvenience, to make any vigorous effort, because nowadays in all situations there are no longer to be found teachers but only...lackeys?

At all events, I propose to deal with the matter differently, I propose to go rather more slowly in counteracting all this falsification and misrepresentation, all these lies and slanders, all this prate and twaddle. Partly because I learn from the New Testament that the occurrence of such things is a sign that one is on the right road, so that obviously I ought not to be exactly in a hurry to get rid of it, unless I wish as soon as possible to get on the wrong road. And partly because I learn from the New Testament that what may temporally may be called a vexation, from which according to temporal concepts one might try to be delivered, is eternally of value, so that obviously I ought not to be exactly in a hurry to try to escape, if I do not wish to hoax myself with regard to the eternal.

This is the way I understand it; and now I come to the consequence which ensues for thee. If thou really hast ever had an idea that I am in the service of something true—well then, occasionally there shall be done on my part what is necessary, but only what is strictly necessary to thee, in order that, if thou wilt exert thyself and pay due attention, thou shalt be able to withstand the falsifications and misrepresentations of what I say, and all the attacks upon my character—but thy indolence, dear reader, I will not encourage. If thou dost imagine that I am a lackey, thou hast never been my reader; if thou really art my reader, thou wilt understand that I regard it as my duty to thee that thou art put to some effort, if thou art not willing to have the falsifications and misrepresentations, the lies and slanders, wrest from thee the idea that I am in the service of something true.

That the task has a double direction

[May 17.]

When Christianity came into the world the task was simply to proclaim Christianity. The same is the case wherever Christianity is introduced into a country the religion of which is not Christianity.

In "Christendom" the situation is a different one. What we have before us is not Christianity but a prodigious illusion, and the people are not pagans but live in the blissful conceit that they are Christians. So if in this situation Christianity is to be introduced, first of all the illusion must be disposed of. But since this vain conceit, this illusion, is to the effect that they are Christians, it looks indeed as if introducing Christianity were taking Christianity away from men. Nevertheless this is the first thing to do, the illusion must go.

This is the task; but the task has a double direction.

It is in the direction of seeing what can be done by way of clarifying men's concepts, teaching them, moving them by means of the ideals, bringing them by pathos into a state of suffering, stirring them up by the gadfly-sting of irony, derision, sarcasm, etc., etc.

There would be no further task, were it not that this illusion, the fact that men imagine they are Christians, is connected with an enormously big illusion which has a purely external side, the illusion that Christianity and State have been amalgamated, in the fact that the State introduces 1000 functionaries who by the instinct of self-preservation have an interest in not letting men learn to know what Christianity is and that they in fact are not Christians. For the very existence of these priests is an untruth. Being completely secularized and in the service of the State (royal functionaries, persons of social position, making a career), they obviously could not very well tell the congregation what Christianity is, for to say this would mean resigning their posts.

Now this illusion is of a different sort from the first one mentioned, which had to do with men's conceptions, the ensnarement of the individuals in the conceit that they were Christians. In the case of this latter illusion one must go to work in another fashion, for the State has the power to do away with it. This then is the other side of the task: to labor in the direction of getting the State to do away with it.

If I were to liken this task to anything, I would say that it resembles the therapeutic treatment of a psychic patient. One must work on psychic lines, says the physician; but it does not follow from this that there may be nothing to do physically.

From what is here set forth there ensues something I must urge upon the reader—and I hope he will bear with me if I do not do as authors commonly do, do not bow and scrape before the reader because I want his money and regard his judgment as the final judgment.

What I would urge upon the reader is, that he will not confine himself to reading the particular number of the *Instant* through, but as each number contains several articles, I urge him to make himself acquainted with the contents by a first cursory reading, and to read later each several article for itself.

The comfortable—and the concern for an eternal blessedness

[April 11.]

It is these two things—one might almost be tempted to say, what the deuce have these two things to do with one another?—and yet it is these two things that official Christianity, or the State by the aid of official Christianity, has jumbled together, and done it as calmly as when at a party where the host wants to include everybody he jumbles many toasts in one.

It seems that the reasoning of the State must have been as follows. Among the many various things which man needs on a civilized plane and which the State tries to provide for its citizens as cheaply and comfortably as possible—among these very various things, like public security, water, illumination, roads, bridge-building, etc., etc., there is also...an eternal blessedness in the hereafter, a requirement which the State ought also to satisfy (how generous of it!), and that in as cheap and comfortable a way as possible. Of course it will cost money, for without money one gets nothing in this world, not even a certificate of eternal blessedness in the other world; no, without money one gets nothing in this world. Yet all the same, what the State does, to the great advantage of the individual, is that one gets it from the State at a cheaper price than if the individual were to make some private arrangement, moreover it is more secure, and finally it is comfortable in a degree that only can be provided on a big scale.

So, to introduce Christianity, first a complete count of the people is made, thereupon the whole population is inscribed in the tax list—exactly as it was when Christianity came into the world—and then 1000 royal functionaries are appointed. "You, my dear subjects"—this might well be the thought of the State—"with respect also to the great and inestimable benefit of an eternal blessedness, ought to have everything as convenient, as comfortable and as cheap as possible. With water on every floor, instead of the bitter toil, as in the old days, of dragging it up stairs, one cannot have things more convenient than you shall have them with respect to an eternal blessedness in the hereafter (in pursuit of which in the uncivilized ages of ignorance men ran to the ends of the world, and on their knees); if you but whistle, it will be at your service, yea, before you whistle; you shall not have to go up and down stairs, good gracious, no, it will be brought to your house—as beer is nowadays[7]—by royally authorized waiters, who surely will prove themselves diligent and attentive, for this is their livelihood, whereas the price is after all so cheap that this cheapness exposes the shamelessness of Catholicism [which exacts so much more].

Far be it from me to speak disparagingly of the comfortable! Let it be applied wherever it can be applied, in relation to everything which is in such a sense a thing that this thing can be possessed irrespective of the way in which it is possessed, so that one can have it either in this way or in the other; for when such is the case, the convenient and comfortable way is undeniably to be preferred. Take water for example: water is a thing which can be procured in the difficult way of fetching it up from the pump, but it can also be procured in the convenient way of high pressure; naturally I prefer the more convenient way.

But the eternal is not a thing which can be had regardless of the way in which it is acquired; no, the eternal is not really a thing, but is the way in which it is acquired. The eternal is acquired in *one* way, and the eternal is different from everything else precisely for the fact that it can be acquired only in one single way; conversely, what can be acquired in only one way is the eternal—it is acquired only in one way, in the difficult way which Christ indicated by the words: "Narrow is the gate and straitened the way, that leadeth unto life, and few are they that find it."

That was bad news! The comfortable—precisely the thing in which our age excels—absolutely cannot be applied with respect to...an eternal blessedness. When, for example, the thing you are required to do is to walk, it is no use at all to make the most astonishing inventions in the way of the easiest carriages and to want to convey yourself in these when the task prescribed to you was...walking. And if the eternal is the way in which it is acquired, it doesn't do any good to want to alter this way, however admirably, in the direction of comfort; for the eternal is acquired only in the difficult way, is not acquired indifferently both in the easy and in the difficult way, but is the way in which it is acquired, and this way is the difficult one.

Thanks be to you, ye Government Clerks, ye Counselors of Chancery, Counselors of Justice, Counselors of State, and Privy Counselors, thanks for the enormous amount of scribbling ye have had to do to arrange for His Majesty's subjects all and sundry in a cheap and comfortable way the attainment of an eternal blessedness; thanks be to you, ye clerical counselors; truly ye have not done it for naught, for ye have your percentage; yet after all it is no more than reasonable that ye should be thanked. Thanks to you all and sundry—if only it is certain that the subjects become blessed, and is not rather true that a certificate from "the State" is a most inauspicious recommendation in the hereafter, where the judgment depends upon whether you have belonged to that kingdom which would not at any price be a kingdom of this world.

The human protects (its *protégé*) the divine!

[April.]

It is easy enough to understand that this thing of the human protecting the divine is an abracadabra. How in the world could a notion like this occur to such a sensible being as the State?

Well, it's a long story; but principally it is due to the fact that in the course of time Christianity came to have less and less men who served it with an appreciation of what it is—the divine.

Imagine a statesman who lived at the time when Christianity came into the world, and say to him, "*Quid tibi vedetur*, don't you think that this would be the religion for the State?" Presumably he would regard you as mad, would hardly condescend to make a reply.

But when Christianity is served by human fear, by mediocrity, by temporal interests—yes, then it makes a rather different appearance, then it really may seem as if Christianity (which with that sort of service had gradually become spavined, knock-kneed, and lame in the shoulder, a pitiful "critter") might be exceedingly glad to be protected by the State and thus brought to honor.[8]

In view of this, the responsibility lies with the clergy, who have made a fool of the State, put into its head the notion that here was something for the State to do—which may end with the State having to pay the piper because it got too highfalutin. For though it is certainly not too high for the State to patronize that sort of thing which people made out Christianity to be, yet as soon as it becomes again what it is, the State seems foolishly highfalutin, and may well wish for its own sake to get down to earth again, the sooner the better.

This thing of Christianity being protected by the State is like a fairy tale or a story: A king, dressed as a common man, lives in a provincial town, and the Burgomaster is so kind as to wish to patronize this burgher—then suddenly there comes an emissary who with a deep bow and then on bended knee addresses this burgher as "Your Majesty." If the Burgomaster is a sensible man, he sees that, though well-meaningly, he was too highfalutin in patronizing this burgher.

Imagine—not what has been talked about so much that it has almost become trivial, that Christ returned to the earth—no, imagine that one of the Apostles were to return. He would shudder at seeing Christianity patronized by the State. Imagine him approaching Christianity so deeply degraded, and bowing low before it—the most narrow-minded statesman would see that he had got in wrong by wanting to treat

Christianity as a *protégé*, that it is a shocking mistake to confuse the fact that the priests want the protection of the State with the notion that this is wanted by Christianity, which, if it had any want whatever, would want to be rid of such priests, who do not know how to bow before Christianity (for to it one bows by willingness to offer sacrifices, to suffer for the doctrine), but only know how to bow before the King, to do homage on receiving a rank equivalent to that of Counselor of State, or for being made a Knight of Dannebrog, etc., which is faithlessness on the part of one who in the character of a teacher of Christianity is bound by an oath upon the New Testament, it is faithlessness to the New Testament.[9] For there Christianity teaches: "Fear God, honor the King." A Christian ought to be if possible His Majesty's best subject. But, *Christianly*, the King is not the prerogative authority, he is and can and must and will *not* be the prerogative authority in relation to a kingdom which is not willing at any price to be of this world, come life, come death, will not be of this world. Faithfulness to the oath upon the New Testament would therefore help one to avert that which a man, precisely if he loves the King, must wish to avert, that His Majesty be put in a wrong light. With its lofty divine seriousness Christianity has always maintained the seriousness of the kingly power; it is only the detestable play at being Christian which, being treasonable to the New Testament, was also treasonable to the King by presenting him in a light which is prejudicial to the dignity and seriousness of the kingly power.

The moment will therefore surely come when a king will rise in his seat and say, "Now I see it; these rascally priests, this is what they have brought me to, the last thing I wanted to become—to become ridiculous. For, by my royal honor, I know, if anybody does, what the King's majesty means, and I know also what I have in my power: gold and goods and rank and dignity and all badges of honor, yea, even kingdoms and lands I can bestow, I who above other kings have crowns to dispose of. But what now is Christianity? Christianity is the renunciation of all this, Christianity is not merely not to pursue such aims; no, it is not being willing at any price to accept them if they are offered, to shun them with greater dread than the earthly mind shuns misery and sufferings, to shun them more passionately than the earthly mind aspires after them. How in the world did I fall into such madness, thinking that with gold and goods and titles and dignities and stars and badges of honor I could patronize...that which shuns all such things more than the pest? I am indeed ridiculous! And who is at fault for it?

Who but these rascally priests that have transformed Christianity into the very opposite of what it was in the New Testament, and thereby put the idea into my head that I could patronize Christianity! Fool that I am! For what is it I have patronized? Verily not Christianity, which for all its lowliness is more lofty than I, but it is a lot of rascals who precisely for this cause are the least deserving of my protection."

A eulogy upon the human race
or
a proof that the New Testament is no longer truth

In the New Testament the Saviour of the world, our Lord Jesus Christ, represents the situation thus: The way that leadeth unto life is straitened, the gate narrow—few be they that find it!

— — now, on the contrary, to speak only of Denmark, we are all Christians, the way is as broad as it possibly can be, the broadest in Denmark, since it is the way in which we all are walking, besides being in all respects as convenient, as comfortable, as possible; and the gate is as wide as it possibly can be, wider surely a gate cannot be than that through which we all are going en masse.

Ergo the New Testament is no longer truth.

All honor to the human race! But Thou, O Saviour of the world, Thou didst entertain too lowly a notion of the human race, failing to foresee the sublime heights to which, perfectible as it is, it can attain by an effort steadily pursued!

To that degree therefore the New Testament is no longer truth: the way the broadest, the gate the widest, and all of us Christians. Yea, I venture to go a step further—it inspires me with enthusiasm, for this you must remember is a eulogy upon the human race—I venture to maintain that, on the average, the Jews who dwell among us are to a certain degree Christians, Christians like all the others—to that degree we are all Christians, in that degree is the New Testament no longer truth.

And since it is in point here to look for whatever contributes to the glorification of the human race, one ought, though taking care not to come out with anything untrue, to be careful also not to overlook anything which in this respect is demonstrative proof or even suggestive. I venture therefore to go a step further, without expressing, however, any definite opinion, seeing that in this respect I lack precise information, and hence submit to persons well informed, the specialists, the question whether among the domestic animals, the nobler ones, the horse, the dog, the cow, there might not be visible some Christian token. That is not unlikely. Just think what it means to live in a Christian state, a Christian nation, where everything is Christian, and we are all Christians, where, however a man twists and turns, he sees nothing but Christianity and Christendom, the truth and witnesses to the truth—it is not unlikely that this may have an influence upon the nobler domestic animals, and thereby in turn upon that which, according to the judgment of both the veterinary and the priest, is the most important thing, namely, the progeny. Jacob's cunning device is well known, how in order to get speckled lambs he laid speckled rods in the watering troughs, so that the ewes saw nothing but speckles and therefore gave birth to speckled lambs. It is not unlikely—although I do not presume to have any definite opinion, as I am not a specialist, and therefore would rather submit the question to a committee composed, for example, of veterinaries and priests—it is not unlikely that it will end with domestic animals in "Christendom" bringing into the world a Christian progeny.

I am almost dizzy at the thought; but then, on the greatest possible scale—to the honor of the human race—will the New Testament be no longer truth.

Thou Saviour of the world, Thou didst anxiously exclaim, "When I come again, shall I find faith on the earth?" and then didst bow Thy head in death; Thou surely didst not have the least idea that in such a measure Thine expectations would be surpassed, that the human race in such a pretty and touching way would make the New Testament untruth and Thine importance almost doubtful. For can such good beings truthfully be said to need, or ever to have needed, a saviour?

We are all Christians

That we are all Christians is something so generally known and assumed that it needs no proof but may even be about to work its way up from being a historical truth to becoming an axiom, one of the eternal intuitive principles with which the babe is now born, so that with Christianity there may be said to have come about a change in man, that in "Christendom" a babe is born with one intuitive principle more than a human being has outside of Christendom, the principle that we are all Christians.

For all that, it never can do any harm to make it clear to ourselves over and over again to what degree it is certain and true that we are all Christians.

Here is an attempt of mine; and I flatter myself that it really does make clear to what a degree we are all of us Christians. We are Christians to such a degree that, if among us there lived a Freethinker who in the strongest terms declared that the whole of Christianity is a lie, *item* in the strongest terms declared that he was not a Christian—there is no help for him, he is a Christian; according to the law he may be punished, that is a different thing, but a Christian he is. "What stuff and nonsense!" says the State. "What would this lead to? If once we allowed a man to declare that he is not a Christian, it soon would come to pass that all would deny that they were Christians. No, *principiis obsta*,[10] and let us hold fast to principles. We now have everything well tabulated, all under proper headings, everything perfectly correct—under the assumption of course that we are all Christians—*ergo* he too is a Christian. Such a conceit, which merely wants to be eccentric, one must not humor, and that's the end of it."

If he dies...and leaves behind him so much that the man of God (the priest), the undertaker man, and several other men, could each get his share—then all his protests are of no use, he *is* a Christian and is buried as a Christian—to that degree it is certain that we all are Christians. If he leaves nothing (for a little is no help: the priest, who as a Christian is always easily contented, is content with little if there is no more), but if he leaves literally nothing—that would be the only case in which his protests might be taken into account, since by being dead he would be prevented from defraying the costs of Christian burial by corporal labor—to that degree it is certain that we are all Christians. It stands firm in "Christendom," stands as firm as the principle of contradiction outside of Christendom, it stands firm, this eternal principle, which no doubt is able to shake: we are all Christians.

A difficulty about the New Testament

In the New Testament everything is planned in noble proportions. The true is represented ideally; but on the other hand errors and aberrations are again on a big scale: we are warned against hypocrisy, against all sorts of false teaching, against presumptuous reliance upon good works, etc., etc.

But strangely enough the New Testament takes no account of the thing there is all-too-great a mass of in this world, which is the content of this world, that is, of twaddle, twattle, patter, smallness, mediocrity, playing at Christianity, transforming everything into mere words. Owing to this it is almost impossible by the aid of the New Testament to punch a blow at real life, at the actual world in which we live, where for one certified hypocrite there are 100,000 twaddlers, for one certified heretic, 100,000 nincompoops.

The New Testament seems to entertain high notions of what it is to be a man. On the one hand it holds up the ideal; on the other hand, when it depicts wrong actions, one sees that it has nevertheless a high notion of what it is to be a man: but twaddling, nincompoopism, mediocrity, are constantly spared its blows.

So from time immemorial twaddle has taken advantage of this to establish itself as the true Christian orthodoxy—hence these countless battalions of millions of Christians. This orthodoxy, so strong in numbers, so weak in mind, takes advantage of the fact that one cannot truthfully denounce it as heterodoxy, hypocrisy, etc. (as indeed one cannot)—*ergo* it is the true Christian orthodoxy.

And this can very well be argued. The fact is that in every situation the highest and the lowest have a certain superficial resemblance to one another, neither of them being a little lower than the high, nor having the intermediate qualification between high and low. Thus these two qualifications, that of being above all criticism, and that of being beneath all criticism, have a certain resemblance to one another. And so it is also with the orthodoxy of these masses and of the priests who live off of them en masse: it resembles true Christianity in so far as it is not heterodoxy or heresy.

In other respects it resembles true Christianity even less than does any heresy or heterodoxy whatsoever. The situation is this: as high as true Christianity stands above all heresy and error and aberration, just so deep below all heresy and error and aberration lies twaddle. But, as has been said, the difficulty about the New Testament is that, requiring as it does ideality and fighting against spirits, it does not once take aim at this immense corpus which in "Christendom" is constantly producing the Christian orthodoxy and the Christian seriousness which expresses itself in the fact that "witnesses to the truth" (what a satirical self-contradiction!) make a career and a success in this world by depicting on Sundays how truth must suffer in this world.

Of this fact one must take due notice. And when one has duly noticed it, one will see that after all the New Testament is in the right, that things do go as the New Testament has foretold. In the midst of this immense population of "Christians," this shoal of Christians, there live here and there some individuals, a single individual. For him the way is narrow (cf. the New Testament), he is hated by all (cf. the New Testament), to put him to death is regarded as a divine service (cf. the New Testament). This after all is a curious book, the New Testament; it really is in the right; for these individuals, this single individual—why, yes, they would be the Christians.

If we really are Christians—what then is God?

If it isn't so—that what we understand by being a Christian is a vain conceit, that all this machinery with a State Church and 1000 spiritual-worldly counselors of chancery, etc., is a prodigious optical illusion which in eternity will not help us in the least, on the contrary will be used as an accusation against us—if it isn't so; for in that case, let us (for eternity's sake!) get rid of it the sooner the better.

— — if it isn't so, if what we mean by being a Christian really is being a Christian—what then is God?

He is the most comical being that ever lived, His Word the most comical book that ever has come to light: to set heaven and earth in motion (as He does in His Word), so threaten with hell, with eternal punishment...in order to attain what we understand by being Christians (and we indeed are true Christians)—no, nothing so comical ever occurred! Imagine that a man with a loaded pistol stepped up to a person and said to him, "I'll shoot you dead," or imagine something still more terrible, that he were to say, "I'll seize upon your person and torture you to death in the most dreadful manner, if you do not (now be on the watch, for here it comes)...make your own life here on earth as profitable and enjoyable as you possibly can." This surely is the most comical speech; for to bring that about one really does not need to threaten with a loaded pistol and the most agonizing kind of death; perhaps neither the loaded pistol nor the most agonizing kind of death would avail to prevent it. And so it is here: by the dread of eternal punishment (frightful menace!), by the hope of an eternal blessedness, to want to bring about...yes, to bring about what we are (for what we call a Christian is indeed to be a Christian), so then to want to bring about what we are: that we may live as we most like to live—for to refrain from civil crimes is nothing but plain shrewdness.

The most dreadful sort of blasphemy is that of which "Christendom" is guilty: transforming the God of Spirit into...ludicrous twaddle. And the stupidest [literally, most spirit-less] divine worship, more stupid than anything that is or was to be found in paganism, more stupid than worshiping a stone, an ox, an insect, more stupid than all that is—to worship under the name of God...a twaddler.

In case we really are Christians, in case it is (Christianly) quite as it should be with "Christendom," a "Christian world"—then the New Testament is *eo ipso* no longer a guide for Christians, cannot be such

Under the assumed conditions, the New Testament neither is nor can be a guide for Christians—for the way is changed, is entirely different from the one in the New Testament.

The New Testament therefore, regarded as a guide for Christians, becomes, under the assumption we have made, a historical curiosity, pretty much like a guidebook to a particular country when everything in that country has been totally changed. Such a guidebook serves no longer the serious purpose of being useful to travelers in that country, but at the most it is worth reading for amusement. While one is making the journey easily by railway, one reads in the guidebook, "Here is Woolf's Gullet where one plunges 70,000 fathoms down under the earth"; while one sits and smokes one's cigar in the snug café, one reads in the guidebook, "Here it is a band of robbers has its stronghold, from which it issues to assault the travelers and maltreat them"; here it is, etc. Here it is; that is, here it *was*; for now (it is very amusing to imagine how it was), now there is no Woolf's Gullet but the railway, and no robber band, but a snug café.

If then we really are Christians, if it is quite as it should be with "Christendom" and a Christian world—then would I shout, loud enough if possible to be heard in heaven, "Thou infinite One, if in other respects Thou hast showed Thyself to be love, this verily was unloving on Thy part, that Thou hast not let men know that the New Testament is no longer a guide [guidebook] for Christians! How cruel, while all has been changed to the very opposite, and yet it is true that we are all Christians, to alarm the weak by the fact that Thy Word has not yet been repealed or altered!"

However this I cannot assume, that God could be like that; and therefore I am compelled to try another explanation, to which also I am much more inclined: this whole thing about "Christendom" and "a Christian world" is a knavish trick on man's part, the notion that we really are Christians is a vain conceit by force of the knavish trick; on the other hand, the New Testament, entirely unchanged, is the guidebook for Christians, for whom things will go in this world as one reads in the New Testament, and who should not let themselves be disturbed by the fact that for knavish Christians things go differently in this world, a knavish world.

How lucky we are not all priests!

[May 11.]

Imagine that a society was formed for the purpose of counteracting the drinking of wine.

To that end the director of the society thought it expedient to engage a number of men who as emissaries, speakers, call them "priests," could travel through the whole land, working to win men and persuade them to join the society.

"But," said the director at the meeting when the thing was decided, "to economize on the priests doesn't do a damn bit of good, to require them not to drink wine leads to nothing, all we get out of that is the watery and fasting talk which doesn't fill anybody with enthusiasm for joining our association. No, we must not economize on the priest, he must have his bottle of wine every day, and in proportion to his zeal something extra, so that he may have a liking for his work, and with warmth, vigor, the whole power of conviction, he will carry people away, so that they will enter our society in countless numbers."

Suppose that all of them became, not members of the society, but priests in the service of this society.

So it is with Christianity and the State. Christianity, the teaching about renunciation, about heterogeneity to this world, a teaching which issues no checks except those payable in another world, this teaching the State wants to have introduced. "But," says the State, "to economize on the priests really doesn't do any good, all we get out of it is a kind of fasting and waterish something which wins nobody for the teaching but rather scares them all away. No, the priest must be remunerated in such a way, his life arranged in such a way, that he can find pleasure, both for himself and with his family, in preaching this doctrine. Thus there can be hope for winning men for the renunciation of the earthly; for the priest will be in the mood to describe to men with warmth, vigor, the whole power of conviction, how blessed this renunciation and suffering is, how blessed it is to get checks payable only in another world, that it is [listen to him!] blessed, blessed, blessed!"

How lucky we are not all priests!

God in heaven behaves in a different way when He wants to introduce Christianity. He assures Himself that in any case at least one man becomes a Christian: the teacher of Christianity. And then off He goes winning men for the doctrine. Well, yes, it goes slowly, and in the same degree that it is certain the teacher is a Christian, the likelihood is that it will end with the teacher being put to death, and the whole outcome would be one: the teacher.

However, God in heaven is entirely lacking in shrewdness, especially the high shrewdness of statesmanship; He is a poor narrow-minded fellow of the old school, simple enough really to believe that when one wants to sew one must knot the thread,[11] He has no notion of that which is the secret of the statesman's shrewdness, no presentiment how much faster it goes if one lets such foolishness alone and takes the matter up seriously, that then with a turn of the hand one has millions of Christians by the help of teachers who are not Christians.

O human nonsense! And this has been called seriousness! Centuries have been thrown away upon that costly foolishness, which has been paid for with money at a dear price, and paid for still more dearly...by having forfeited eternity!

WHAT CHRIST'S JUDGMENT IS
about
OFFICIAL CHRISTIANITY

By

S. Kierkegaard

Copenhagen
Published by C. A. Reitzel's Estate and Heirs
Bianco Luno's Press
1855

June 1855.
[Published June 16.]

What Christ's judgment is about official Christianity

IT MIGHT seem strange that not till now do I come out with this; for Christ's judgment after all is surely decisive, inopportune as it must seem to the clerical gang of swindlers who have taken forcible possession of the firm "Jesus Christ" and done a flourishing business under the name of Christianity.

It is not without reason, however, that I educe this testimony now, and he who has followed with attention my whole work as an author will not have failed completely to observe that there is a certain method in the way I set to work, that in the first place it is determined by the fact that this whole thing about "Christendom" is, as I have said, a criminal case, corresponding to what ordinarily is known as forgery, imposture, except that here it is religion which is thus made use of; and in the second place by the fact that I really have, as I have said, a talent for detective work.

Consider this a moment, so that thou mayest be able to follow the course of the development. I began by giving myself out to be a poet, aiming slyly at what I thought might well be the real situation of official Christianity, that the difference between a Freethinker and official Christianity is that the Freethinker is an honest man who bluntly *teaches* that Christianity is poetry, *Dichtung*,[12] whereas official Christianity is a forger who solemnly protests that Christianity is something quite different, and by this means conceals the fact that for its part it does actually turn Christianity into poetry, doing away with the following of Christ, so that only through the power of imagination is one related to the Pattern, whilst living for one's own part in entirely different categories, which means to be related poetically to Christianity or to transform it into poetry which is no more morally binding than poetry essentially is; and at last one casts the Pattern away entirely and lets what it is to be a man, mediocrity, count pretty nearly as the ideal.

Under the name of a poet I then drew out a number of ideals, brought forth that to which—yes, to which 1000 royal functionaries are bound by an oath. And these good men noticed nothing whatever, they felt perfectly secure, to such a degree was everything spiritlessness [i.e. stupidity] and worldliness; these good men had no presentiment that anything was hidden behind the poet—that the line of action was that of a detective's shrewdness in order to make the person concerned feel secure, a method the police use precisely for the sake of having a chance to get a profounder insight.

Then some time elapsed. I even stood on very good terms with these perjured men—and quite quietly I managed to introduce the ideals, and at the same time got acquainted with the men with whom I had to deal.

But at last these good men became impatient with the poet, he was too impertinent for them. This was occasioned by the article against Bishop Martensen about Bishop Mynster. Feeling perfectly secure as they did, they then made a great outcry (as one will recall from that time), saying that it was "far too great a standard which was being applied,"[13] etc.—feeling themselves perfectly secure.

Then this poet suddenly transformed himself, threw away the guitar, if I may speak thus, brought out a book which is called *The New Testament of Our Lord and Saviour Jesus Christ,* and—I may say, with a detective's eye upon them—put it up to these good perjured teachers whether this is not the book to which they were bound by an oath, this book whose standard is a good deal higher than that which the "poet" had employed.

From that instant there supervened, as one knows, profound silence. So prompt in raising a warning, so ready in declaiming, as long as they thought they not only could slip out of it but could show themselves off by saying, "It is a poet we have before us, his ideals are extravagant, the standard is far too great"—then they were silent from the moment that book and the oath came into the game. The first thing is to make the person in question feel secure; a police agent, though he were in possession of all other talents, if he has no virtuosity in the art of making people feel secure, is nothing of a "detective talent." In that condition the opposite party inverts the whole relationship: it is he, precisely he who is the honest man, and it looks almost as if the detective had got into a dilemma. But then when the detective, by this making the opposite party feel secure, has learned what he wanted to know, he alters his procedure, goes bluntly about it—and then suddenly the opposite party becomes silent, bites his lips, and likely thinks, This is a pretty pickle.

So then I brought forward the New Testament, took the liberty of respectfully calling to mind that these respected witnesses to the truth were bound by an oath to the New Testament—and then silence followed. Was not this strange?

Nevertheless I thought it best to keep them if possible in obscurity about how well posted I was and to what degree I have the New Testament on my side; and in that too I succeeded, though it could not occur to me to boast of it.

I spoke then in my own name; each time more decisively, it is true, since I saw that they steadily disdained the effort I first made to state the case for the opponent as favorably as I could possibly do it; and at last I undertook in my own name to say that it is a crime, a great crime, to take part in the public worship of God as it now is. That was in my own name. Now of course they no longer could escape by representing that I am a poet while it was the others who could even plume themselves upon being the truth. Yet there is always something reassuring in the fact that I speak in my own name, so in view of this reassurance I succeeded again in making the opponents feel a little secure, in order to have an opportunity of knowing them better, to see whether they were inclined to harden themselves against the accusation. For doubtless conscience must have smitten these perjured men at hearing this word which altered everything: It is a crime, a great crime, to take part in the public worship of God as it now is; for this is at the greatest possible remove from being divine worship.

But, as I have said, the reassuring thing was that I spoke in my own name. For though it is true that I know with God that I have spoken truly and spoken as I ought to speak, and though what I have said is true and ought to be said, even if there were no words to this effect from Christ himself, yet it is always a good thing that we know from the New Testament how Christ judges official Christianity.

And that we do know from the New Testament, His judgment is found there. But naturally I am fully convinced that thou, whoever thou art, if thou knowest nothing about what Christianity is except what is to be learned from the Sunday sermons of the "witnesses to the truth," thou mayest go year after year to three churches every Sunday, hear, broadly speaking, every one of the royal functionaries—and never hear the words of Christ which I have in view. Presumably the witnesses to the truth think about it in this way: The proverb says not to speak of rope in the house of a man that was hanged; so also it would be madness to bring forward in the church these words from God's Word which bear witness before high heaven against the juggling tricks of the priests. Indeed I might be tempted to make the following requirement, which, equitable and mild as it is, is yet the only punishment I desire to inflict upon the priests. Certain passages from the New Testament would be selected, and the priest be obliged to read them aloud before the congregation. Of course I should have to make one stipulation, that after he had knocked off reading such a passage from the New Testament the priest should not, as he usually does, put the New Testament aside and proceed thereupon to "explain" what he had read. No, many thanks. No, what I might be tempted to propose is the following order of service: the congregation assembles; a prayer is said at the church door; a hymn is sung; then the priest goes up to the speaker's seat, takes out the New Testament, pronounces the name of God, and thereupon reads from it before the congregation that definite passage, loudly and distinctly, whereupon he has to be silent and to remain standing silently for five minutes in the pulpit, and then he can go. This I would regard as exceedingly profitable. I am not thinking of making the priest blush. He who is conscious of willing to understand by Christianity what he understands by Christianity, and without blushing has been capable of taking an oath upon the New Testament, is not a man one can easily cause to blush; and it may indeed be said to be an essential part of the preparation of an official priest that he has weaned himself from the childish habits of youth and innocence, like blushing, etc. But I assume that the congregation would blush on behalf of the priest.

And now for the words of Christ to which I refer.

They are found in Matthew 23:29-33; Luke 11:47, 48; and they read as follows:

Woe unto you, scribes and Pharisees, hypocrites! for ye build the sepulchers of the prophets and garnish the tombs of the righteous, and say, If we had been in the days of our fathers, we should not have been partakers with them in the blood of the prophets. Wherefore ye witness to yourselves, that ye are sons of them that slew the prophets. Fill up then the measure of your fathers. Ye serpents, ye offspring of vipers, how shall ye escape the judgment of hell?

Woe unto you! for ye build the tombs of the prophets, and your fathers killed them. So ye are witnesses and consent unto the works of your fathers: for they killed them, and ye build their tombs.

But what then is "Christendom"? Is not "Christendom" the most colossal attempt at serving God, not by following Christ, as He required, and suffering for the doctrine, but instead of that, by "building the sepulchers of the prophets and garnishing the tombs of the righteous" and saying, "If we had been in the days of our fathers, we should not have been partakers with them in the blood of the prophets"?

It is of this sort of divine service I used the expression that, in comparison with the Christianity of the New Testament, it is playing Christianity. The expression is essentially true and characterizes the thing perfectly. For what does it mean to play, when one reflects how the word must be understood in this connection? It means to imitate, to counterfeit, a danger when there is no danger, and to do it in such a way that the more art is applied to it, the more delusive the pretense is that the danger is present. So it is that soldiers play war on the parade grounds: there is no danger, one only pretends that there is, and the art essentially consists in making everything deceptive, just as if it were a matter of life and death. And thus Christianity is played in "Christendom." Artists in dramatic costumes make their appearance in artistic buildings—there really is no danger at all, anything but that: the teacher is a royal functionary, steadily promoted, making a career—and now he dramatically plays Christianity, in short, he plays comedy. He lectures about renunciation, but he himself is being steadily promoted; he teaches all that about despising worldly titles and rank, but he himself is making a career; he describes the glorious ones ("the prophets") who were killed, and the constant refrain is: If we had been in the days of our fathers, we should not have been partakers with them in the blood of the prophets—we who build their sepulchers and garnish their tombs. So they will not go so far even as to do what I have constantly, insistently and imploringly proposed, that they should at least be so truthful as to admit that they are not a bit better than those who killed the prophets. No, they take advantage of the circumstance that they are not in fact contemporary with them to assert mendaciously of themselves that they are far, far better than those who killed the prophets, entirely different beings from those monsters—they in fact build the sepulchers of the men so unjustly killed and garnish their tombs.

However, this expression, "to play Christianity," could not be used by the Authoritative Teacher; He has a different way of talking about it.

Christ calls it (O give heed!), He calls it "hypocrisy." And not only that, but He says (now shudder!), He says that this guilt of hypocrisy is as great, precisely as great a crime as that of killing the prophets, so it is blood-guilt. Yea, if one could question Him, He would perhaps make answer that this guilt of hypocrisy, precisely because it is adroitly hidden and deliberately carried on through a whole lifetime, is a greater crime than theirs who in an outburst of rage killed the prophets.

This then is the judgment, Christ's judgment upon "Christendom." Shudder; for if you do not, you are implicated in it. It is so deceptive: must not we be nice people, true Christians, we who build the sepulchers of the prophets and garnish the tombs of the righteous, must not we be nice people, especially in comparison with those monsters who killed them? And besides, what else shall we do? We surely cannot do more than be willing to give of our money to build churches, etc., not be stingy with the priest, and go ourselves to hear him. The New Testament answers: What thou shalt do is to follow Christ, to suffer, suffer for the doctrine; the divine service thou wouldst like to carry on is hypocrisy; what the priests, with family, live on is that thou art a hypocrite, or they live by making thee a hypocrite, by keeping thee a hypocrite.

"Your fathers killed them, and ye build their tombs: so ye are witnesses and consent unto the works of your fathers." Luke 11:48.

Yes, Sunday Christianity and the huge gang of tradesmen-priests may indeed become furious at such a speech, which with one single word closes all their shops, quashes all this royally authorized trade, and not only that, but warns against their divine worship as against blood-guilt.

However, it is Christ who speaks. So profoundly does hypocrisy inhere in human nature that just when the natural man feels at his best, has got a divine worship fixed up entirely to his own liking, Christ's judgment is heard: This is hypocrisy, it is blood-guilt. It is not true that while on weekdays thy life is worldliness, the good thing about thee is that after all on Sundays thou goest to church, the church of official Christianity. No, no, official Christianity is much worse than all thy weekday worldliness, it is hypocrisy, it is blood-guilt.

At the bottom of "Christendom" there is this truth, that man is a born hypocrite. The Christianity of the New Testament was truth. But man shrewdly and knavishly invented a new kind of Christianity which builds the sepulchers of the prophets and garnishes the tombs of the righteous, and says, "If we had been in the days of our fathers." And this is what Christ calls blood-guilt.

What Christianity wants is...the following of Christ. What man does not want is suffering, least of all the kind of suffering which is properly the Christian sort, suffering at the hands of men. So he dispenses with "following," and consequently with suffering, the peculiarly Christian suffering, and then builds the sepulchers of the prophets. That is one thing. And then he says, lyingly before God, to himself and to others, that he is better than those who killed the prophets. That is the second thing. Hypocrisy first and hypocrisy last—and according to the judgment of Christ...blood-guilt.

Imagine that the people are assembled in a church in Christendom, and Christ suddenly enters the assembly. What dost thou think He would do?

He would turn upon the *teachers* (for of the *congregation* He would judge as He did of yore, that they were led astray), He would turn upon them who "walk in long robes," tradesmen, jugglers, who have made God's house, if not a den of robbers, at least a shop, a peddler's stall, and would say, "Ye hypocrites, ye serpents, ye generation of vipers"; and likely as of yore He would make a whip of small cords and drive them out of the temple.

Thou who readest this, if thou knowest nothing more about Christianity than is to be learned from the Sunday twaddle—I am thoroughly prepared for thee to be shocked at me, as though I were guilty of the cruelest mockery of God by representing Christ in this way, "putting such words into His mouth: serpents, generation of vipers. That is so dreadful. These indeed are words one never hears from the mouth of a cultivated person; and to make Him repeat them several times, that is so dreadfully common; and to turn Christ into a man who uses violence."

My friend, thou canst look it up in the New Testament. But when what has to be attained by preaching and teaching Christianity is an agreeable, a pleasurable life in a position of prestige, then the picture of Christ must be altered considerably. As for "garnishing"—no, there will be no sparing on that: gold, diamonds, rubies, etc. No, the priest is glad to see that and makes men believe that this is Christianity. But severity, the severity which is inseparable from the seriousness of eternity, that must go. Christ thus becomes a languishing figure, the impersonation of insipid human kindliness. This is related to the consideration that the plate must be passed during the sermon and the congregation must be in a mood to spend something, to shell out freely; and above all it is related to the desire prompted by fear of men to be on good terms with people, whereas the Christianity of the New Testament is: in the fear of God to suffer for the doctrine at the hands of men.

But "woe unto you, who build the sepulchers of the prophets" (teaching the people that this is the Christianity of the New Testament) "and garnish the tombs of the righteous" (constantly setting Money and Christianity together by the ears) and say, "If we"—yea, if ye had lived in the time of the prophets, ye would have put them to death, that is, ye would have done, as actually was done, hiddenly prompted the people to do it and bear the guilt. But in vain ye hide yourselves behind "Christendom," for what is hidden becomes revealed when the Truth pronounces the judgment: "Wherefore ye bear witness to yourselves that ye are the sons of them that killed the prophets, and ye fill up the measure of your fathers; for they killed the prophets, and ye garnish their tombs." In vain ye set yourselves up as holy, in vain ye think that precisely by building the tombs of the righteous ye prove yourselves better than the ungodly men who put them to death. Ah, the impotence of hypocrisy to hide itself! Ye are seen through and through. Precisely the building of the tombs of the righteous and saying, "If we," precisely this is to kill them, to be the true children of those ungodly men, doing the same thing as they, it is to bear witness to the fathers' deeds and to consent to them, to fill up the measure of your fathers, that is, to do what is far worse.

THE INSTANT

No. 3

CONTENTS

June 27, 1855. S. Kierkegaard.

Copenhagen

Published by C. A. Reitzel's Estate and Heirs

Bianco Luno's Press

From the Journal

THE NEW TESTAMENT

I might be tempted to make to Christendom a proposal different from that of the Bible Society. Let us collect all the New Testaments we have, let us bring them out to an open square or up to the summit of a mountain, and while we all kneel let one man speak to God thus: "Take this book back again; we men, such as we now are, are not fit to go in for this sort of thing, it only makes us unhappy." This is my proposal, that like those inhabitants in Gerasa we beseech Christ to depart from our borders. This would be an honest and human way of talking—rather different from the disgusting hypocritical priestly fudge about life having no value for us without this priceless blessing which is Christianity.

XI[1] A 347

State / Christianity

THE State is directly proportionate to number (the numerical); therefore when a state is decreasing, its numbers may gradually become so small that the State ceases to exist, the concept is snuffed out.

Christianity stands in a different relation to number: one single true Christian is enough to justify the assertion that Christianity exists. In fact, Christianity is inversely proportionate to number; for the concept "Christian" is a polemical concept, one can only be a Christian in contrast or contrastedly. So it is also in the New Testament: to God's desire to be loved, which essentially is a relationship of contrast or opposition in order to raise love to a higher power, corresponds the fact that the Christian who loves God in contrast and opposition to other men has to suffer from their hate and persecution. As soon as the opposition is taken away, the thing of being a Christian is twaddle—as it is in "Christendom," which has slyly done away with Christianity by the affirmation that we are all Christians.

So then the concept "Christianity" is inversely proportionate to number / "State" is directly proportionate: and for all that they have made Christianity and State divisible into one another——to the advantage of twaddle and the priests. For to set State and Christianity together by the ears in this fashion makes just as good sense as to talk of a yard of butter, or if possible there is less sense in it, since butter and a yard are merely things which have nothing to do with one another, whereas State and Christianity are inversely related to or rather from one another.

This, however, is with difficulty understood in "Christendom," where one naturally has no presentiment of what Christianity is, and where it never could occur to anyone, nor when it is affirmed could one get it into one's head, that Christianity has been *abolished* by *expansion,* by these millions of name-Christians, the number of which is surely meant to conceal the fact that there is not one Christian, that Christianity simply does not exist. For as one speaks of chattering oneself away from a subject by a long talk, so has the human race, and the individual within it, wanted to chatter itself out of being a Christian and sneak out of it by the help of this shoal of name-Christians, a Christian state, a Christian world, notions shrewedly calculated to make God so confused in His head by all these millions that He cannot discover that He has been hoaxed, that there is not one single...Christian.

Is the State justified, Christianly, in seducing a part of the youth engaged in study?

"Seducing"—commonly the word is used in relation to the feminine. One speaks of seducing a young girl, reflecting that at an age when the longings of the heart are directed to vain and earthly things, a way is opened to the poor child which leads to what she desires, but, alas, at the cost of her innocence. And the seduction of a young girl seems so unjustifiable precisely because at her age the longing for pleasure and the vanity of life is so strong in her own breast that she has special need of an influence from without in an opposite direction. As the proverb says, it is easy to get one to prance who likes to dance; and precisely for this reason it is so unjustifiable to take advantage of her.

Christianly, it may be said of the State that it is guilty of precisely the same thing with respect to the young men engaged in theological studies. For Christianity's view of life is so high that what commonly is called innocence and purity suffices by no means to meet its requirements. According to the Christianity of the New Testament, being a Christian, not to speak of being a teacher of Christianity, is sheer renunciation and suffering, and the lot of being a teacher is for the natural man the least attractive lot.

But precisely at the moment when the young man's longing after the things of this world may be only too strong, precisely at that moment when he is especially in need of the strongest influence in the opposite direction, either to frighten him back from taking that path, or, if he really has a call, to make him ripe to tread it—precisely of that moment the State takes advantage, spreading its toils to entangle him, to "seduce" him, so that to the youth whose mind is beguiled by seduction it looks as if being a teacher of Christianity is precisely the path which will lead him to all that he desires, to a reward for his labor not only ample and secure but increasing with the lapse of years, to a cosy home in the bosom of his family, perhaps to a career, perhaps even to a brilliant career—but only too surely, alas, only too surely, at the cost of his innocence. For after all there is an oath he has to make upon the New Testament, an oath which then opens to him, the seduced man, entrance to the things desired, but revenges itself later.

What is required might, Christianly, be stated thus: Whether the State might not be so good as to make known as soon as possible that from a given date it no longer undertakes to appoint teachers who have perjured themselves upon the New Testament. With the clergy now actually appointed the State has made a contract, to my way of thinking it has even contracted with all the young men now actually engaged in theological study. Let it therefore indicate a definite year after which it will no longer have anything to do with the appointment of such teachers.

Is the State justified in receiving an oath which not only is not kept but in the taking of which there is a self-contradiction?

One need not be very old, if only one has an eye for such things and has made use of it, to have convinced oneself that men have a decided partiality for illusion, find the best repose in illusion.

If there is one thing or another of importance for the community, men generally concentrate their effort in getting a committee appointed. When it is appointed people are reassured, do not much concern themselves whether the committee does anything, and finally forget the whole affair.

So also when something is to be seriously undertaken, men think there must be an oath, an oath which reassures us that the thing is serious and remains serious—whether the oath is kept or not concerns them less.

Indeed for sheer seriousness they sometimes do not observe whether the taking of the oath does not involve a self-contradiction.

This is the case with the priest's oath upon the New Testament, which the State nevertheless receives. If it should turn out that the oath is not kept, that would be not the most suspicious circumstance; but the truth is that it involves a self-contradiction. Yet it is likely that neither society nor the individual would feel reassured if in relation to something so serious as being a teacher of Christianity the seriousness is not secured by...an oath, the taking of which certainly involves a self-contradiction, so that one who is reassured by such an oath is reassured by...an illusion.

Christianity is related to a kingdom which is not of this world—and then the State receives an oath from teachers of Christianity, which oath signifies therefore that the man swears loyalty precisely to that which is the opposite to the State. Such an oath is a self-contradiction, like making a man swear by laying his hand upon the New Testament, where it is written, Thou shalt not swear.

In case the priest should be by any manner of means what the oath upon the New Testament obliges him to be, namely, a disciple of Christ, and his life an imitation of Christ, then his engagement as a royal functionary is the greatest obstacle. At the very moment when he should move in the direction in which his oath upon the New Testament requires him to move, he must break with his position as a royal functionary. That is, by an oath as a royal functionary they bind him in such a way that if he is to keep the oath they require him to make upon the New Testament, he must break with the first relationship. What a self-contradiction! And what a strange sort of seriousness, that an oath is taken (how solemnly!), an oath the taking of which is...a self-contradiction! And how pernicious both to the State and to Christianity!

The Christian demand upon the State must be to the following effect: Whether the State, the sooner the better, might not be so good as to dispense all the clergy from their oath upon the New Testament, give them back the oath, as an expression of the fact that the State had got into something it cannot meddle with, which at the same time will express what is true, that God, if I may venture to say so, discharges the whole actual garrison of priests, gives them back their oath.

Is the State justified, Christianly, in misleading the people, or in misleading their judgment as to what Christianity is?

[May 18.]

When we talk of the merely human, and leave the divine (Christianity) out of account, the situation is this: the State is the highest instance of authority, it is humanly the highest authority.

The people as a whole and the individuals among them live therefore in the assurance that everything which bears a special mark of being legalized, sanctioned, authorized by the State, everything which in a monarchical state is marked "royal," is to be regarded as something more than the same thing without this adjective which by the intervention of the State provides an assurance (guarantee) that here is something one can rely upon, something one has to respect.

Thus it is the people live, and it is desirable that they should live in this assurance; for this serves to make quiet and tranquil subjects who place their trust confidently in the State. But then the people live in such a way that from morning to night the individual gets an impression of this, all his thinking is ingrafted with the notion of what is royal, what is authorized by the State. Even in the least important concerns this way of thinking intrudes; business and professional men think that by getting permission to use the adjective "royal" they count for more than those who do not have this adjective.

Let us now turn to Christianity. It is the divine, and that instance of the divine which precisely because it truly is the divine would not at any price be a kingdom of this world; on the contrary, it would that the Christian might venture life and blood to prevent it from becoming a kingdom of this world.

Nevertheless the State takes it upon itself to introduce 1000 royal functionaries under the guise of teachers of Christianity.

Christianly, how misleading! The people, as was said, live and breathe in the thought that what is royally authorized is something more, more than what is not royally authorized. Then the people apply the notion to this instance also, have more respect for a royally authorized teacher of Christianity than for one who is not that, and then again with regard to the royally authorized teachers they have more respect in proportion as they are distinguished by the State, have higher rank, more orders of knighthood, bigger incomes.

What a fundamental confusion! In the same sense as one speaks of murdering a language, this is murdering Christianity, turning it round about, standing it on its head, or in a polite fashion shuffling it out. Under the color of Christianity the people live as pagans!

No, inasmuch as Christianity is the antithesis to the kingdoms of this world, is heterogeneous, not to be royally authorized is the truer thing. So to be royally authorized may be more easy, comfortable, convenient...for the priest; but Christianly it is a discommendation, precisely in the degree that, according to the State's order of precedence, one is in a higher station, has more orders, a bigger income.

Let the State test the reckoning, and it will be found that the reckoning is radically wrong

[June 16.]

The test is quite simple: let the State (and this is the one and only Christian demand, and also the only reasonable thing), let the State make all preaching of Christianity a private practice—

—and it will soon be evident whether there are in this land one and a half million Christians, and likewise whether there is in this land employment for 1000 priests with families.

The truth will prove to be that perhaps there is not really employment for 100 priests, and the truth will also prove to be that perhaps there is not a single one of all these bishops, deans and priests who is capable of undertaking a private practice.

Just as when the mother tongue was introduced in examinations[14] it was a sharpening of the test because the examinee had then no pretext that it was the language which hindered from betraying how much he knew, so is a private practice in the religious field very much more serious than this silly business of having royal functionaries, which does not so much as require one to have a religion for oneself, but merely to lecture *qua* royal functionary, paid by the State, protected by the State, insured of respect...*qua* royal functionary.

What keeps up the illusion about a Christian nation is partly the universal human indolence and love of ease which prefers to remain in the old ruts—but principally it is these 1000 self-interested men, among whom there is not a single one who is not pecuniarily interested in maintaining the illusion. If the illusion were removed, it is likely that 900 would be entirely without any means of earning their living; and the 100 who are capable of carrying on a private practice understand only too well that this is something entirely different from the present service in gaiters, with steady promotion insured by the State which may amount to a salary of many thousands. That a man needs medical help is something which makes itself physically so understandable that the State does not need in this instance to help people to understand it. But when men are made free religiously, a person may have trouble enough in making clear to them their spiritual need. Here it is that the State helps—but no doubt very unchristianly. "What! You feel no need of Christianity? Perhaps you need to go to the Reformatory!" "What! You feel no need of Christianity? Then perhaps you feel a need of becoming nothing; for unless you become a Christian all paths in society are closed to you!" Ah, that helped the priests' practice; and it is upon this in great part the priest lived, as one of Peder Paar's characters said of himself, "I live Christianly...by bankruptcy."[15]

That is no use; we must get rid of all disguises, mystifications and pompousness in order to get at the fact—that the stability of the Established Church is a money question, that the solemn silence of the clergy has a perfectly simple explanation, corresponding to what happens in business when a man is dunned for money and perhaps first tries to get out of it by pretending he did not hear. The clergy therefore had far better admit the true situation; things will only become worse for them by the help of this sort of silence. When a man with gravely measured tread walks with great gravity down the street, people are prompted to think, This must be something uncommon; but when one chances to learn the explanation of this gravity, that the man is a little tight, that for this reason (to counteract the tendency to gravitate directly towards the curbstone) he must hold himself with such gravity—he might far better stagger a bit, people would perhaps smile, perhaps not notice his condition at all. On the other hand, by his gravity he prompts an interest, and now cannot escape the banter, which only becomes more unmerciful in proportion as he makes an effort to walk with more and more gravity. So it is with the silence of the clergy. An open, frank, direct word would have been infinitely more serviceable to them than this silence, which solemnly, with high uplifted solemnity, conceals the fact that it is...a money question. For now the sarcasm acquires interest, the situation of the clergy becomes by this solemn and pretentious silence so very interesting.

If the State truly would serve Christianity, let it take away the 1000 livings

[May 12.]

As long as here in Denmark there exist 1000 livings for teachers of Christianity, the best is being done that can be done to hinder Christianity.

As long as there are 1000 livings, there continually will be a corresponding number of men who propose in this way to earn their bread.

Among these there will be some few who nevertheless had perhaps a call to preach Christianity. But precisely at the moment when it should have been a serious matter for them, in reliance only upon God and at their own risk, to undertake to come forward as teachers—precisely then the State opens to them the convenience of accepting a royal office, whereby these few are botched.

The far greater number will have no call at all to preach Christianity, but regard it simply as a living.

In this way the State succeeds in filling the whole land with Christianity in a badly spoiled condition, which creates the greatest difficulty for the introduction of true Christianity, far greater than complete paganism.

Take an example. If the State had a mind to put a stop to all true poetry, it would need merely (and remember that poetry is not so heterogeneous to this world as Christianity is), it would need merely to introduce 1000 livings for royal poetic functionaries. In this way the aim will soon be attained, the land will be overfilled continually with badly spoiled poetry, to such a degree that all true poetry becomes as good as impossible. The few who really had a call to become poets will precisely at the critical moment spring away from the effort required to venture out at one's own risk—and into the comfort of a royal office. But that effort is precisely the condition without which nothing can come of their call to be a poet. The many will see nothing but a living in this thing of being a poet, a living which is assured to them by the pain of going through with the course of reading for examination.

THE INSTANT

No. 4

CONTENTS

July 7, 1855. S. Kierkegaard.

Copenhagen
Published by C. A. Reitzel's Estate and Heirs
Bianco Luno's Press

From the Journal

CHRISTIANITY A FORTRESS

Imagine a fortress, absolutely impregnable, provisioned for an eternity. There comes a new commandant. He conceives that it might be a good idea to build bridges over the moats—so as to be able to attack the besiegers. *Charmant!* He transforms the fortress into a countryseat, and naturally the enemy takes it.

So it is with Christianity. They changed the method—and naturally the world conquered.

In my *Short Life of K.*, p. 234

Medical diagnosis

1.

THAT a proper diagnosis and prognosis of an illness is more than half the battle, every physician will admit, and likewise that no ability, no care and vigilance, is of any avail when the case has not been correctly diagnosed.

So it is also in relation to the religious.

This thing of "Christendom," the notion that we are all Christians, people have allowed to prevail and wish to do so; and then they bring forward now one aspect of the teaching, now another.

But the truth is that not only are we not Christians but we are not so much as pagans, to whom the Christian doctrine could be preached without embarrassment; but by an illusion, a monstrous illusion ("Christendom," a Christian state, a Christian land, a Christian world), we are even prevented from becoming as receptive as the pagans were.

And so people want the illusion to be undisturbed, its power to remain intact, and on the other hand they want someone to furnish a new presentation of Christian doctrine.[16]

That is what they want; and in a certain sense it is quite natural, precisely because they are ensnared in the illusion (not to raise the query whether they are personally interested in the illusion), precisely for this cause they want what must feed the disease—a thing quite universal, that what the sick man most desires is just what feeds the disease.

2.

Think of a hospital. The patients are dying like flies. The methods are altered in one way and another. It's no use. What does it come from? It comes from the building, the whole building is full of poison. That the patients are registered as dead, one of this disease, and that one of another, is not true; for they are all dead from the poison that is in the building.

So it is in the religious sphere. That the religious situation is lamentable, that religiously men are in a pitiable state, nothing is more certain. So one man thinks that it would help if we got a new hymnal,[17] another a new altar-book, another a musical service, etc., etc.

In vain—for it comes from...the building. This whole lumberroom of a State Church, which from time immemorial has not been ventilated, spiritually speaking—the air confined in this lumberroom has developed poison. And for this reason the religious life is sick or has died out. For, alas, precisely that which worldliness regards as health is, Christianly considered, disease; and inversely, what Christianly considered as health is regarded by worldliness as disease.

Let it collapse, this lumberroom, get rid of it, shut all these shops and booths, the only ones which the severe Sunday ordinance[18] exempted, make this official ambiguity impossible, put all these men out of commission and make provision for them, these quacks. For if it is true that the royally authorized physician is the proper physician and the unauthorized a quack, in Christianity it is the other way around; precisely the royally authorized teacher is the quack, is such by being royally authorized. And let us again serve God in simplicity, instead of treating him as a fool in magnificent buildings. Let the thing again become seriousness, and stop playing a game. For a Christianity preached by royal functionaries who are paid and made secure by the State and employ the police against other people, such a Christianity has the same relation to the Christianity of the New Testament as swimming with a cork float or with a bladder has to swimming,[19] that is to say, it is play.

Yea, let this come to pass. What Christianity needs is not the suffocating protection of the State; no, it needs fresh air, it needs persecution, and it needs...God's protection. The State only works disaster, it wards off persecution, and it is not the medium through which God's protection can be conducted. Above all, save Christianity from the State. By its protection it smothers Christianity to death, as a fat lady with her corpus overlies her baby. And it teaches Christianity the most disgusting bad habits, as for example, under the name of Christianity to employ the power of the police.

3.

A man becomes thinner and thinner day by day; he is wasting away. What can the matter be? He does not suffer want. "No, certainly not," says the physician, "it doesn't come from that, it comes precisely from eating, from the fact that he eats out of season, eats without being hungry, uses stimulants to arouse a little bit of appetite, and in that way he ruins his digestion, fades away as if he were suffering want."

So it is religiously. The most fatal thing of all is to satisfy a want which is not yet felt, so that without waiting till the want is present, one anticipates it, likely also uses stimulants to bring about something which is supposed to be a want, and then satisfies it. And this is shocking! And yet this is what they do in the religious sphere, whereby they really are cheating men out of what constitutes the significance of life, and helping people to waste life.

For this is the aim of the whole machinery of the State Church, which under the form of care for men's souls cheats them out of the highest thing in life, that in them there should come into being the concern about themselves, the want, which verily a teacher or priest would find according to his mind; but now, instead of this, the want (and precisely the coming into being of this want is life's highest significance for a man) does not come into being at all, but having been satisfied long before it came into being, it is prevented from coming into being. And this is thought to be the continuation of the work which the Saviour of the human race completed, this bungling of the human race! And why? Because there are now as a matter of fact so and so many royal functionaries who, with families, have to live off of this, under the name of...the cure of souls!

What really is shocking

[April 10.]

That the Christianity of the New Testament is a thing most repugnant to us men (to the Jews a stumbling block, to the Greeks foolishness), that it is as though calculated to stir us men up against it, that as soon as it is heard it is the signal for the most passionate hate and the cruelest persecution, of this the New Testament makes no concealment; on the contrary, it affirms it as distinctly and decisively as possible. It is heard constantly when Christ is talking with the Apostles, saying that they must not be offended; it is emphasized again and again that they must be well prepared for what awaited them. And the Apostles' talk bears sufficient witness to the fact that they had to experience the truth of what was foretold.

It therefore never could occur to anyone who understands himself Christianly, that he might be angry at a man if he were to become the object of his hate and resentment for telling him what Christianity really is. By no means, for when he understands himself Christianly he must find this quite natural.

But even the man who is most exasperated against him must agree with him on one point and understand why he finds it shocking that there is a whole family of parasites (called to be teachers of Christianity and bound by an oath upon the New Testament) who support themselves by palming off in the name of Christianity what is after their own taste (the absolutely decisive proof that it is not the Christianity of the New Testament), support themselves by preaching under the name of Christianity what is exactly the opposite of the Christianity of the New Testament, pluming themselves upon a royal commission, which is just as ridiculous as in a game of cards to want to take a trump with a simple card, or as wanting to legitimate oneself as a shepherd by a testimonial from the wolf.

This is the shocking thing. Perhaps too it is without an analogy in history that a religion has been abolished by...flourishing. But note that in saying "flourishing" Christianity is understood as the opposite of what the New Testament understands by Christianity. The religion of suffering has become the religion of mirth, but it retains the name unchanged.

This is the shocking thing, that the situation is if possible made twice as difficult for Christianity as it was when it came into the world, because now it is confronted, not by pagans and Jews, whose whole resentment must be aroused, but by *Christians* whom the clerical gang of swindlers has made to believe that they are Christians, and that Christianity is set to the melody of a drinking song, only still merrier than such a song, which after all is constantly accompanied by the sad reflection that it soon is over and "in a hundred years is all forgotten";[20] whereas the merry Christian drinking song, according to the assurance of the priests, "lasts an eternity."[21]

Truth and a living

[April 13.]

Herr Zierlich, in the play by State Counselor Heiberg,[22] possesses, as everyone knows, the sense of decency to such a degree that he finds it indecent for men's and women's garments to be hung in the same closet.

We will leave that to Herr Zierlich. But on the other hand, what for us in our characterless age it is necessary to practice is separation, discrimination, between the infinite and the finite, between a striving for the infinite and for the finite, between living for something and living by something, which our age—most indecently!—has put together in the closet, got them to curdle together or coalesce into one, which Christianity on the contrary, with the passion of eternity, with the most dreadful either/or, holds apart from one another, separating them by a yawning abyss.

Christianity, which also has after all some acquaintance with man and knows what a fine chap he is, how easy it is to get him to engage in and take an oath upon whatsoever cause it may be, if only it is a way to a living, a way of making a career, of being able to get himself a wife, etc.—Christianity therefore, as warily as possible, as warily as the police can act, has erected a barrier with a view to preventing these things from coalescing completely into one: Christianity and a living, Christianity and a career, Christianity and a fiancée, etc.

It is quite different with the State, which has managed to make synonymous the notions of Christianity and a living, a bachelor of theology and an engagement, etc., etc. And therefore an entirely different kind of thing has been got out of Christianity from the moment the State took hold. Instead of the bagatelle which was all it came to, with Christ especially, but also with the Apostles, when only some few Christians were produced, it now went into the millions, millions of Christians and 100,000 livings—Christianity is completely triumphant.

Yes, or else under the name of Christianity a prodigious piece of knavery is triumphant. For like that well-known inscription, "This is supposed to be Troy,"[23] instead of the simple word "Troy," or like the title stamped upon the binding of an empty volume, so it is with all this about "Christendom." In this way one can introduce any religion whatsoever into the world, and Christianity introduced in this way is unfortunately exactly the opposite of Christianity. Might there in these shrewd times be found even a youth who does not easily understand that, if the State got the notion, for example, of wanting to introduce the religion that the moon is made out of a green cheese, and to that end were to arrange for 1000 livings for a man with family, steadily promoted, the consequence would be—if only the State held to its purpose—that after a few generations a statistican would be able to affirm that this religion (the moon is made out of a green cheese) is the prevailing religion in the land?

A living—oh, these proofs which are advanced for the truth of Christianity, these devilish learned and profound and perfectly convincing proofs which have filled folios, upon which "Christendom" plumes itself as the State does upon the army, what do they all amount to in comparison with...a living, and the possibility of a career thrown into the bargain?

A living—and then Juliana, that Frederick and Juliana can come together. Oh, these proofs which are advanced for the truth of Christianity, these devilish learned and profound and perfectly convincing proofs, what do they all amount to in comparison with Juliana and the fact that in this way Frederick and Juliana can come together? If at any moment the thought should struggle in Frederick, "I myself do not really believe this doctrine, and then to have to preach it to others"—if such thoughts should struggle in Frederick, go to Juliana, she can drive such thoughts away. "Sweet Frederick," says she, "only let us manage to come together. Why go and torment thyself with such thoughts? There are surely 1000 priests like thee; in short, thou art a priest like the others."

In fact Juliana plays a great role in procuring clergy for the State. And hence they should have been wary about introducing Juliana, and also about introducing livings. For it may be, as Don Juan says to Zerline,[24] that only in the soft arms of a blameless wife does true felicity reside, and possibly it is true, as both poets and prose writers have affirmed, that in these soft arms one forgets the world's alarms; but the question is whether there is not also something else one can only too easily forget in these soft arms—namely, what Christianity is. And the older I grow the clearer it becomes to me that the twaddle into which Christianity has sunk, especially in Protestantism, and more especially in Denmark, is due in part to the fact that these soft arms have come to interfere a little too much, so that for the sake of Christianity one might require the respective proprietors of these soft arms to retire a little more into the background.

To get an opportunity to know what the true situation of Christianity is in this land, it would be very important if we could manage to thrust aside the livings and Juliana so as to be able to see. How desirable it would be if the State understood it in this way, if it were to proclaim that it felt under obligation to pay the priests with whom it had already contracted, in case they thought they must resign from their office! There are doubtless many upright and honest men who would feel their consciences greatly relieved. And after all it is really the State which bears the responsibility, the State which, beckoning seductively, has pointed out to inexperienced young bachelors of theology and their fiancées a something which, Christianly, is without justification. Afterwards (when one has once become *pater familias*, etc.), yes, then it is too late, then one hasn't the power to break with this wrong situation one innocently got into, but remains in it...with a troubled conscience.

True Christians / Many Christians

[April 9.]

The interest of Christianity, what it wants, is—true Christians.

The egoism of the priesthood, both for pecuniary advantage and for the sake of power, stands in relation to—many Christians.

"And that's very easily done, it's nothing at all: let's get hold of the children, then each child is given a drop of water on the head—then he is a Christian. If a portion of them don't even get their drop, it comes to the same thing, if only they imagine they got it, and imagine consequently that they are Christians. So in a very short time we have more Christians than there are herring in the herring season, Christians by the millions, and then, by the power of money as well, we are the greatest power the world has ever seen. That thing about eternity is definitely the cleverest of all inventions, when it gets into the right hands, the hands of practical people; for the Founder, unpractical as he was, had a wrong notion of what Christianity is."

No, rather than this let us stick to what by comparison is angelic purity, though the State punishes it with the penitentiary; let us stick to enriching ourselves by counterfeiting the custom-house stamps or by using abusively the marks of celebrated factories! But to become a power and to win the earthly by the use of a false label with reference to that which was served by suffering unto the end, to the utmost, to the point of being forsaken by God, to use a false label with reference to that cause which He in dying upon the cross entrusted to human honesty evinced by imitation, and then to do this unmoved by the thought that it was Love which suffered, and Love which in dying entrusted its cause to human honesty, and unmoved by the thought that there would be millions of men who in this way would be swindled out of the highest and holiest, would be swindled by being made to believe that they were Christians. No, this is horrible. It is true, generally speaking, that the greatness of a crime, its meanness, its wide ramifications, inflames the policeman, gives him increased zeal; but there is a limit, and if the crime exceeds that, the policeman may well have the experience, like a man in a swoon, of grasping for something to support him, desiring to escape and find in tears relief from what he had never before experienced.

So then this accounts for the millions of Christians, the Christian states, kingdoms, lands, a Christian world. But this is only the first half of the criminal story; we come now to the refinement. The refinement is unique in its genre, altogether without analogy; for those who enrich themselves by counterfeiting the custom-house stamps or the marks of celebrated factories at least do not lay claim to be regarded as the most faithful friends of the custom-house or of those factories. This is reserved to the Christian counterfeiters. That zeal, the zeal of egoism, for making many Christians in a way which is precisely the most repugnant to Christianity in its inmost heart, that zeal is bedizened as true Christian zeal and jealously for the spread of the doctrine, as though it were Christianity one were serving in this way and not rather Christianity one was betraying by serving oneself. Nevertheless this egoistic zeal was by falsification stamped as Christian zeal, these counterfeiters claimed to be regarded as the most faithful friends of Christianity. And those unfortunate millions who were cheated out of their money and misused as a physical power, while as a recompense they were cheated out of the eternal by being put off with some sort of galimatias—these millions worshiped and adored the Christian counterfeiters as the true servants of Christianity.

There are pranks of a child, a boy, which are punished by a box on the ear; and it would be pronounced madness if for such a prank the father or teacher were to require the child to be punished by a sentence to the penitentiary for life. On the other hand, in the case of crimes which the State reasonably punishes by a life sentence to the penitentiary, it would be pronounced madness to think that they would be expiated by a box on the ear. But what we never hear a word about in our days, in these Christian states and lands, where all priests are witnesses to the truth, is that there are crimes with respect to which (on other grounds than in the case of the child) it would be a sort of madness to apply the punishment of the penitentiary for life, because here again the punishment would bear no proportion to the crime. The longer I live, the clearer it becomes to me that the real crimes are not punished in this world. The child's prank is punished; but that after all is not really a crime. The State punishes crimes; but the real crimes, in comparison with which the crimes the State punishes can hardly be called crimes, are not punished...in Time.

In "Christendom" all are Christians; when all are Christians, the New Testament *eo ipso* does not exist, yea, it is impossible

[April.]

The Christianity of the New Testament rests upon the assumption that the Christian is in a relationship of *opposition*, that to be a Christian is to believe in God, to love Him, in a relationship of opposition. While according to the Christianity of the New Testament the Christian has all the effort, the conflict, the anguish, which is connected with doing what is required, dying from the world, hating oneself, etc., he has at the same time to suffer from the relationship of opposition to other men, which the New Testament speaks of again and again: to be hated by others, to be persecuted, to suffer for the doctrine, etc.

In "Christendom" we are all Christians—therefore the relationship of opposition drops out. In this meaningless sense they have got all men made into Christians, and got everything Christian—and then (under the name of Christianity) we live a life of paganism. They have not ventured defiantly, openly, to revolt against Christianity; no, hypocritically and knavishly they have done away with it by falsifying the definition of what it is to be a Christian. It is of this I say that it is: (1) a criminal case, (2) that it is playing Christianity, (3) taking God for a fool.

Every hour this lasts the crime is continued; every Sunday that divine worship is conducted in this manner Christianity is played as a game and God is taken for a fool; everyone who participates is participating in playing Christianity and taking God for a fool, and is thus implicated in the Christian criminal case.

Yea, O God, if there were no eternity—the most untruthful word that ever was spoken in the world, Thou, O God of truth, hast spoken: Be not deceived, God will not be mocked.

The difficulty of my task

[April 18.]

That the official Christianity, what we call Christianity, is not the Christianity of the New Testament, is not a striving after it, has not the remotest resemblance to it—nothing is easier to see, and to get men to see this clearly I should count a small matter, if there were not a very peculiar sort of difficulty involved in it.

Assuming that what the New Testament understands by Christianity and by being a Christian were something quite according to a man's taste, something which might thoroughly please and appeal to the natural man, almost as if it were his own invention, as though it talked to him out of his own heart—well, yes, then we soon shall have everything as it ought to be.

But, but, but here lies the difficulty. Precisely what the New Testament understands by Christianity and by being a Christian is—and this the New Testament makes no effort to conceal but emphasizes decisively—what most of all is repugnant to the natural man, is an offense to him, against which with wild passion and defiance he must revolt, or else cunningly try at any price to be rid of it, as for example by the help of a knavish trick, calling Christianity what is the exact opposite of Christianity, and then thanking God for Christianity and for the great and inestimable privilege of being a Christian.

So then, when I would make known that what we call Christianity, the official Christianity, is not at all the Christianity of the New Testament, and when to that end I would point out what the New Testament understands by Christianity and by being a Christian, that this is sheer anguish, misery, wretchedness (but then true enough it is sure of eternity), whereas what we call Christianity is pleasant and merry (but then true enough without any assurance of eternity but that of the priest)—when I do this, it is unavoidable that most people will confuse two things which are totally different: that what I prove to be Christianity does not please them; and that the question whether it pleases them or not has nothing whatever to do with the question what the Christianity of the New Testament is. Yea, the fact that it does not please them might be regarded as a token that what I call the Christianity of the New Testament is the Christianity of the New Testament, since the New Testament itself says again and again that it does not please man, that it is an offense to him.

It is verily not for naught I have called this thing about "Christendom" a criminal case. The preaching of official Christianity has of course, as one might expect, not been negligent but has gone about its falsification thoroughly—to win men is thus the important thing, Christianity is less important. The mode of procedure is this: They set human passions in motion, and then what they know appeals to the passions they call Christianity, they get that to be Christian—and thus they win men to Christianity.

The Christianity of the New Testament on the contrary is what displeases and shocks man in the highest degree. When it is truly preached it neither wins men by the millions nor wins reward and profit. In every generation that man is a rarity who exercises such a power over himself that he can *will* what is not pleasant to him, that he can hold fast *that* truth which does not please him, hold that it is the truth although it does not please him, hold that it is the truth precisely because it does not please him, and then nevertheless, in spite of the fact that it does not please him, can commit himself to it. With most men the situation is at once confused; what they must go in for must be something which is shown to please them, to appeal to them.

This is what the Christian counterfeiters aim at. In explaining to men what Christianity is they constantly give this turn to the thing: That this and this is Christianity you can assure yourself by the fact that it appeals to you; conversely, that this and this could not be Christianity you can assure yourselves by the fact that it offends you in your heart of hearts.

In this way the priestly corporation which speculates in human numbers has won men, made them believe they are Christians by making them believe something under the name of Christianity, something which appeals to them! And with that the millions have found themselves content—to be able to be Christians too in such a cheap and agreeable way; in a half-hour, and with a turn of the hand, to get the whole thing about eternity settled, in order to be thoroughly able to enjoy this life.

Behold, here lies the difficulty. The difficulty by no means consists in making it clear that the official Christianity is not the Christianity of the New Testament, but in the fact that the Christianity of the New Testament and what the New Testament understands by being a Christian is the last thing of all to be pleasing to a man.

And think then what it means to have to make men who are demoralized by this knavish preaching of Christianity, coddled by the notion that the token for distinguishing Christianity is that it appeals to one, to have to get them to be willing to see what the New Testament understands by Christianity, to get them to that point while thousands of "pastors of souls" want to set everything in motion so as not to lose the sheep, and set in motion all passions on the part of the sheep, saying that this cannot possibly be Christianity, as you can easily convince yourselves, for you feel indeed how it offends you.

Yea, ye pastors of souls, ye have populated heaven! How empty it would have been in the beyond, if ye had not been! And these millions whom your care for souls has dispatched to heaven, how they one day will thank you and bless you! In German they use the expression "soul-selling" for the white-slave trade. In that sense it is figuratively used, for really it is bodies that are sold. In the literal sense "soul-selling" is appropriately reserved for the pastors of souls. This soul-selling in the literal sense is not punished in this world but is honored and revered! The greatness of a crime has also a relation to its duration in time; the real crimes cannot be punished in time because they need the whole of time's duration to become what they are, and if they were punished in time, they would be prevented from becoming the real crimes that they are—they are punished only by eternity.

The personal / The official

Thou who readest this, imagine the following case. There comes to thee a man who, without in any way suggesting that he is crazy, says to thee quietly, earnestly, but with deep emotion, "Pray for me, O pray for me." This likely would make upon thee an almost terrifying impression. And why? Because thou thyself personally didst get an impression of a human personality who must presumably be engaged in the severest struggle with a personal God, forasmuch as it could occur to him to say to another man, Pray for me, O pray for me.

On the other hand, when thou readest, for example in a "*Pastoral Letter*,"[25] "Brethren, include Us in your prayers, as We unceasingly, night and day, pray for you and embrace you in Our petitions"—how does it come that this presumably makes upon thee no impression at all? Surely it comes from the fact that thou hast conceived a suspicion that this is a formula, official patter, out of a handbook or a musicbox. Ah, of the official one cannot say that it leaves a bad taste in the mouth; no, the disgusting thing about the official is that one finds it so insipid because it tastes of nothing at all, because one gets no more taste from it than (to use an old Danish expression) by putting the tongue out of the window to see what the weather is like.

And so now when the last man the State has engaged as a shepherd to walk in velvet to preach that Jesus Christ lived in poverty and commanded, "Follow me," i.e. since Bishop Martensen has presumably resolved to fight with all his might...for the official, against sects and heresies, etc.,[26] and since besides him there are hundreds in the service of the official—there may well be need of one man who devotes some attention to the official. I dare not on this account expect any preferment on the part of the State, perhaps rather (be it said between us) on the part of our Lord. For believe me that there is nothing, no heresy, no sin, nothing whatever so abhorrent to God as the official. And that thou canst well understand; for since God is a personal being, thou canst well conceive how abhorrent it is to Him that people want to wipe His mouth with formulas, to wait upon Him with official solemnity, official phrases, etc. Yea, precisely because God is personality in the most eminent sense, sheer personality, precisely for this cause is the official infinitely more loathsome to Him than it is to a woman when she discovers that a man is making love to her...out of a book of etiquette.

THE INSTANT

No. 5

CONTENTS

July 27, 1855. S. Kierkegaard.

Copenhagen

Published by C. A. Reitzel's Estate and Heirs

Bianco Luno's Press

From the Journal

EMPTY NUTSHELLS

. . . God would be loved. Therefore He wants Christians. To love God is to be a Christian. . . .

Now "man's" knavish interest consists in creating millions and millions of Christians, the more the better, all men if possible; for thus the whole difficulty of being a Christian vanishes, being a Christian and being a man amounts to the same thing, and we find ourselves where paganism ended.

Christendom has mocked God and continues to mock Him—just as if to a man who is a lover of nuts, instead of bringing him one nut with a kernel, we were to bring him tons and millions...of empty nuts, and then make this show of our zeal to comply with his wish.

XI^2 A 390

We are all Christians—without having so much as a suspicion what Christianity is

LET me illustrate this from merely one point of view.

When Christianity requires us to love our enemies, one might say in a certain sense that it had good reason to require this, for God would be loved, and (speaking merely in a human way) God is man's most redoubtable enemy, thy mortal enemy; He would that thou shouldst die, die unto the world, He hates precisely that wherein thou naturally hast thy life, to which thou dost cling with all thy joy in living.

The men who have entered into no relation with God enjoy now—frightful irony!—the privilege that God does not torment them in this life. No, it is only the men whom He loves, who have entered into relation with God, whose mortal enemy (speaking merely in a human way) God may be said to be—but for all that out of love.

But He is thy mortal enemy. He Who is love would be loved by thee. This signifies that thou must die, die unto the world, for otherwise thou canst not love Him.

So there He sits, omnipresent and omniscient as He is, and watches thee, knowing the least thing that transpires in thee, that indeed He does, thy mortal enemy! Beware then of wishing anything, beware of fearing anything; for what thou wishest will not be fulfilled, but rather the contrary, and what thou fearest, and the more thou fearest only the sooner, shall fall upon thee. For He loves thee and would be loved by thee, both out of love. But as soon as there is something thou dost wish think not of Him, and so also if there is something thou dost fear; or if thou dost associate Him with thy wishing and fearing, thou art not thinking of Him in and for Himself, that is, thou dost not love Him—and He would be loved, out of love He wills it.

Take an example. Take a prophet. Think then first what it means to be a prophet, how severely tried and sacrificed is the life of such a man, by the renunciation of pretty much everything we men count valuable. Think of the prophet Jonah! Such a severely tried and tormented man has the modest wish to rest awhile under the shade of a tree. He finds this tree, this shade; it was so grateful a relief to him that presumably he *wished* he might hold on to this refreshment, *feared* that it might be taken from him. He scores a hit! God the almighty at once fixes His attention upon this tree, a worm is commanded to sap its root.

How dreadful (speaking merely in a human way) is God in His love, so dreadful it is (speaking merely in a human way) to be loved of God and to love God. In the declaration that God is love, the subordinate clause is, He is thy mortal enemy.

— — — and here we are playing the game that we are all Christians, that all love God, whereas by God being love and by loving God we nowadays understand nothing else but the nauseating syrupy sweets in which falsehood's witnesses to the truth are wont to deal.

Assuming that no God exists, no eternity, no accounting, then the official Christianity is a perfectly charming and elegant invention for very sensibly making this life as enjoyable as possible, more enjoyable than the pagan could have it. For it is well known that what constantly troubled the pleasure-loving pagan was this thing of eternity; but the official Christianity put such a slant upon this thing of eternity that eternity exists precisely for the sake of giving us a thorough relish and zest for enjoying this life.

Just as if one of the composers who compose variations upon one or more movements of a funeral march were to take occasion to compose with free poetic license a dashing gallop—so has the official Christianity taken occasion from some sentences in the New Testament (this doctrine of a cross and anguish and horror and shuddering before eternity) to compose with free poetic license a lovely idyl, with procreating of children and waltzes, where everything is "so joyful, so joyful, so joyful," where the priest (a kind of leader of the town band) is willing, for money, to let Christianity (the doctrine of dying unto the world) furnish the music for weddings and christenings, where everything is joy and mirth in this (according to the teaching of Christianity, a vale of tears and a penitentiary), this glorious world (yea, according to the New Testament it is a time of probation related to an accounting and judgment), a foretaste of the still more joyful eternity which the priest guarantees to those families which by their devotion to him have evinced a sense for the eternal.

A genius / a Christian

That a genius is not something every man is, surely is something every man will concede. But that a Christian is something still more rare than a genius—this has been clean forgotten, or rather knavishly consigned to oblivion.

The difference between a genius and a Christian is that a genius is nature's extraordinary, no man being able to make himself a genius, whereas a Christian is freedom's extraordinary, or, more properly, freedom's ordinary, for though it is found extraordinarily seldom, it is what everyone ought to be. Therefore God wills that Christianity should be preached to all men absolutely, therefore the Apostles are very simple men, and the Pattern is in the lowly form of a servant, all this in order to indicate that this extraordinary is the ordinary, is accessible to all—but for all that a Christian is a thing even more rare than a genius.

Only be not deceived by the fact that it is accessible to all, possible to all, as if from this it followed that it must be an easy sort of thing and that there were many Christians. No, it must be possible for all, otherwise it would not be freedom's extraordinary, but, for all that, a Christian is a thing even more rare than a genius.

Assuming that it is all as it should be with these battalions of millions × millions of Christians, there emerges here an objection which is really significant, namely, that the case of Christianity is entirely without analogy in the rest of existence. Everywhere else we see the monstrous disproportions of existence: the possibility of millions of plants is carried away by the wind as the pollen of flowers, millions of possibilities of living beings are wasted, etc., etc., thousands × thousands of men go to make one genius, etc., always this enormous prodigality. Only in the case of Christianity is it different: in the case of what is even more rare than a genius it holds good that everyone that is born is a Christian.

Still another objection acquires great significance, if this thing about millions of Christians is to be taken as truth. The earth is only a little point in the universe—and Christianity would be reserved solely for it, and at such an absurdly low price that any and everybody that is born is a Christian.

The matter presents itself in a different light when we perceive that to be a Christian is so high an ideality that, instead of the twaddle about Christendom and the eighteen centuries of Christian history and the claim that Christianity is perfectible, the thesis must be proposed that

Christianity never came into the world, that it stopped with the Pattern, or at the most with the Apostles—but after all they preached it so strongly in the direction of extension that the trouble began there. For it is one thing to work for extension in such a way that incessantly, early and late, one preaches the doctrine to all men; and it is another thing to be too hasty in permitting people by hundreds and thousands to assume the name of Christians, to give themselves out to be Christians.[27] The Pattern's way of preaching was rather different. Absolutely as He preached the doctrine to all men, living only for this, just so absolutely did He hold back when it was a question of being a disciple or of being allowed to call oneself such. Though an assembly of the nation had suffered itself to be carried away by Christ's discourse, He certainly would not at once have allowed these thousands to call themselves disciples of Christ. No, He would have held back more stoutly. Therefore in three and a half years[28] He won only eleven—whereas one Apostle in one day, maybe in one hour, wins three thousand disciples of Christ. Either the disciple is in this instance greater than the master, or the truth is that the Apostle is a little too hasty in striking a bargain, a little too hasty in the direction of extension, so that the trouble already begins here.

Only divine authority could impress the human race in such a way that the thing of absolutely willing the eternal became absolute seriousness. Only the God-Man can unite these two things: to work absolutely for extension, and absolutely to hold back on the question what is to be understood by being a disciple. Only the God-Man would be able to hold out (if you can imagine it) for a thousand years, and then another thousand years, working for the spread of the doctrine by preaching it, though He did not get a single disciple, if He could get them only by altering the terms. After all, the Apostle feels some selfish need of the relief of getting adherents, of becoming many, which the God-Man does not feel, Who has no need of adherents and therefore has only the price of eternity, no market price.

So the matter stood when Christ preached Christianity. The human race was absolutely impressed.

But *naturam furca expellas*,[29] yet it comes back. Man has a tendency to invert the situation. Just as a dog which is compelled to walk on two feet has every instant a tendency to go again on all four, and does so as soon as it sees its chance, waiting only to see its chance, so is Christendom an effort of the human race to go back to walking on all fours, to get rid of Christianity, to do it knavishly under the pretext that this is Christianity, claiming that it is Christianity perfected.

First they turned out the other side of the Pattern, the Pattern becomes no longer the Pattern but the Mediator, they dwelt upon His kind deeds and wished they were in their stead to whom they were shown, which is just as preposterous as if when a man is represented as a pattern of kindness, one were not willing to look upon him with the idea of imitating his kindness but with a view to wishing to be in their stead to whom the kindness was shown.

So then the Pattern passed out. Then they did away also with the Apostles as patterns, and thereupon also with the first Christian age as a pattern. And so at last they succeeded in getting to the point of going again on all fours, and making out that this, precisely this, was true Christianity. By the help of dogmas they secured themselves against everything which with any semblance of truth could be called a Christian pattern, and then they went with full sail in the direction of...perfectibility.

The Christianity of the spiritual man / the Christianity of us men

When I thus confront one Christianity with another, it surely could not occur to anyone to misunderstand this, as though now I were in agreement with the veterinary surgeon Pastor Fog[30] that there are two sorts of Christianity. No, I confront them with the unaltered conviction that the Christianity of the New Testament is Christianity, the other being a knavish trick, and that they no more resemble one another than a square resembles a circle. But my purpose in confronting them is to illustrate in a few words the question I raised in an article in the *Fatherland*, whether we, i.e. the human race, are not so degenerate that men no longer are born who are able to endure this divine thing which is the Christianity of the New Testament. If this is so, it erects in the simplest possible way an obstacle to the proof offered by the perjured priests that the official Christianity is the Christianity of the New Testament and that Christianity exists.

There are two points of difference between the spiritual man and us men, to which I would especially draw attention, and thereby in turn illustrate the difference between the Christianity of the New Testament and the Christianity of "Christendom."

(1) The spiritual man differs from us men in the fact that (if I may so express it) he is so heavily built that he is able to endure a duplication in himself. In comparison with him we men are like frame walls in comparison with the foundation wall, so loosely and frailly built that we cannot endure a duplication. But the Christianity of the New Testament has to do precisely with a duplication.

The spiritual man is able to endure a duplication in himself; by his understanding he is able to hold fast to the fact that something is contrary to the understanding, and then will it nevertheless; he is able to hold fast with the understanding to the fact that something is an offense, and yet to will it nevertheless; that, humanly speaking, something makes him unhappy, and yet to will it, etc. But the New Testament is composed precisely in view of this. We men on the other hand are not able to support or endure a duplication within ourselves; our will alters our understanding. Our Christianity therefore, the Christianity of "Christendom," takes this into account; it takes away from Christianity the offense, the paradox, etc., and instead of that introduces, probability, the plainly comprehensible. That is, it transforms Christianity into something entirely different from what it is in the New

Testament, yea, into exactly the opposite; and this is the Christianity of "Christendom," of us men.

(2) The spiritual man differs from us men in being able to endure isolation, his rank as a spiritual man is proportionate to his strength for enduring isolation, whereas we men are constantly in need of "the others," the herd; we die, or despair, if we are not reassured by being in the herd, of the same opinion as the herd, etc.

But the Christianity of the New Testament is precisely reckoned upon and related to this isolation of the spiritual man. Christianity in the New Testament consists in loving God, in hatred to man, in hatred of oneself, and thereby of other men, hating father, mother, one's own child, wife, etc., the strongest expression for the most agonizing isolation.—And it is in view of this I say that such men, men of this quality and caliber, are not born any more.

The Christianity of us men is, to love God in agreement with other men, to love and be loved by other men, constantly the others, the herd included.

Let us take an example. In "Christendom" this is what Christianity is: a man with a woman on his arm steps up to the altar, where a smart silken priest, half educated in the poets, half in the New Testament, delivers an address half erotic, half Christian—a wedding ceremony. This is what Christianity is in "Christendom." The Christianity of the New Testament would be: in case that man were really able to love in such a way that the girl was the only one he loved and one whom he loved with the whole passion of a soul (yet such men as this are no longer to be found), then, hating himself and the loved one, to let her go in order to love God.—And it is in view of this I say that such men, men of such quality and caliber, are not born any more.

The Christianity of the New Testament / the Christianity of "Christendom"

The thought of Christianity was to want to change everything.

The result of the Christianity of "Christendom" is that everything, absolutely everything, has remained as it was, only everything has assumed the name of "Christian"—and so (musicians, strike up the tune!) we live a life of paganism: Merrily, merrily, merrily, here we go round and round; or rather we live a pagan life which is refined by eternity, or by the help of the thought that the whole thing is Christian.

Try it, take what you will, and you shall find that it corresponds to what I say.

What Christianity wanted was chastity—to do away with the whorehouse. The change is this, that the whorehouse remains exactly what it was in paganism, lewdness in the same proportion, but it has become a "Christian" whorehouse. A whoremonger is a "Christian" whoremonger,[31] he is a Christian exactly like all the rest of us; to exclude him from the means of grace—"Good God," the priest will say, "what would be the end of it if once we were to begin by excluding one contributing member!" He dies, and exactly in proportion as he pays he gets his eulogy at the grave. And after having earned his money in so mean and despicable a way (for Christianly considered the priest might better have stolen it) the priest hies him home, he is in a hurry, he has to go into the church to declaim, or, as Bishop Martensen says, to bear witness.

What Christianity wanted was honesty and fair dealing, to do away with swindling—the change effected was this: swindling remained exactly as in paganism, the adage is, "In business every man's a thief"—every Christian! But swindling assumed the predicate "Christian," it became "Christian swindling"—and the "priest" pronounced a blessing upon this Christian society, this Christian state, where they swindle just as in paganism, and do it also by paying the "priest," who by this mark is the biggest swindler, they swindle themselves into the notion that this is Christianity.

What Christianity wanted was earnestness in living, and to do away with vain honors and glories—everything remained as it was, the change being that it assumed the predicate Christian: the gewgaws of knightly orders, titles, rank, etc., became Christian—and the priest (of all equivocal characters the most indecent, of all comical things the most comical hodgepodge), he is tickled to death when he himself is decorated with...the Cross. The Cross! Yes, in the Christianity of "Christendom" the Cross has become something like the child's hobby-horse and trumpet.

And so in everything. If in the natural man there is any instinct so strong as the instinct of self-preservation, it is the instinct for the propagation of the race, which therefore Christianity tried to cool off, teaching that it is better not to marry, yet, if worse comes to worst, it is better to marry than to burn. But in "Christendom" the propagation of the race has become the serious business of life, together with Christianity; and the priest (this epitome of nonsense enveloped in long robes), the priest, the teacher of Christianity, of the Christianity of the New Testament, has even got his income fixed in proportion to his activity in promoting the propagation of the race, getting a definite amount for each child.

As I have said, just try it, and in everything you will find that it is as I have affirmed: the change from paganism is this: that everything has remained unchanged, but has assumed the predicate "Christian."

When all are Christians, Christianity *eo ipso* does not exist

When once it is pointed out, this is very easily seen, and once seen it can never be forgotten.

Any determinant which applies to all cannot enter into existence but must either underlie existence or lie outside as meaningless.

Take the determinant man. We are all men. This determinant therefore does not enter into human existence, for the human race as a whole is subsumed under the generic term "man." This determinant lies before the beginning, in the sense of underlying. We are all men—and then it begins.

This is an example of a determinant which applies to all and is underlying. The other alternative was that a determinant which applies to all, or by the fact that it applies to all, is meaningless.

Assume (and let us not haggle over the fact that it is a strange assumption, we shall have the explanation), assume that we are all thieves, what the police call suspicious characters—if that's what we all are, this determinant will *eo ipso* have no effect upon the situation as a whole, we shall be living just as we are living, each will then count for what he now counts, some (suspicious characters) will be branded as thieves and robbers, i.e. within the definition that we are all suspicious characters; others (suspicious characters) will be highly esteemed, etc.; in short, everything even to the least detail will be as it is, for we are all suspicious characters, and so the concept is annulled (Hegel's *aufgehoben*); when all are that, then to be that = 0; this is not to say that it does not mean anything much; no, it means nothing at all.

It is exactly the same with the definition that we are all Christians. If we are all Christians, the concept is annulled, being a Christian is something which lies before the beginning, outside—and then it begins, we live then the merely human life, exactly as in paganism; the determinant Christian cannot in any way manage to enter in, for by the fact that we all are this it is precisely put outside.

God's thought in introducing Christianity was, if I may venture to say so, to pound the table hard in front of us men. To that end He set "individual" and "race," the single person and the many, at odds, set them against one another, applied the determinant of dissension; for to be a Christian was, according to His thought, precisely the definition of dissension, that of the "individual" with the "race," with the millions, with family, with father and mother, etc.

God did it that way, *partly* out of love; for He, the God of love, wanted to be loved but is too great a connoisseur of what love is to want to have to order men to love Him by battalions or whole nations, as the command, "One, two, three," is given at the church parade. No, the formula constantly is: the individual in opposition to the others. And *partly* He did it as the ruler, in order to keep men in check and educate them. This was His thought, even though we men might say, if we dared, that it was the most annoying caprice on the part of God to put us together in this way, or cut us off in this way from what we animals regard as the true well-being, from coalescing with the herd, everyone just like the others.

God succeeded in this, he really overawed men.

But gradually the human race came to itself, and, shrewd as it is, it saw that to do away with Christianity by force was not practicable—"So let us do it by cunning," they said. "We are all Christians, and so Christianity is *eo ipso* abolished."

And that is what we now are. The whole thing is a knavish trick; these 2000 churches, or however many there are, are, Christianly considered, a knavish trick; these 1000 priests in velvet,[32] silk, broadcloth, or bombazine, are a knavish trick—for the whole thing rests upon the assumption that we are all Christians, which is precisely the knavish way of doing away with Christianity. Therefore it is a very peculiar sort of euphemism too when we reassure ourselves with the thought that we all will attain blessedness, or say, "I shall become blessed, just like all the others"; for when forwarded to heaven with this address, one is not received there, does no more go to heaven than one reaches New Holland by land.

A revolt in defiance / a revolt in hypocrisy

or

about apostasy from Christianity

That man is a defiant and refractory creature we know well enough, but that in a very high degree he is a shrewd creature—when it comes to a question of flesh and blood and earthly well-being—we do not always perceive. It is so nevertheless, though at the same time it is true that we have reason to deplore man's stupidity.

When there is something which is distasteful to man, he looks to see if the power which commands him is not too great for him to pit his power against it. If he is convinced that it is not too great, he revolts in defiance.

But if the power which commands what is distasteful to man is so superior to him that he absolutely despairs of making a revolt in defiance, he resorts to hypocrisy.

This applies to Christianity. The fact that the apostasy from Christianity occurred long ago has not been noticed because the apostasy came about, the revolt was made, in hypocrisy. Precisely Christendom is the apostasy from Christianity.

In the New Testament, according to Christ's own teaching, to be a Christian is, humanly speaking, sheer anguish, an anguish in comparison with which all other human sufferings are hardly more than child's-play. What Christ speaks of (for he makes no disguise of it) is about crucifying the flesh, hating oneself, about suffering for the doctrine, weeping and wailing while the world rejoices, about the most heart-rending sufferings due to hating father, mother, wife, one's own child, about being what the Scripture says of the Pattern (and surely to be a Christian must mean corresponding to the Pattern), that He is a worm and no man. Hence the reiterated warnings not to be offended, not to be offended at the fact that what in the highest, the divine understanding of it is salvation and help is, humanly speaking, so frightful.

This is what it is to be a Christian. That, however, is hardly a thing for us men, such things we might rather pray to be dispensed from. Indeed if such exactions had occurred to any human power, man would at once have revolted in defiance. But unluckily God is a power against which man cannot rebel in defiance.

So man resorted to hypocrisy. People had not so much as the courage and honesty and truth to say to God bluntly, "That I cannot agree to," they resorted to hypocrisy and thought they were perfectly secure.

They resorted to hypocrisy, they falsified the definition of being a Christian. To be a Christian, they said, is sheer blessedness. "What would I be, O what would I be, if I were not a Christian! Yea, to be a Christian is the only thing which gives real significance to life, gives a relish to joys, and to sufferings assuagement."

In that way we all became Christians. And then everything went gaily, with fine words and grandiloquent phrases and heavenly glances and torrents of tears, all by the artists engaged for this purpose, who could not find words to thank God enough for the great privilege that we are all Christians, etc.—and the secret was that we have falsified the concept of what it is to be a Christian, but hope by knavish and hypocritical flattery and sweet words, giving thanks again and again that we are...the opposite of what God understands by being a Christian—by this hoping, deluding ourselves, to put a wax nose on God's face; by so heartily thanking Him that we are that, we hope to get out of being that.

Behold, for this reason the church is the most equivocal place. For doubtless there are other places which are called "equivocal places" but are not really that, the fact that they are called "equivocal" prevents them from being really equivocal. A church, on the other hand, that is indeed an equivocal place, a royally authorized Christian church in "Christendom" is the most equivocal thing that has ever existed.

For to make a fool of God is not equivocal, but to do that under the name of worshiping Him is equivocal; to want to do away with Christianity is not equivocal, but it is equivocal to do away with Christianity under the name of spreading it; to give money to work against Christianity is not equivocal, but it is equivocal to take money for working against Christianity under the name of working for it.

The taking of an oath
or
the official / the personal

Let me relate a little anecdote from the criminal world which is not without some psychological interest.

It was a case where a man could, as the phrase is, "free himself" by an oath, that is, free himself temporally by binding himself eternally with a perjury. The person in question was sufficiently well known to the magistrate and had often been punished. The magistrate did not have it in his power to prevent a resort to an oath, but morally was fully convinced that it was a false oath. So the man took the oath.

When the case was concluded his Honor visited the man who had been tried, entered into personal conversation with him and said, "Wouldst thou dare to give me thy hand on it that what thou hast sworn is true?" "No," he replied, "no, your Honor, that I will not do."

Here is an example of the difference between the official and the personal. For one who belongs essentially to the criminal world to clear himself by an oath is something official, something he cannot for an instant hesitate to do, or harbor the least doubt that it is justifiable, for it is something he knows all about by long continued practice; for him it is a matter of course, people do such things officially, impersonally, the trick consists in being deft at giving the case such a turn that one can clear oneself by an oath, the taking of an oath is no more than saying "Prosit" to one who sneezes, or adding Esq. to a letter. In vain the solemnity of an oath seeks to make an impression upon him as a personal matter; in vain, for this is a business affair, he himself is official, is officially armed against every impression he knows in advance they will try to make upon him, and so he officially takes the oath. The whole thing, as he understands it, is *ex officio*.

But personally, no; personally he cannot make up his mind to confirm solemnly a lie. "Wouldst thou dare to give me thy hand on it?" "No, your Honor, that I will not do."

Everyone who has the least practice will surely concede the truth of the assertion that (passing over to an entirely different world) this case occurs not too rarely, that one will be able to get a priest to acknowledge in private conversation (especially if he is personally touched) that he has a different conviction from that which he officially pronounces, or perhaps that he is personally dubious about what he publicly pronounces with "full conviction." And yet the priest is in fact bound by an oath, he has taken an oath which is supposed to give assurance that what he publicly pronounces is his sincere conviction. Ah, yes, but in the priest-world this thing about taking an oath belongs definitely to the official—the thing must be done if one is to get into the living. One takes the oath officially, and preaches officially what one is bound to by the oath. "But answer me honestly, Pastor B., wilt thou give me thy hand on it that this is thy conviction, or wilt thou confirm it upon the memory of thy deceased wife—for to me, for my own sake, in order that I may put an end to my doubt, it is so important for me to learn to know thy true opinion?" "No, my friend; no, that I cannot do, thou must not require it of me."

The taking of an oath—that surely should give complete assurance that the thing is personal! However, the oath (the oath which is the condition of getting into a living etc., O God, lead us not into temptation), the oath is perhaps taken officially. "But is it really thy conviction thou dost teach? I adjure thee by the memory of thy deceased wife that to help me thou wilt tell me thy honest opinion." "No, my friend, that I cannot do."

Newfangled religious assurances (guarantees)

Once upon a time, long, long ago, this was the way people understood it: they required of a man who would be a teacher of Christianity that his life too should furnish guarantees for what he taught.

Now they have got far away from that, the world has become shrewder, more serious, has learned to disdain all this petty, morbid concern about the personal, has learned to desire only the objective[33]—now it is required that the teacher's life shall furnish guarantees that what he says is a pleasantry, a dramatic flourish, a *divertissement*, altogether objective.

A few examples. If what you would talk about is that Christianity, the Christianity of the New Testament, has a preference for the single state, and you yourself are a single man—my dear fellow, that is no subject for you to talk about, the congregation might in fact believe that it was seriousness, become uneasy, or might feel offended that in this way, so unbecomingly, you brought your own personality into it. No, it will be a long time before you will be in a position to talk seriously about that, in such a way as to content the congregation. Wait till you already have your first wife under the sod and are a good piece along with the second; that is the time for you, then you will step before the congregation to teach and "witness" that Christianity has a preference for the single state—and you will content the people perfectly; for your life furnishes guarantees that this is foolery, a jollification, or that what you say is interesting. Yes, how interesting! For just as in a marriage, if it is to be assured against boredom, if it is to be interesting, the husband must be unfaithful to the wife, and the wife to the husband, so too the truth only becomes interesting, immensely interesting, when a person in an exalted mood lets himself be gripped by it, carried away, enchanted—but of course does exactly the opposite and is cunningly secured by letting it stop at that.

If you would talk about the Christian contempt for titles, decorations and the tomfoolery of glory...and you yourself are neither a person of rank nor anything resembling it—my dear fellow, that is no subject for you to talk about, the congregation might in fact believe that it was seriousness, or feel offended at your lack of breeding in obtruding your own personality. No, wait till you yourself have laid up a store of decorations, wait till you are dragging with you such a rigmarole of titles that for the multitude of them you hardly know what your name is—then is the time, then you will step forward to preach and "witness"; for your life furnishes guarantees that this is dramatic entertainment, an interesting morning's recreation.

If you would talk about preaching Christianity in poverty, affirming that this is the genuine Christian preaching...and you literally are a poor devil—my dear fellow, this is no subject for you to talk about, the congregation might in fact believe that it was seriousness, become fearful, feel quite put out and in the highest degree uncomfortable at having poverty come to such close quarters with them. No, first procure a fat living, and then when you have had that so long that you soon will be promoted to a still fatter one, that is the appropriate time, then you will appear before the congregation to preach and "witness," and you will completely content them; for your life furnishes guarantees that the whole thing turns out to be a jest, such as serious men might desire once in a while at the theater or in church, in order to gather new strength...to make money.

And this is the way they worship God in the churches! And there silken and velvet orators weep, they sob, their voice is stifled by tears! Oh, in case it is true (and so it is, for God himself says it) that God counts the tears of the suffering and puts them in a bottle—then woe to these orators, if God has also counted their Sunday tears and kept them in a bottle![34] Yea, woe to us all, in case God really notices these Sunday tears, especially those of the orators, but of the audience, too! For a Sunday orator would be right in saying (and oratorically it would certainly make a brilliant effect, especially when supported by tears and that stifled sob), he would be right in saying to the audience, "I will collect all the useless tears you have shed in church, and with them I will appear accusingly before God at the Day of Judgment"—he is right, only do not forget that the orator's own dramatic tears were far more pernicious than the light-minded tears of the audience.

"Beware of them that like to walk in long robes"

(Mark 12:38; Luke 20:46)

June 15, 1855.

Since "witnesses to the truth," as "genuine witnesses," instead of uttering a warning against me openly, prefer to be, as they think, all the more effective by secrecy, then I shall undertake their business and *witness* aloud, aloud before the whole nation: Beware of the priests!

Above all beware of the priests! It is a mark of being a Christian (if one is to be a Christian in such a sense that it will hold good in the Judgment) that one has suffered for the doctrine. But believe me, as sure as my name is Søren Kierkegaard, you can get no official priest to say that. Of course not, for that would be suicide. The very instant it is said that to suffer for the doctrine is required for being even an ordinary Christian, that same instant the whole machinery with the 1000 livings and functionaries is thrown into confusion, all these wassailers [*Levebrødre*—whereas a "living" is *Levebrød*] are left destitute. Hence you get no official priest to say it. On the other hand, you may be fully assured that with all his might he will preach the opposite, prevent you from entertaining that thought, so that you may be kept in the state which he understands as that of a Christian, a sheep good for shearing, an inoffensive mediocrity, to whom eternity is closed.

Pray believe me. I tender you with my life the security you can demand; for I am not dealing with you in a finite interest, I am not seeking to draw you to me in order to found a party, etc. No, I am merely doing religiously my duty, and in a certain sense, if only I do it, it is indifferent to me, entirely indifferent, whether you comply with what I say or not.

"Beware of them that walk in long robes." It is not necessary to say that with these words Christ has no intention of criticizing their dress; no, it certainly is not an observation about clothes. Christ had no objection to their clothes being long. If the professional attire for priests had been short, Christ would have said, "Beware of them that walk in short clothes." And if you insist that I go to the extreme to show that this is not a criticism of clothes—if the professional attire for priests had been to walk without clothes, Christ would have said: "Beware of them that walk without clothes." It is the professional dress He would swat, indicating it as a distinctive costume—for he understands something altogether different by being a teacher.

Beware of them that *like* to walk in long robes. A Bible interpretation over the teacups will at once seize upon the word "like" and explain that Christ had in view only individuals in the professional class, those who take vain pride in long robes, etc. No, my good long-robed man, that perhaps by great solemnity in the pulpit you can make women and children believe, it also corresponds perfectly with the picture of Christ which is presented in the Sunday services. But you cannot make me believe it; and the Christ of the New Testament does speak in this way. He always speaks about the whole order and does not resort to the meaningless gabble that there are some members of the order who are depraved, which is true at all times of all classes, so that obviously nothing whatever is said. No, He conceives the order as a whole and says that the order as a whole is depraved, so that the order as a whole has a depraved liking for walking in long robes, because to be a priest in the official sense is exactly the opposite of what Christ understood by being a teacher, the latter meaning to suffer for the teaching, the former meaning to enjoy the earthly as it is refined by the glory of being God's representative. So it is no wonder they like to walk in long robes; for all other official positions in life are rewarded only by the earthly, but the official clergy take along with them a little of the heavenly as a refinement.

So then in itself it is entirely indifferent whether the professional dress is long or short. The decisive point is that when the teacher acquires "canonicals," a peculiar dress, professional attire, you have official worship—and that is what Christ will not have. Long robes, splendid churches, etc., all this hangs together, and it is the human falsification of the Christianity of the New Testament, a falsification which shamelessly takes advantage of the fact that unfortunately the human mass only too easily lets itself be deluded by sense-impressions, and therefore (exactly in opposition to the New Testament) is prone to judge true Christianity by sense-impressions. It is the human falsification of the Christianity of the New Testament, and it is not true of the clerical order as it is of other orders, that there is nothing evil about the order; no, the clerical order is, Christianly considered, in and for itself of the Evil, is a demoralization, a human egoism, which inverts Christianity to exactly the opposite of that which Christ had made it.

But now that long robes have in fact become the official dress for priests, one can be sure that there is something in it, and I believe that by observing what it implies one can form a very significant conception of the nature of official Christianity.

By long robes one's thought is involuntarily led to the suspicion that there is something to be concealed; when one has something to conceal, long robes are very convenient—and official Christianity has a prodigious lot to conceal, for from first to last it is an untruth, which therefore had best be hidden...in long robes.

And long robes—in fact that is feminine attire. Thereby thought is led on to something which also is characteristic of official Christianity, the unmanliness of using cunning, untruth and lies as its power. That again is very characteristic of official Christianity, which, being itself an untruth, uses a prodigious amount of untruth, both to hide what truth is, and to hide the fact that it is untruth.

And this womanish quality is also in another way characteristic of official Christianity. The feminine trait of willing and yet resisting, this coquetry which in woman is unconscious, has its unpardonable parallel in official Christianity, which so keenly wills the earthly and the temporal, but because of a sense of shame must make out that it does not will it, is on the alert to get it, yet secretly, for one must make out—God save us!—one must faint, fall into a swoon, when one has to accept a high and fat post, which one is so reluctant to assume that only from a sense of duty, solely and simply from a sense of duty, one has been able to resolve to assume such a post, and that only when one has—alas, in vain—sighed upon one's knees before God and begged Him to take this cross, this bitter cup, from one — — and one would find oneself perhaps in desperate embarrassment if the government were ironical enough to excuse one.

Finally, there is something equivocal about men in women's clothes. One might be tempted to say that it conflicts with the police ordinance which forbids men to appear in women's clothes and vice versa. But in any case, there is something equivocal—and equivocal is the more descriptive term for what official Christianity is, descriptive of the change Christianity has undergone in the course of time, that from being what it was in the New Testament, namely, simplicity, it has (presumably by the aid of its perfectibility) become something more, namely, duplicity, an equivocation.

Beware therefore of them that like to walk in long robes! According to Christ (who surely must know best about the way, since He is the Way) the gate is strait, the way is narrow—and few there be that find it. And what perhaps most of all has brought it about that the number of these few is so small, smaller proportionately with every century, is the monstrous illusion which official Christianity has conjured up. Persecution, maltreatment, bloodshedding, has by no means done such injury, no, it has been inestimably beneficial in comparison with the radical damage done by official Christianity, which is designed to serve human indolence, mediocrity, by making men believe that indolence, mediocrity and enjoyment of life is Christianity. Do away with official Christianity, let persecution come—that very instant Christianity again exists.

THE INSTANT

No. 6

CONTENTS

August 23, 1855. S. Kierkegaard.

Copenhagen

Published by C. A. Reitzel's Estate and Heirs

Bianco Luno's Press

From the Journal

PLAYING CHRISTIANITY

We all know what it is to play warfare in mock battle, that it means to *imitate* everything just as it is in war. The troops are drawn up, they march into the field, seriousness is evident in every eye, but also courage and enthusiasm, the orderlies rush back and forth intrepidly, the commander's voice is heard, the signals, the battle cry, the volley of musketry, the thunder of cannon—everything exactly as in war, lacking only one thing...the danger.

So also it is with playing Christianity, that is, imitating Christian preaching in such a way that everything, absolutely everything is included in as deceptive a form as possible—only one thing is lacking...the danger.

XI^1 A 70, XI^2 A 289

Short and sharp

1.

CHRISTIANITY is capable of being perfected (it is perfectible); it advances; now perfection has been attained. What was striven after as the ideal, but which even the first age could only approximately attain, the ideal that the Christians are a nation of priests, that has now been perfectly attained, especially in Protestantism, more especially in Denmark.

That is to say, in case what we call a priest is what it really is to be a priest...then we are all priests.

2.

In the magnificent cathedral the Honorable and Right Reverend Geheime-General-Ober-Hof-Prädikant, the elect favorite of the fashionable world, appears before an elect company and preaches *with emotion* upon the text he himself elected: "God hath elected the base things of the world, and the things that are despised"—and nobody laughs.

3.

When a man has a toothache the world says, "Poor man"; when a man's wife is unfaithful to him the world says, "Poor man"; when a man is in financial embarrassment the world says, "Poor man"—when it pleased God in the form of a lowly servant to suffer in this world the world says, "Poor man"; when an Apostle with a divine commission has the honor to suffer for the truth the world says, "Poor man" — — poor world!

4.

"Had the Apostle Paul any official position?" No, Paul had no official position. "Did he then earn much money in other ways?" No, he didn't earn money in any way. "Was he at least married?" No, he was not married. "But then really Paul is not a serious man." No, Paul is not a serious man.

5.

It is related of a Swedish priest[35] that, profoundly disturbed by the sight of the effect his address produced upon the auditors, who were dissolved in tears, he said soothingly, "Children, do not weep; the whole thing might be a lie."

Why does the priest say that no more? No need to, we know it—we're all priests.

But in spite of that we well may weep; both his and our tears may be in no way hypocritical, but well-meaning, genuine...as in the theater.

6.

When paganism was in dissolution there were a lot of priests, called augurs. Of them it is reported that one augur could not look at another without smiling.[36]

In "Christendom" before long no one can see a priest, or indeed no man look at another, without smiling—but indeed we are all of us priests, too.

7.

Is this the same teaching, when Christ says to the rich young man, "Sell all that thou hast, and give it to the poor";

and when the priest says, "Sell all that thou hast and...give it to me"?

8.

Geniuses are like a thunderstorm[37]: they go against the wind, terrify people, cleanse the air.

The Established Church has invented sundry lightning-conductors.

And it succeeded. Yes indeed, it suceeded; it succeeded in making *the next thunderstorm* all the more serious.

9.

One cannot live off of nothing. This one hears so often, especially from priests.

And precisely the priests perform this trick: Christianity actually does not exist—yet they live off of it.

A measure of distance
and
therewith again about the peculiar difficulty I have to contend with

My dear reader!

In order to call thy attention to where we are, Christianly, in order to give thee an opportunity to measure the distance from the Christianity of the New Testament and the primitive age, allow me to make use for this purpose of two men who are regarded, each for his own sake but in different ways, as representatives of true Christianity, and who are universally known.

Take first Bishop *Mynster*. In the opinion of pretty much the whole population he was regarded as true Christian earnestness and wisdom.

However, this is the way things stood with Bishop Mynster. All his earnestness reached no further than the thought: in a humanly allowable and honest way, or indeed in a humanly honorable way also, to get through this life happily and well.

But this view of life is not at all that of the New Testament or of primitive Christianity. Primitive Christianity has such a militant attitude towards the world that its view is: not to want to slip through this world happily and well, but precisely to be on the alert to conflict with this world in dead earnest, so that after having thus fought and suffered, one might be able to face the Judgment, where the Judge (whom, according to the New Testament, one can love only by hating this world and one's own life in this world) will judge whether one has accomplished His will.

So there is a difference as wide as the earth, as wide as heaven, between the Mynsterish life-view (which properly is Epicureanism, enjoyment of life and the lust for life, belonging to this world) and the Christian view, which is that of suffering, of enthusiasm for death, belonging to the other world; yea, there is such a difference between these two life-views that the latter (if it were taken seriously, and not at the very most expressed rarely in a quiet hour) must appear to Bishop Mynster as a kind of madness.

Measure now, and thou wilt see that what under the name of Mynster thou art wont to regard as Christian earnestness and wisdom is, Christianly measured, lukewarmness and indifferentism. For thus indeed it is the difference must be described, as the difference between the will to contend in mortal combat with this world, not to be willing at any price to make friendship with this world (the Christian requirement), and, on the other hand, the will to slip through this world happily and well, at the utmost contending a little bit when this might contribute to slipping through this world happily and well.

Then take Pastor *Grundtvig*. G. is in fact regarded as a "sort of an Apostle,"[38] representing enthusiasm, the courage of faith which fights for a conviction.

Let us now look more closely. The highest thing he has fought for is to get leave for himself and those who want to join him to state what he understands by Christianity. For this cause he would throw off the yoke which the State Church laid upon him. It shocked him that they wanted to use the police power to prevent him from exercising his freedom.

Good. But, if then G., for himself and his party, had attained what he wanted, it also was his notion to let the whole monstrous illusion remain in force, that the State makes itself out to be Christian, the people imagine that they are Christians, in short, that every blessed day an insult is offered to God, the crime of lèse-majesté is committed by falsifying the conception of what Christianity is. To fight on that front surely never occurred to G. No, freedom for himself and whoever might be in agreement with him, freedom to state what he and those with him understood by Christianity, that is the utmost he has willed—and then he would be tranquil, tranquillized in this life, belonging to his family, and in other respects living like those who are essentially at home in this world, and perhaps would call his tranquillity tolerance, tolerance towards the others...the other Christians.

Think now what passion there was in primitive Christianity, without which it never would have come into the world; propose to one of those figures the question, "Dare a Christian tranquillize himself in this way?" "Abominable," he would reply, "horrible, that a Christian, if only he might be allowed for himself to live as he would, that a Christian should tranquilly keep silent in the face of the fact that God every day is mocked by people pretending by millions to be Christians and worshiping Him by taking Him for a fool, that in the face of that he should keep silent, and not instantly—for the honor of God—venture sufferingly in among those millions, gladly suffering for the doctrine!" For let us not forget that whereas in one sense Christianity is doubtless the most tolerant of all religions, inasmuch as most of all it abhors the use of physical power, it is in another sense the most intolerant, inasmuch as its true confessors recognize no limit with respect to compelling others by suffering themselves, compelling others by suffering their ill-treatment and persecution.

Measured by this measure, it is easily seen that G. can never properly be said to have fought for Christianity; he really only fought for something earthly, civil freedom for himself and his adherents; and he has never fought with Christian passion. No, in comparison with the passion of primitive Christianity G.'s passion is lukewarmness and indifferentism.

What deceives us with respect both to Mynster and to Grundtvig is that, living in an age which had no notion whatever of primitive Christianity, they have by comparison with such an age attained respectively a reputation for earnestness and wisdom, and for enthusiasm and the courage of faith.

But if it is true that in a given age the two most prominent representatives of Christianity, who are regarded as earnestness and wisdom, enthusiasm and the courage of faith, must when measured by the measure of primitive Christianity be said to be lukewarmness and indifferentism, one gets from this a conception of the whole age and of the peculiar difficulty I have to contend with.

The difficulty consists in the fact that the whole age has sunk into the profoundest indifferentism, has no religion whatever, is not even in a condition for religion.

The misleading thing is that they call themselves "Christians," and that the people are not conscious of what indifferentism properly is, or that this is the most pernicious form of indifferentism.

By indifferentism one commonly understands having no religion at all. But resolutely and definitely to have no religion at all is something passionate, and so is not the most dangerous sort of indifferentism. Hence too it occurs rather rarely.

No, the most dangerous sort of indifferentism and the most common is to have a particular religion, but a religion which is watered down and garbled into mere twaddle, so that one can hold this religion in a perfectly passionateless way. That is the most dangerous sort of indifferentism; for precisely by having this trumpery under the name of religion, a person, so he thinks, is secured, made inaccessible, against the reproach of having no religion.

All religion has to do with passion, with having passion. It will be true therefore of every religion, especially in ages of rationalism or common sense, that it has only very few genuine adherents. On the other hand, there are thousands who take a little something out of that religion, and then dispassionately (i.e. irreligiously, indifferently) have... that religion. That is to say, by having that religion they are (though they are completely indifferent) assured against the reproach of having no religion.

Herein lies the difficulty I have to contend with, a difficulty like that of punting a boat off a shoal where the ground on all sides is quaking bog, so that when the pole is thrust down it gives way and offers no resistance.

What I have before me is indifferentism, the profoundest, the most pernicious and the most dangerous sort of indifferentism. It is a society of which the Apostle Paul would say, "Christians! These men Christians! Why, they have no religion at all, they are not even in a condition to have religion!" A society of which Socrates would say, "They are not men, but inhumanized by being the public."

They all of them are...the public. This human question, whether in and for itself an opinion is true, does not concern them; what concerns them is, how many hold this opinion. Aha! For number decides whether an opinion has physical might; and that is what concerns them through and through, down to the individual in the nation—ah, there is no individual, every individual is the public.

So in the end it becomes a sort of sensual pleasure, corresponding to the pleasure it must have been to be a spectator of the fights of wild beasts in the Roman circus, it becomes a sort of sensual pleasure to witness in the capacity of "the public" this fight, where a single man who only has strength of spirit and at no price would have any other, is fighting for that religion which is the religion of sacrifice against this gigantic corpus of 1000 tradesmen-priests, who decline with thanks the offer of spirit, but heartily thank the Government for salary, titles, decorations, and the congregation for...their sacrifice, the offering.

And because the situation on the whole is this, namely, the profoundest indifference, it is made in turn all too easy for the individual who is a trifle more advanced to become self-important, as though he were the earnest man, a man of character, etc.—There is a young man—he feels indignant about the general lukewarmness and indifference, he an enthusiast and would also express his enthusiasm, he ventures...to express it anonymously. Well-meaning as he doubtless is, and that's the pleasing part about it, it perhaps escapes his notice that this is rather weak, and he lets himself be deluded by the consideration that in comparison with the prevailing lukewarmness this appears to be something.—Or it is an older man, an earnest citizen, he is shocked at the lukewarmness and indifference of many people who would rather hear nothing about religion. He on the contrary reads, procures whatever is published, talks about it, declaims zealously...in the parlor; and it perhaps escapes his notice that, Christianly, this is not really earnestness, that it is earnestness only in comparison with that which never ought to be used for comparison if one would go forward; for that forward striving only becomes possible by comparison with what is ahead, the more advanced.

"Yea, O God, if Thou wert not omnipotence which is able omnipotently to compel, and if Thou wert not love which is able irresistibly to move the heart! . . . But Thy love moves me, the thought of daring to love Thee prompts me to accept my lot joyfully and thankfully, to be a sacrifice, sacrificed on behalf of a generation," etc. Cf. "This Has To Be Said" [the last paragraph].

Fear most of all to be in error

This, as everyone knows, is a saying of Socrates: he feared most of all to be in error.

Doubtless in one sense Christianity does not teach men to fear, it even teaches them not to fear those who are able to kill the body; yet in another sense it inculcates a still greater fear than that of Socrates, it teaches us to fear him who is able to cast both soul and body into hell.

First, however, that which is first, namely, to become mindful of the Christianity of the New Testament, and to this thou wilt be helped by that Socratic fear, fearing most of all to be in error.

If thou hast not that fear, or (not to pitch the note too high) if it is not thus with thee, if this is not what thou wilt, if thou wilt not strive to pluck up courage to "fear most of all to be in a delusion"—then have nothing to do with me. No, remain then with the priests, let them convince thee firmly, the sooner the better, that what I say is a kind of madness (for the fact that it stands in the New Testament is completely a matter of indifference—when the priest is bound by an oath upon the New Testament, thou art perfectly insured that nothing which stands in the New Testament is suppressed), remain with the priests, try with all thy might to fix it in thy mind that Bishop Mynster was a witness to the truth, one of the genuine witnesses, a link in the holy chain, Bishop Martensen ditto, ditto, likewise every priest, and that the official Christianity is the saving truth; that the reason why Christ suffered the most frightful agony upon the cross, even being forsaken by God, breathing out His life upon the cross, was in order that we might be encouraged to spend our time, our effort, our powers, in enjoying this life wisely and in good taste; that the purpose of His coming into the world was really to encourage the procreation of children, wherefore it is said also that "it is not convenient that any man be made a priest who is unmarried"; that the never to be forgotten significance of His life is that by His death (*Des einen Tod, des andern Brot!*) He made possible a new way of livelihood, that of the priests, which may be considered one of the most profitable, seeing that it also offers employment to the greatest number of tradesmen, forwarding agents, shippers, whose *Geschäft* (in return for an almost incredibly reasonable compensation, considering the importance of the journey, the length of the way, the glory of the place of arrival, and the duration of the stay) is to ship people to the blessedness of eternity, a *Geschäft* which, unique in its kind, has in comparison with all exportations to

America, Australia, etc., the inestimable advantage which secures the shipping agents against even the mere possibility of falling into discredit for the fact that one has absolutely no advice that the goods have reached their destination.

If on the contrary thou hast courage to will to have this courage which fears most of all to be in error, then thou wilt also be able to know the truth concerning what it is to become a Christian. The truth is that to become a Christian is to become unhappy for this life. The situation is this: the more thou hast to do with God, and the more He loves thee, the more wilt thou become, humanly speaking, unhappy for this life, the more thou wilt have to suffer in this life.

And this thought, which to be sure casts a rather disturbing light (as the Christianity of the New Testament is bound to do) upon the jocund traffic of this cheerful, child-begetting, career-making gang of priests, and like a flash of lightning illuminates through and through this fantastic deception, masquerade, the society game, the foolery about "Christendom" (the stronghold of all the illusions), Christian states, lands, a Christian world—this thought for a poor man is so frightful, deadly, almost superhumanly taxing to his strength. This I know by experience, in two ways. First for the reason that I am unable to endure this thought, and therefore merely investigate this true definition of what it is to become a Christian,* whereas for my part I help myself to endure sufferings by a much easier thought, one which is Jewish, not in the highest sense Christian, the recognition that I suffer for my sins. And in the second place, by the conditions of my own life I was led in a very special way to observe it. If it were not for that, I should never have observed it, and still less should I have been able to endure the pressure of that thought; but, as has been said, I was helped by the conditions of my own life.

The conditions of my own life, as has been said, were the rudiments of my learning; by the help of them, in proportion as I was developed in the course of years, I became more and more observant of Christianity and of the definition of what it is to become a Christian. For according to the New Testament what is it to become a Christian? whereto the oft repeated warnings not to be offended? whence the

* Therefore neither do I call myself yet a Christian, I am still far behind. But one advantage I have over all official Christianity (which moreover is bound by an oath upon the New Testament), that I report truly what Christianity is, and so do not take the liberty of altering what Christianity is, and I report truly how I am related to what Christianity is, and so do not take part in altering what Christianity is in order to win millions of Christians.

frightful collisions (hating father, mother, wife, child, etc.), in which the New Testament lives and breathes? Surely both are accounted for by the fact that Christianity knows well that to become a Christian is, humanly speaking, to become unhappy for this life, yet blissfully expectant of an eternal blessedness. For according to the New Testament what is it to be loved by God? It is to become, humanly speaking, unhappy for this life, yet blissfully expectant of an eternal blessedness—in no other way can God Who is spirit love a man. He makes thee unhappy, but He does it out of love—blessed is he who is not offended! And according to the New Testament what is it to love God? It is to *will* to become, humanly speaking, unhappy for this life, yet blissfully expectant of an eternal blessedness—in no other way can a man love God who is spirit. And only by the help of this canst thou see that the Christianity of the New Testament does not exist, that the little religiousness there is in the land is at the very most...Judaism.

That we ("Christendom") cannot in any wise appropriate Christ's promises to ourselves, for we are not in the place where Christ and the New Testament require one to be in order to be a Christian

Imagine that there was a mighty spirit who had promised to certain men his protection, but upon the condition that they should make their appearance at a definite place where it was dangerous to go. Suppose that these men forbore to make their appearance at that definite place, but went home to their parlors and talked to one another in enthusiastic terms about how this spirit had promised them his potent protection, so that no one should be able to harm them. Is not this ridiculous?

So it is with "Christendom." Christianity and the New Testament understood something perfectly definite by believing; to believe is to venture out as decisively as it is possible for a man to do, breaking with everything a man naturally loves, breaking, in order to save his own soul, with that in which he naturally has his life. But to him who believes is promised also assistance against all danger.

But in "Christendom" we play at believing, play at being Christians; as far as possible from any breach with what we love, we remain at home, in the parlor, in the old grooves of finiteness—and then we go and twaddle with one another, or let the priest twaddle to us, about all the promises which are found in the New Testament, that no one shall harm us, that the gates of hell shall not prevail against us, against the Church, etc.

"That the gates of hell shall not prevail against His Church," are words of Christ which recently have been cited again and again against me[39] and my affirmation that Christianity simply does not exist.

My answer is that this promise does not help us in the least, for the twaddle we are living in, as though that is what it means to be a Christian, is not at all what Christ and the New Testament understand by being Christians.

Venture out so decisively that thou breakest with all the temporal and the finite, with all a man commonly lives for and in, venture out so decisively in order to become a Christian, and then wilt thou (this is the teaching of Christianity), then (this is the first thing) thou wilt thereby come into conflict with the devil and the powers of hell (which the "Christendom" of nincompoops does to be sure avoid). But then also God the Almighty will not let thee out of His hand but will help thee marvelously; and be thou convinced that the gates of hell shall never prevail over the Church of Christ.

But "Christendom" is not the Church of Christ, neither do I say that the gates of hell have prevailed against the Church of Christ. Not by any means. No, I say that "Christendom" is twaddle which has clung to Christianity like a cobweb to a fruit, and now is so polite as to want to be mistaken for Christianity, just as if the cobweb were to think it was the fruit because it is a thing not nearly so nice which hangs on the fruit. The sort of existence which the millions of "Christendom" give evidence of has absolutely no relation to the New Testament, it is an unreality which has no claim upon the promises which apply to believers; yes, an unreality, for true reality is only there where a man has ventured as Christ requires—and then too the promises at once apply to him. But "Christendom" is the disgusting foolery of willing to remain wholly in finiteness and then...allege the promises of Christ.

If it were not a matter so easily checked, these legions of Christians or the priestly patter which is preached to them would presumably affirm also that these Christians are able to perform miracles; for this indeed was promised by Christ to believers, He left the world precisely with the words (Mark 16:17, 18) that these signs should follow them that believe, "In My name they shall cast out devils, they shall speak with new tongues, they shall take up serpents, and if they drink any deadly thing, it shall in no wise hurt them; they shall lay hands on the sick, and they shall recover." But this is exactly the way it stands also with the promise that the gates of hell shall not prevail over Christ's Church. Both promises apply only to what the New Testament understands by believers, not to the priestly swindle with these battalions of Christians, which, corresponding to the distinction between "Sunday-hunters" and real hunters, may be called Sunday-Christians. But for this sort of beings Satan doesn't take the trouble to fish, he sees very well that twaddle has caught them. In view of this it is no less than ludicrous that in reliance upon Christ's promises they think themselves secured against the gates of hell.

What says the Fire Chief?[40]

That when in any way one has what is called a cause, something he earnestly wishes to promote—and then there are others who propose to themselves the task of counteracting it, hindering it, harming it, that he then must take measures against these enemies of his, this everyone is aware of. But not everyone is aware that there is such a thing as honest good-intention which is far more dangerous and as if especially calculated with a view to preventing the cause from becoming truly serious.

When a man suddenly falls ill, well-meaning persons hasten at once to lend aid, one proposes one thing, and one another, if all of them had leave to advise at once, the patient's death would be certain; the well-meant advice of the individual may in itself be dangerous, in any case their bustling, flurried presence is injurious for the fact that it impedes the physician.

So also in the case of a fire. Hardly is the cry of "Fire!" heard before a crowd of people rush to the spot, nice, cordial, sympathetic, helpful people, one has a pitcher, another a basin, the third a squirt, etc., all of them nice, cordial, sympathetic, helpful people, so eager to help put out the fire.

But what says the Fire Chief? The Fire Chief, he says—yes, generally the Fire Chief is a very pleasant and polite man; but at a fire he is what one calls coarse-mouthed—he says, or rather he bawls, "Oh, go to hell with all your pitchers and squirts." And then, when these well-meaning people are perhaps offended and require at least to be treated with respect, what then says the Fire Chief? Yes, generally the Fire Chief is a very pleasant and polite man, who knows how to show everyone the respect that is due him; but at a fire he is rather different—he says, "Where the deuce is the police force?" And when some policemen arrive he says to them, "Rid me of these damn people with their pitchers and squirts; and if they won't yield to fair words, smear them a few over the back, so that we may be free of them and get down to work."

So then at a fire the whole way of looking at things is not the same as in everyday life. Good-natured, honest, well-meaning, by which in everyday life one attains the reputation of being a good fellow, is at a fire honored with coarse words and a few over the back.

And this is quite natural. For a fire is a serious thing, and whenever things are really serious, this honest good-intention by no means suffices. No, seriousness applies an entirely different law: either/or. Either thou art the man who in this instance can seriously do something, and seriously has something to do/or, if such be not thy case, then for thee the serious thing to do is precisely to get out. If by thyself thou wilt not understand this, then let the Fire Chief thrash it into thee by means of the police, from which thou mayest derive particular benefit, and which perhaps may after all contribute to making thee a bit serious, in correspondence with the serious thing which is a fire.

But as it is at a fire, so also it is in matters of the mind. Wherever there is a cause to be promoted, an undertaking to be carried out, an idea to be introduced—one can always be sure that when he who really is the man for it, the right man, who in a higher sense has and must have command, he who has seriousness and can give to the cause the seriousness it truly has—one can always be sure that when he comes (if I may so put it) to the spot, he will find there before him a genial company of twaddlers who under the name of seriousness lie around and bungle things by wanting to serve the cause, promote the undertaking, introduce the idea; a company of twaddlers who of course regard the fact that the person in question will not make common cause with them (precisely indicating his seriousness) as a certain proof that he lacks seriousness. I say, when the right man comes he will find things thus. I can also give this turn to it: the fact that he is the right man is really decided by the way he understands himself in relation to this company of twaddlers. If he has a notion that it is they who are to help, and that he must strengthen himself by union with them, he *eo ipso* is not the right man. The right man sees at once, like the Fire Chief, that this company of twaddlers must get out, that their presence and effect is the most dangerous assistance the fire could have. But in matters of the mind it is not as at a fire, where the Fire Chief merely has to say to the police, "Rid me of these men."

So it is in all matters of the mind, and so it is also in the religious field. History has so often been compared with what the chemists call a process. The metaphor may be quite suggestive, if only it is understood aright. They speak of a filtering process: water is filtered, and in the process it deposits impure ingredients. It is precisely in an opposite sense that history is a process. The idea is introduced—and with that it enters into the process of history. But unfortunately this does not (as one ludicrously assumes) result in the purification of the idea, which never is purer than in its primary form. No, it results, with steadily increasing momentum, in garbling the idea, in making it hackneyed, trite, in wearing it out, in introducing the impure ingredients which originally were not present (the very opposite of filtering), until at last, by the enthusiastic cooperation and mutual approbation of a series of successive generations the point is reached where the idea is entirely extinguished and the opposite of the idea has become what they now call the idea, and this they maintain has been accomplished by the historical process in which the idea has been purified and refined.

When at last the right man comes, he to whom in the highest sense the task belongs, who perhaps was early selected and slowly educated for this task, which is to let in light upon the affair, to set fire to this wilderness which is the asylum of all twaddle, all illusions, all knavish tricks—when he comes he will already find there before him a company of twaddlers who with cheerful cordiality have a sort of a notion that things are wrong, or are prepared to chatter about things being dreadfully wrong, and to be self-important for chattering about it. In case he, the right man, for a single instant sees amiss and thinks that it is this company that is to be a help, he is *eo ipso* not the right man. In case he makes a mistake and has anything to do with them, divine governance will instantly let go of him as unfit. But the right man sees with half an eye, as does the Fire Chief, that this company which well-meaningly would help to put out a fire with pitchers and squirts, that this same company which in the present instance, where it is not a question of extinguishing a fire but precisely of lighting a fire, would lend aid with a sulphur match without the sulphur, or with a damp paper-lighter, must get out, that he must not have the least thing to do with this company, that he must be as coarse-mouthed with them as possible, he who perhaps is usually anything but that. But everything depends upon getting rid of that company; for the effect of it is, in the form of hearty sympathy, to eradicate the real seriousness from the cause. Naturally the company will then rave against him, against this frightful pride,[41] etc. But to him this must make no difference. Wherever there truly must be seriousness the law is this: either/or; either I am the one who seriously has to deal with the matter, is thereto called and is absolutely willing to venture decisively/or, if such is not my case, then seriousness is, not to engage in it at all. Nothing is more detestable and more vile, both betraying and bringing about a deeper demoralization, than this: to want to have somehow a little part in that which must be *aut / aut; aut Caesar / aut nihil,*[42] to want to have somehow a little part, and then with good-hearted moderation to prate about it, and so by this prattle to pretend mendaciously that one is better than those who have nothing to do with the whole concern—pretend to be better, and make the thing more difficult for him who properly has the task to do.

Brief observations

1.

The Biblical interpretation of mediocrity.

The Biblical interpretation of mediocrity goes on interpreting and interpreting Christ's words until it gets out of them its own spiritless [trivial] meaning—and then, after having removed all difficulties, it is tranquillized, and appeals confidently to Christ's words!

It quite escapes the attention of mediocrity that hereby it generates a new difficulty, surely the most comical difficulty it is possible to imagine, that God should let himself be *born*, that the Truth should have come into the world...in order to make trivial remarks. And likewise the new difficulty as to how one is to explain that Christ could be crucified. For it is not usual in this world of triviality to apply the penalty of death for making trivial remarks, so that the crucifixion of Christ becomes both inexplicable and comical, since it is comical to be crucified because one has made trivial remarks.

2.

The theater / The church.

The difference between the theater and the church is essentially this, that the theater honestly and honorably acknowledges itself to be what it is; on the other hand the church is a theater which dishonestly tries in every way to hide what it is.

For example. On the theater-board is always plainly written: "Money will not be returned." The church, this solemn sanctity, would shudder at the scandal, the offensiveness, of writing this over the church door, or having it printed under the list of preachers for Sundays. But yet the church does not shudder at insisting, perhaps more strictly than the theater, that money will *not* be returned.

It is lucky therefore that the church has the theater alongside of it; for the theater is a wag, really a sort of witness to the truth, which gives the secret away. What the theater says openly, the church does secretly.

3.

God / The world.

If two men were to eat nuts together, and the one liked only the shell, the other only the kernel, one may say that they match one another well. What the world rejects, casts away, despises, namely, the sacrificed man, the kernel—precisely upon that God sets the greatest store, and treasures it with greater zeal than does the world that which it loves with the greatest passion.

THE INSTANT

No. 7

Contents

August 30, 1855. S. Kierkegaard.

Copenhagen

Published by C. A. Reitzel's Estate and Heirs

Bianco Luno's Press

From the Journal

PAYING THE PRIESTS

. . . The punishment I could wish to inflict upon the priests would be: to provide each one of them ten times the income he now has...but not a person in the church. But naturally I must fear that neither the world nor the priests would understand this punishment, ideal as it would be.

If somebody—let us make the thought-experiment—if somebody were able to prove conclusively that Christ never existed at all, nor the Apostles either, that the whole thing was a fabrication—in case on the part of the State and the congregation there was no hint of suppressing the livings—I should like to see how many priests would lay down their office.

The machine with the 1000 livings goes buzzing on quite calmly. This is perfectly possible when it is a question of "spirit." The fact that one lacks an arm or a leg cannot pass unnoticed; but the "spirit" may perfectly well have vanished—and the machine continues to go.

XI² A 22, X⁴ A 571

Why does "man" love the "poet" above all?
and
why, speaking in a godly sense, is precisely the "poet" the most dangerous?

ANSWER: Precisely for this reason is the poet the most dangerous, in a godly sense, because man loves the poet above all.

And for this reason man loves the poet above all, because he is the most dangerous. For it is an ordinary accompaniment of illness to desire most vehemently, to love most of all, precisely that which is injurious to the sick man. But, spiritually understood, man in his natural condition is sick, he is in error, in an illusion, and therefore desires most of all to be deceived, so that he may be permitted not only to remain in error but to find himself thoroughly comfortable in his self-deceit. And a deceiver capable of rendering him this service is precisely the poet; therefore man loves the poet above all.

The poet has to do only with the imaginative powers, he depicts the good, the beautiful, the noble, the true, the sublime, the unselfish, the magnanimous, etc., in a mood as remote from reality as imagination is. And at this distance how charming is the beautiful, the noble, the unselfish, the magnanimous! On the other hand, if it is brought so close to me that it would compel me as it were to make it reality, because he who depicted it was not a poet but a man of character, a witness to the truth, who himself made it reality—frightful! That would be unendurable!

In every generation there are very few so hardened and depraved that they would have the good, the noble, etc., clean done away with; but also in every generation there are only very few so serious and honest that they truly wish to make the good, the noble, etc., a reality.

"Man" does not desire that the good be so far away as those first few, but neither would he have it so near as those last few.

Here is the place of the poet, the beloved foundling of the human heart. That he is, and how can we wonder at it? For the human heart, among other qualities, has one which, to be sure, is rather rarely mentioned (but this after all is obviously the effect of the same quality), the quality of refined hypocrisy. And the poet is the fellow who can play the hypocrite with men.

That which, if it is made into reality, is the most dreadful suffering, the poet is able to transform dexterously into the most refined enjoyment. To renounce the world in reality...is no joke. But, while secure in the possession of this world, to revel in sentiment along with the poet in a "quiet hour," that is the most refined enjoyment.

— — And it is by this kind of worship we have reached the point of being all Christians. That is to say, all this thing about "Christendom," Christian states, lands, State Church, National Church, etc., is removed from reality by the whole distance of imagination, it is...a conceit, and, Christianly, a conceit so pernicious that we may apply to it the proverb which says, "Conceit is worse than pestilence."

Christianity is renunciation of this world. This is the theme of the professor's lecture, and then he makes lecturing his career, without so much as admitting that this after all is not Christianity. If it is Christianity, where then is the renunciation of this world? No, this is not Christianity, it is a poet's relation to Christianity—The priest preaches, he "witnesses" (No, I thank you kindly!), that Christianity is renunciation, and then makes preaching his remunerative profession; he does not so much as admit to himself that this is not Christianity. But where is the renunciation? Is not this then also a poet-relationship?

But the poet plays the hypocrite with men—and the priest is a poet, as we have seen. So then the official worship is to play hypocrite—and to attain this great blessing the State naturally does not hesitate to spend money.

If hypocrisy is to be checked, the mildest form in which this can come about is for the "priest" to make the admission that this after all is not Christianity—otherwise we have hypocrisy.

What therefore is stated in the title is not quite true, that the poet is the most dangerous thing. *The far more dangerous thing is that one who is only a poet is for that called a priest, gives himself out to be something far more serious and true than the poet, and yet is only a poet. This is hypocrisy in the second degree (raised to the second power)*. Hence there is needed a police expert who, merely by pronouncing this word, by saying that he was only a poet, could get in behind the scenes of all this mummery.

Fishers of men

These are Christ's own words: "Follow me, and I will make you fishers of men." (Matthew 4:19).

So off went the Apostles.

"But what was that likely to amount to, with these few men, who moreover understood Christ's words to mean that it was they who had to be sacrificed in order to catch men? It is easy to see that if things had gone on that way, it would have amounted to nothing. That was God's notion, perhaps a pretty one, but—as every practical man must surely admit—God is not practical. Or can one think of anything more topsy-turvy than that sort of fishing, where fishing means being sacrificed, so that it is not the fishermen who eat the fish but the fish who eat the fishermen? And that is what they call fishing! It is almost like Hamlet's madness when he says of Polonius that he is at a supper, not where he eats, but where he is eaten.[43]

Then man undertook God's cause.

"Fishers of men! What Christ meant is something quite different from what these honest Apostles achieved, in defiance of all linguistic usage and linguistic analogy, for in no language is this what is understood by fishing. What He meant and intended was the origination of a new branch of business, i.e. man-fishery, preaching Christianity in such a way that it will amount to something to fish with this fishing company."

Attention now, and you will see that it does amount to something!

Yes, my word, it did amount to something! It amounted to "established Christendom" with millions and millions and millions of Christians.

It was quite simply arranged. Just as one company is formed to speculate in the herring-fishery, another in cod-fishing, another in whaling, etc., so man-fishing was carried on by a stock company which guaranteed its members a dividend of such and such a per cent.

And what was the result of it? If you haven't done it yet, don't fail to take advantage of this opportunity to admire man! The result was that they caught a prodigious number of herring, or what I mean is men, Christians; and of course the company was in a brilliant financial condition. It proved indeed that even the most successful herring company did not make nearly so big a profit as did man-fishery. And one thing further, an extra profit, or at least a piquant seasoning on top of the profit, namely, that no herring company is able to quote words of Scripture when they send boats out for the catch.

But man-fishery is a godly enterprise, the stockholders in this company can appeal to words of Scripture for themselves, for Christ says, "I will make you fishers of men." They can tranquilly go to meet the Judgment, saying, "We have accomplished Thy word, we have fished for men."

The sort of person they call a Christian

First picture.

It is a young man—let us think of it so, reality furnishes examples in abundance—it is a young man, we can imagine him with more than ordinary ability, knowledge, interested in public events, a politician, even taking an active part as such.

As for religion, his religion is...that he has none at all. To think of God never occurs to him, any more than it does to go to church, and it is certainly not on religious grounds he eschews that; he almost fears that to read God's Word at home would make him ridiculous.

When it turns out that the situation requires him to express himself about religion and there is some danger in doing it, he gets out of the difficulty by saying, as is the truth, "I have no opinion at all, such things have never concerned me."

This same young man who feels no need of religion feels the need of being...paterfamilias. He marries, then he has a child, he is...presumptive father. And then what happens?

Well, our young man is, as they say, in hot water about this child; in the capacity of...presumptive father he is compelled to have a religion. And it turns out that he has the Evangelical Lutheran religion.

How pitiful it is to have a religion in this way. As a man he has no religion; when there might be danger connected with having even an opinion about religion, he has no religion—but in the capacity of...presumptive father he has (*risum teneatis!*) that religion precisely which extols the single state.

So they notify the priest, the midwife arrives with the baby, a young lady holds the infant's bonnet coquettishly, several young men who also have no religion render the presumptive father the service of having, as godfathers, the Evangelical Christian religion, and assume obligation for the Christian upbringing of the child, while a silken priest with a graceful gesture sprinkles water three times on the dear little baby and dries his hands gracefully with the towel— —

And this they dare to present to God under the name of Christian baptism. Baptism—it was with this sacred ceremony the Saviour of the world was consecrated for His life's work, and after Him the disciples,[44] men who had well reached the age of discretion and who then, dead to this life (therefore were immersed three times, signifying that they were baptized into communion with Christ's death), promised to be willing to live as sacrificed men in this world of falsehood and evil.

The priests, however, these holy men, understand their business, and understand too that if (as Christianity must unconditionally require of every sensible man) it were so that only when a person has reached the age of discretion he is permitted to decide upon the religion he will have—the priests understand very well that in this way their trade would not amount to much. And therefore these holy witnesses to the truth insinuate themselves into the lying-in room, where the mother is weak after the suffering she has gone through, and the paterfamilias is...in hot water. And then under the name of baptism they have the courage to present to God a ceremony such as that which has been described, into which a little bit of truth might be brought nevertheless, if the young lady, instead of holding the little bonnet sentimentally over the baby, were satirically to hold a night cap over the presumptive father. For to have religion in that way is, spiritually considered, a pitiful comedy. A person has no religion; but by reason of family circumstances, first because the mother got into the family way, the paterfamilias in turn got into embarrassment owing to that, and then with the ceremonies connected with the sweet little baby—by reason of all this a person has...the Evangelical Lutheran religion.

Second Picture.

It is a tradesman. His motto is: Every man's a thief in his business. "It is impossible," says he, "to be able to get through this world if one is not just like the other tradesmen, who all pay homage to the maxim that every man is a thief in his business."

As for religion—well, really his religion is this: Every man's a thief in his business. He also has a religion in addition to this, and his opinion is that especially every tradesman ought to have one. "A tradesman," says he, "even if he has no religion, ought never to let that be noticed, for that may readily be harmful to him by casting possibly suspicion upon his honesty; and preferably a tradesman ought to have the religion which prevails in the land." As to the last point, he explains that the Jews always have the reputation of cheating more than the Christians, which, as he maintains, is by no means the case; he maintains that the Christians cheat just as well as the Jews, but what injures the Jews is the fact that they do not have the religion which prevails in the land. As to the first point, namely, the profit it affords to have a religion, with a view to the countenance it gives to cheating—with regard to this he appeals to what one learns from the priests; he maintains that what helps the priests to cheat more than any other class in society is precisely the fact that they are so closely associated with religion. If such a thing could be done, he would gladly give a good shilling to obtain ordination, for that would pay brilliantly.

So two or four times a year this man puts on his best clothes...and goes to communion. Up comes a priest, a priest (like those that jump up out of a snuffbox when one touches a spring) who jumps up whenever he sees "a blue banknote."[45] And thereupon the priest celebrates the Holy Communion, from which the tradesman, or rather both tradesmen (both the priest and the honest citizen), return home to their customary way of life, only that one of them (the priest) cannot be said to return home to his customary way of life, for in fact he had never left it, but rather had been functioning as a tradesman.

And this is what one dares to offer to God under the name of the Sacrament of the Lord's Supper, the Communion in Christ's body and blood!

The Sacrament of the Lord's Supper! It was at the Last Supper that Christ, Who from eternity had been consecrated to be the Sacrifice, met for the last time before His death with His disciples, who also were consecrated to death or to the possibility of death if they truly followed Him. Hence for all the festal solemnity it is so shudderingly true, what is said about His body and blood, about this blood-covenant which has united the Sacrifice with His few faithful...blood-witnesses, as they surely were willing to be.

And now the solemnity is this: to live before and after in complete worldliness—and then a ceremony. However, for good reasons the priests take care not to enlighten people about what the New Testament understands by the Lord's Supper and the obligation it imposes. Their whole business is based upon *living off of* the fact that others are sacrificed, their Christianity is, *to receive sacrifices.* If it were proposed to them that they themselves should be sacrificed, they would regard it as a strange and unchristian demand, conflicting violently with the *wholesome* doctrine of the New Testament, which they would prove with such colossal learning that the span of life of no individual man would suffice for studying all this through.

"*First* the kingdom of God"[46]

A kind of novel.

The theological candidate Ludvig From—is seeking. And when one hears that a "theological" candidate is seeking, one need not have a specially vivid imagination to understand what it is he seeks, of course it is the kingdom of God, which indeed one must seek first!

No, it is not that after all. What he seeks is a royal appointment to a living. And before he got that far there *first* occurred a great many things, which I shall indicate with a few strokes.

First he went to high school, from which he eventually graduated. Thereupon he *first* took two examinations, and after four years of reading he *first* took the professional examination.

With that he is a theological candidate, and one would perhaps suppose that after he had *first* passed all this, he would finally have reached the point of working for Christianity. Oh, yes, if it were for an artisans' guild. But, no, *first* he must go to the Seminary for half a year,[47] and when that is finished it means that eight years have *first* gone by during which there was no question of being able to seek.

And now we have reached the beginning of the novel: the eight years are past, he seeks.

His life, which hitherto cannot be said to have had any relation to the absolute, suddenly assumes such a relation: he seeks absolutely everything; he writes one sheet after another of officially stamped paper,[48] filling four pages of each; he runs from Herod to Pilate; he recommends himself to the ministers of state and to the porters; in short, he is entirely in the service of the absolute. Indeed, one of his acquaintances, who for the past few years has not seen him, thinks to his amazement that he discovers a decrease in his size, which perhaps may be explained by supposing that it happened to him as to Münchausen's dog, which was a greyhound, and by much running became a dachshund.

Thus three years pass. Our theological candidate really is in need of repose, after such prodigious exertion in running on commissions, he needs to be put out of commission or else to come to rest in a living and be nursed a little by his future wife—for meanwhile he *first* became engaged.

Finally, as Pernille says to Magdalone,[49] the hour of his "redemption" strikes, so with the whole power of conviction he will be able from his own experience to "bear witness" before the congregation that in Christianity there is salvation and redemption—he is appointed to a living.

What happens? By procuring more precise information about the revenues of the living, he discovers that they are about 150 dollars less than he had supposed. The game is up. The unfortunate man is almost in despair. He already has bought stamped paper in order to approach the Cultus Minister with the petition that he may be allowed to be regarded as not called (and then to begin all over again from the beginning),[50] when one of his acquaintances persuades him to give this up. So it remains at that, he keeps the call.

He is ordained—and the Sunday arrives when he is to be presented to the congregation. The Dean, by whom he is presented, is more than an ordinary man; he not only has what all priests have (and all the more developed, the higher their rank), an unprejudiced eye for earthly profit, but he also has a speculative eye for universal history,[51] which he does not keep to himself but allows the congregation to share. By a stroke of genius he chooses for his text the words of the Apostle Peter: "Lo, we have left all and have followed Thee," and he then explains to the congregation that precisely in times such as ours there must be men like that as teachers, and in connection therewith he recommends this young man, of whom he knows how near he has been to drawing back for the sake of 150 dollars.

The young man himself now mounts the pulpit—and, strangely enough, the Gospel for the Day is: "Seek *first* the kingdom of God." He delivers his sermon. "A very good sermon," says the Bishop, who himself was present, "a very good sermon; and it produced a proper effect, that whole part about 'first' the kingdom of God, and the way he stressed this word *first*." "But does it not seem to your Lordship that in this instance a correspondence between speech and life would be desirable? Upon me this word *first* made an almost satirical impression." "What an absurdity! He is called to preach the doctrine, the sound, unadulterated doctrine of seeking first the kingdom of God, and that he did very well."

This is the sort of divine service one dares—under oath!—to offer unto God—the most dreadful mockery.

Whoever thou art, think merely on this word of God, "First the kingdom of God," and then think on this novel, which is so true, so true, so true—and thou wilt not need more to make it clear to thee that the whole official Christianity is an abyss of falsehood and illusion, something so profane that the only thing that with truth can be said about it is: By ceasing to take part (if usually thou dost) in the public worship of God as it now is, thou hast constantly one sin the less, and that a great one: thou dost not take part in treating God as a fool (cf. "This has to be said, so be it then said").

God's Word reads, "First the kingdom of God," and the interpretation of it, perhaps a way of completing and "perfecting" it (for one wants to do the thing handsomely) is: first everything else, and *last* the kingdom of God; after a long while the earthly is *first* attained, and then finally comes at last a sermon about seeking first the kingdom of God, then one becomes a priest; and the priest's whole profession is a constant practice of this: first the earthly...and then the kingdom of God, first regard for the earthly, whether the thing pleases the Government or the majority, or whether a man is himself a big enough bug to do it, i.e. first regard for what the fear of man bids or forbids...and then the kingdom of God, first money...and then thou canst get thy child baptized, first money...then there will be earth thrown on and a funeral oration corresponding to the tariff, first money...then I will visit the sick, first money...and then, *virtus post nummos* (first money, then virtue[52]), then the kingdom of God, the last being in such a degree last that it doesn't come at all, and the whole thing stops with the first, with money—the only case where one does not feel the need of "going further."[53]

Such at every point and in all respects is the relation of official Christianity to the Christianity of the New Testament. And furthermore this is not what people themselves admit is a pitiable situation; no, they impudently brave it out that Christianity is perfectible, that one cannot stop with the first form of Christianity, that this is merely a phase, etc.

Therefore there is nothing so displeasing to God as official Christianity and taking part in it with the claim that this is worshiping Him. If thou dost believe, as surely thou dost, that to steal, rob, plunder, commit adultery, slander, gormandize, is displeasing to God, then official Christianity and its worship is infinitely more abhorrent to Him; that man can be sunk in such a brutish stupidity and spiritlessness as to offer God worship of this sort where everything is thoughtlessness, spiritlessness and torpor—and then that man can impudently regard this as a stage of progress in Christianity!

It is this which it is my duty to say: "Whoever thou art, whatever in other respects thy life may be, by ceasing to take part (if usually thou dost) in the public worship of God as it now is, thou hast one sin the less, and that a great one." The responsibility is thine, and thou shalt bear it, for the way thou dost act, but thou hast been warned.

That "Christendom" is from generation to generation a society of non-Christians; and the formula in accordance with which this comes about

The formula is this: when the individual has reached the age when there might be any question of his becoming a Christian in the New Testament sense, his notion then is that he can't thoroughly make up his mind to it. On the other hand, he thoroughly desires...to get married. Aha! He then indulges in the following reflection: "I am already too old to become a Christian [the basic falsehood of "Christendom," for according to the New Testament it must be as a man one becomes a Christian]. No, one must become a Christian as a child, it must be taken from childhood up. So now I shall marry and beget children, and they shall be Christians."

Abracadabra! Amen, amen, world without end, amen! All honor to the priests!

This is the secret of "Christendom," an unparalleled impudence by way of putting a wax nose on God, an impudence which, under the name of being Christianity, is blessed by the priests, these perjured teachers, this shady company which (as anyone with any experience must know and perceive, though not everyone is well enough acquainted with the New Testament to be properly disgusted by it) keeps on good terms with the midwives. Look alertly, and thou shalt see that it is as I say, that there is a secret understanding between every priest and the midwives; they understand among themselves that to the priest it is of the utmost importance to stand well with the midwives, and they understand among themselves that they share after all in a common livelihood—and the priest is bound by an oath upon the New Testament which extols the single life. But that is a matter of course, for the Christianity of "Christendom" is also exactly the opposite of the Christianity of the New Testament, and therefore these petticoats (I mean the priests, not the midwives), as importunate as panderesses, haunt the lying-in rooms.

The Christianity of "Christendom" sees that everything depends upon establishing the maxim that one becomes a Christian as a child, that if one is rightly to become a Christian, one must be such from infancy. This is the basic falsehood. If this is put through, then good-night to the Christianity of the New Testament! Then "Christendom" has won the game—a victory which is most fitly celebrated by a regular gorge of meats and drinks, a wild carouse with bacchants and bacchantes (priests and midwives) at the head of the procession.

The truth is, one cannot become a Christian as a child; that is just as impossible as for a child to beget children. Becoming a Christian presupposes (according to the New Testament) being fully a man, what one might call in a physical sense maturity of manhood—in order then to become a Christian by breaking with everything to which one naturally clings. Becoming a Christian presupposes (according to the New Testament) a personal consciousness of sin and of oneself as a sinner. So one readily sees that this whole thing about becoming a Christian as a child, yea, about childhood being above all other ages the season for becoming a Christian, is neither more nor less than puerility, which these puerile priests, presumably by virtue of their oath upon the New Testament, put into people's heads in order that the priests' trade and career may be established.

Let us go back to the beginning. The individual said, "I am already too old to become a Christian, but I shall marry, and my children shall," etc. If he had really been serious about becoming a Christian, he would have said, "Now I am at an age when I can become a Christian. Consequently it could not of course occur to me to marry. Even were it not true that Christianity recommends the single state, which the Pattern exemplifies, although the Apostle, clearly enough against his will, finds himself compelled to yield a little to the uxorious multitude, and, like one who is tired of hearing the everlasting twaddle about the same thing, finally makes the little concession that, if worse comes to worst, it is better to marry than to burn—even if this were not so, it nevertheless could never occur to me to marry. The task of becoming a Christian being so prodigious, why should I charge myself with this impediment, although people, especially when they are at a certain age, represent it and regard it as the greatest felicity? Honestly, I am unable to comprehend how it can occur to any man to unite being a Christian with being married. Note that with this I am not thinking of the case of a man who was already married and had a family, and then at that age became a Christian; no, I mean to say, how one who is unmarried and says he has become a Christian, how it could occur to him to marry. A Saviour comes to the world to save...whom? The lost. Of them there are surely enough, for all are lost, and everyone that is born is by being born a lost soul. For to every individual the Saviour says, 'Wilt thou be saved?' So even if the Saviour said nothing about the single state, it seems to me a matter of course that it was not necessary to say that a Christian does not marry. Surely it was the least one could require of a man who was himself saved, and redeemed at so dear a price that it was accomplished by another man's agonizing life and death, it was after all the least one could require that he should not engage in begetting children, in producing more lost souls, for of them there are really enough. By the propagation of the race the lost are poured out as from a cornucopia. And should then the man who is saved, as though in thanksgiving for his salvation, also take part in the propagation of the race, making his contribution to the number of the lost?"

So then the individual who was really serious about becoming a Christian stopped with himself (seriousness consists precisely in this), he stopped with himself and understood that the task was for him to become a Christian; he stopped with himself to such a degree that it absolutely could not occur to him to marry; he gave expression to the opposite of that which every man naturally may be said to express, the possibility of a race which perhaps through long ages would be descended from him, he expressed the opposite of this by coming there to a stop; he assumed an inverse relation (therefore Christianly the right one) to the "mass of perdition," did not any longer engage in increasing it, but stood in a negative relation to it. In the Christianity of "Christendom" it is different: battalions of breeders and womenfolks are brought together, whereby millions of children are produced—and this, as is maintained by the priests (who must know it, for they have taken an oath upon the New Testament), it is maintained by the priests (but what will not the priests do, even more than the Germans, for money?[54]), this the priests maintain is Christianity, the priests, these holy men, of whom it cannot be said, as it is said of others, that the priest is a thief in his business; the priest is an exception, he is...a liar in his business.

"As a child one must become a Christian, one must take it from childhood up." That is to say, the parents want to be exempted from being Christians; but one would like to have a pretext, and this one serves: to bring up one's children as true Christians. The priests understand the secret very well, and hence there is so much talk about the Christian upbringing of children, about the serious task...which would leave the parents free for what they count the serious business of life. The relation of the parents to their children is like that between the priests and their congregations: the priests too have not exactly an inclination to become Christians—but their congregation, that must become truly Christian. Their waggishness always consists in putting away seriousness (that of becoming Christians themselves) and introducing instead of that the profound seriousness of making others Christians.

Thus people bring up their children as Christians, so called; that is to say, they fill up the children with childish sweets, which are not the Christianity of the New Testament at all; and from these childish sweets, which no more resemble the teaching about a cross and agony, about dying from the world, about hating oneself, than jam resembles cream of tartar, from these childish sweets the parents lick off a little and become so sentimental at the thought that they, alas, are no longer such Christians as they were when they are children, for only as a child can one really be a Christian.

And to all this galimatias the priests of course agree; yes, of course! One thing only is important to the priest, namely, in every way (by virtue of his oath upon the New Testament) to do exactly the opposite of that which the New Testament does, in every way to preserve in man, to cultivate and to encourage, the desire for the propagation of the race, in order that there may constantly be provided battalions of Christians, which are a vital necessity if thousands of priests who are strong breeders are to live off of them with their families. Moreover the "priest" knows also what every politically wise government knows (and what the lovers only discover afterwards), that man is reduced to insignificance by marriage, that therefore it is important, by cattle shows, by prizes for begetting the most children, and in other ways, e.g. by representing this as Christianity, to encourage the propagation of their kind, which is what recalls most strongly man's kinship with God. Finally, the "priest" thereby avoids serious collisions with the multitude of men. Christianity's view of life is high and therefore may easily be an offense to the multitude of men. If on the other hand Christianity amounts only to begetting children, it becomes as popular and comprehensible as possible. And, as the priest says, we ought not to frighten people away from religion, one ought to win them for it, e.g. by making the satisfaction of their lusts religion. In this way one wins them in masses, and then in turn wins (profits oneself) by the fact that men are won for religion—but in that way one does not win heaven.

From generation to generation "Christendom" is a society of non-Christians; and the formula in accordance with which that comes about is this: the individual himself is not willing to be a Christian but undertakes to beget children who shall become Christians; and these children in their turn behave in the same way. God sits in heaven . . . like a fool. But His perjured servants upon earth, the priests, take enjoyment in life and in this comedy. Hand in hand with the midwives they are the assistants in the propagation of the race—the true Christian seriousness.

Confirmation and the wedding: a Christian comedy—or something worse

Conscience (in so far as there can be any question of that in this connection) seems to have smitten "Christendom" with the reflection that this thing after all was too absurd, that this purely bestial nonsense wouldn't do—the notion of becoming a Christian by receiving as an infant a drop of water on the head administered by a royal functionary, the family then arranging a party, a banquet, for the occasion, to celebrate this festivity.

This won't do, thought "Christendom," there must also be an expression of the fact that the baptized individual *personally* undertakes to perform the baptismal vow.

This is the purpose of confirmation—a splendid invention, if one makes a double assumption: that divine worship is in the direction of making a fool of God; and that its principal aim is to provide an occasion for family festivities, parties, a jolly evening, and a banquet which differs in this respect from other banquets that this banquet (what a refinement!) has "also" a religious significance.

"The tender infant," says "Christendom," "cannot personally take the baptismal vow, for which a real *person* is requisite." And so (is this genius or ingenious?) they have chosen the period from fourteen to fifteen years of age, the age of boyhood. This real person—there can be no objection, he's man enough to undertake to perform the baptismal vows made in behalf of the tender infant.

A boy of fifteen! In case it were a question of ten dollars, the father would say, "No, my boy, that can't be left to your discretion, you're not yet dry behind the ears." But as for his eternal blessedness, and when a real personality must concentrate the seriousness of personality upon what in a deeper sense could not be called seriousness, namely, that a tender infant is bound by a vow—for that the age of fifteen years is the most appropriate.

The most appropriate—ah, yes, if, as was previously remarked, divine worship is assumed to have a double aim: in a delicate way (if one can call it that) to treat God as a fool; and to give occasion for family festivities. Then it is extraordinarily appropriate, as is everything else on that occasion, including the Gospel appointed for the day, which, as everyone knows, begins thus: "When the doors were shut"[55]—and is peculiarly appropriate on a Confirmation Sunday, it is with true edification one hears a priest read it aloud on a Confirmation Sunday.

Confirmation then is easily seen to be far deeper nonsense than infant baptism, precisely because confirmation claims to supply what was lacking in infant baptism: a real personality which can consciously assume responsibility for a vow which has to do with the decision of an eternal blessedness. On the other hand, this nonsense is in another sense shrewd enough, ministering to the egoism of the priesthood, which understands very well that, if the decision with regard to religion is postponed to the mature age of man (the only Christian and the only sensible thing), many would perhaps have character enough not to want to be feignedly Christian. Hence the priest seeks to take possession of people in young and tender years, so that in maturer years they might have the difficulty of breaking a "sacred" obligation, imposed to be sure in boyhood, but which many perhaps may feel superstitious about breaking. Therefore the priesthood takes possession of the child, the boy, receives from him sacred vows, etc. And what the "priest," this man of God, proposes to do is surely a godly undertaking. Otherwise analogy might require that, just as there is a police ordinance prohibiting the sale of liquor to boys, so there might also be issued a prohibition against taking solemn vows concerning an eternal blessedness...from boys, a prohibition to insure that the priests, because they are perjurers, should not for this reason be allowed to work in the direction of bringing about (for their own consolation) the greatest possible *comune naufragium*,[56] namely, that the whole community should become perjured; and letting boys of fifteen take a solemn vow concerning an eternal blessedness is as though calculated to this end.

So then confirmation is in itself far deeper nonsense than infant baptism. But not to neglect anything which might contribute to make confirmation the exact opposite of that which it gives itself out to be, this ceremony has been associated with all finite and civil ends, so that the significance of confirmation really is the certificate issued by the priest, without which the boy or girl in question cannot get along at all in this life.

The whole thing is a comedy—and taking this view of it, perhaps something might be done to introduce more dramatic illusion into this solemnity, as, for example, if a prohibition were published against anyone being confirmed in a jacket, *item* an ordinance that upon the floor of the church male confirmants must wear a beard, which of course could fall off at the family festivities in the evening, and perhaps be used for fun and jest.

By what I am writing I do not attack the congregation; they have been led astray, one cannot blame them if, being left to their own devices and deceived by the fact that the priests have taken an oath upon the New Testament, they think well of this sort of worship. But woe unto the priests, woe unto these perjured liars! I know it well, there have been mockers of religion who would have given—yea, what would they not have given?—to be able to do what I can do, but did not succeed because God was not with them. Otherwise with me, originally kindly disposed towards the priests as rarely anyone has been, just desiring to help them, they have brought upon themselves the opposite. And with me is the Almighty; and He knows best how the blows must be dealt so that they are felt, so that laughter administered in fear and trembling may be the scourge—it is for that I am used.

The Wedding

True worship of God consists quite simply in doing God's will.

But this sort of worship was never to man's taste. That which in all generations men have been busied about, that in which theological learning originated, becomes many, many disciplines, widens out to interminable prolixity, that upon which and for which thousands of priests and professors live, that which is the content of the history of "Christendom," by the study of which those who are becoming priests and professors are educated, is the contrivance of another sort of divine worship, which consists in...having one's own will, but doing it in such a way that the name of God, the invocation of God, is brought into conjunction with it, whereby man thinks he is assured against being ungodly—whereas, alas, precisely this is the most aggravated sort of ungodliness.

An example. A man is inclined to want to support himself by killing people. Now he sees from God's Word that this is not permissible, that God's will is, "Thou shalt not kill." "All right," thinks he, "but that sort of worship doesn't suit me, neither would I be an ungodly man." What does he do then? He gets hold of a priest who in God's name blesses the dagger. Yes, that's something different.

In God's Word the single state is recommended. "But," says man, "that sort of worship doesn't suit me, and I am certainly not an ungodly man either. Such an important step as marriage [which, be it noted, God advises against, and thinks that not taking this "important step" is the important thing] I surely ought not to take without assuring myself of God's blessing. [Bravo!] That is what this man of God, the priest, is for; he blesses this important step [the importance of which consists in not doing it], and so it is well pleasing to God"—and I have my will, and my will becomes worship, and the priest has his will, he has ten dollars, not earned in the humble way of brushing people's clothes or serving beer or brandy at the bar; no, he was employed in God's service, and to earn ten dollars in that way is...divine worship. [Bravissimo!]

What an abyss of nonsense and abomination! When something is displeasing to God, does it become well pleasing by the fact that (to make bad worse) a priest takes part who (to make bad worse) gets ten dollars for declaring that it is well pleasing to God?

Let us stick to the subject of the wedding. In his Word God recommends the single state. Now there is a couple that want to get married. This couple, of course, since they call themselves Christians, ought to know well what Christianity is—but let that pass. The lovers apply to... the priest—and the priest is bound by an oath upon the New Testament which recommends the single state. If then he is not a liar and a perjurer who in the basest manner earns paltry dollars, he must act as follows. At the most he can say to them with human sympathy for this human thing of being in love, "My little children, I am the last man to whom you should apply; to apply to me in such a contingency is as if one were to apply to the chief of police to inquire how one should comport oneself when stealing. My duty is to employ every means to restrain you. At the utmost I can say with the Apostle (for they are not the words of the Master), Yes, if it comes to that, and you have not continency, then get together, 'it is better to marry than to burn.' And I know very well that you will shudder inwardly when I talk thus about what you think the most beautiful thing in life; but I must do my duty. And for this reason I said that I am the last man to whom you should apply."

In "Christendom" it is different. The priest—if only there are some he can splice together, he's the man for it. If the couple had applied to the midwives, perhaps they would not be so sure of being confirmed in the notion that their project is a thing well pleasing to God.

So they are wed, i.e. "man" has his will, but this thing of having his will is refined to being also divine worship, for God's name is brought into conjunction with it. They are wed...by the priest. Ah, the fact that the priest takes part is the reassuring thing. This man who by an oath is bound to the New Testament, and then for ten dollars is the most complaisant man one can have to deal with—this man vouches for it that this act is true divine worship.

Christianly one must say that precisely the fact that the priest takes part is the worst thing in the whole affair. If you want to marry, seek rather to be married by a blacksmith; then it might perhaps (if one may speak thus) escape God's notice; but when a priest takes part it cannot possibly escape God's notice. Remember what was said to a man who in a tempest invoked the gods: "Don't for anything let the gods observe that you are in the party!"[57] And in the same way one might say, "Take care at all events not to have a priest take part." The others, i.e. the blacksmith and the lovers, have not taken an oath to God upon the New Testament, so (if I may speak thus) the thing goes better than when the priest intervenes with his...holy presence.

What every religion in which there is any truth aims at, and what Christianity aims at decisively, is a total transformation in a man, to wrest from him through renunciation and self-denial all that, and precisely that, to which he immediately clings, in which he immediately has his life. This sort of religion, as "man" understands it, is not what he wants. The upshot therefore is that from generation to generation there lives—how equivocal!—a highly respected class in the community, the priests. Their métier is to invert the whole situation, so that what man likes becomes religion, on the condition, however, of invoking God's name and paying something definite to the priests. The rest of the community, when one examines the case more closely, are seen to be egoistically interested in upholding the estimation in which the priests are held—for otherwise the falsification cannot succeed.

To become a Christian in the New Testament sense is such a radical change that, humanly speaking, one must say that it is the heaviest trial to a family that one of its members becomes a Christian. For in such a Christian the God-relationship becomes so predominant that he is not "lost" in the ordinary sense of the word; no, in a far deeper sense than dying he is lost to everything that is called family. It is of this Christ constantly speaks, both with reference to himself when he says that to be his disciple is to be his mother, brother, sister, that in no other sense has he a mother, a brother, a sister; and also when he speaks continually about the collision of hating father and mother, one's own child, etc. To become a Christian in the New Testament sense is to loosen (in the sense in which the dentist speaks of loosening the tooth from the gums), to loosen the individual out of the cohesion to which he clings with the passion of immediacy, and which clings to him with the same passion.

This sort of Christianity was never—no more now, precisely no more than in the year 30—to man's taste, but was distasteful to him in his inmost heart, mortally distasteful. Therefore the upshot is that from generation to generation there lives a highly respected class in the community whose métier is to transform Christianity into the exact opposite.

The Christianity of the priests, by the aid of religion (which, alas, is used precisely to bring about the opposite), is directed to cementing families more and more egoistically together, and to arranging family festivities, beautiful, splendid family festivities, e.g. infant baptism and confirmation, which festivities, compared for example with excursions in the Deer Park and other family frolics, have a peculiar enchantment for the fact that they are "also" religious.

"Woe unto you," says Christ to the "lawyers" (the interpreters of Scripture), "for ye took away the key of knowledge, ye entered not in yourselves [i.e. into the kingdom of heaven, cf. Matthew 23:13], and them that were entering in ye hindered." Luke 11:52.

This is the highly respected profession of the priests, a way of livelihood which prevents men from entering the kingdom of heaven. As a compensation for this the "priest" does his best in the way of performances (such performances, e.g. as Manager Carstensen with notable talent produces at our Tivoli[58]), beautiful, splendid performances with (just as a little wine tastes good in lemonade) a little religious tang to them, which Carstensen to be sure cannot provide...but after all perhaps he might be ordained.

That the Christian education of children in the Christian home, which is so much extolled, especially in Protestantism, is based upon a lie, a sheer lie

Of course in "Christendom" people generally are living in such a way that parents do not concern themselves at all about being Christians except in name, have really no religion. The education of the children consists in a formal training, in learning a few things, but one does not undertake to convey any religious and still less any Christian view of life, to talk to the child about God, still less to speak of Him in accordance with the concepts and ideas which are peculiar to Christianity.

It is different in the families which like to assume an air of importance for being earnest Christians, and who know how to talk a great deal about the significance of the education of children in Christianity, from earliest childhood, as they put it.

The truth, however, is that this (the pride of Protestantism!), this Christian education of children in the Christian home is, Christianly speaking, based upon a lie, a sheer lie.

And this can very easily be proved.

In the first place. The parents cannot talk Christianly and truly about how the child's coming into existence is to be *Christianly* understood. The parents are egoistic enough—and that under the name of Christianity!—to bring up the child in the view that it was an extraordinary act of beneficence on the part of the parents that the child exists, that this master-stroke of the parents whereby the child came into existence was peculiarly well pleasing to God. That is to say, under the name of the Christian education of children they turn Christianity topsy-turvy and transform its view of life into exactly the opposite of what it is. *Christianly* it is anything but the greatest benefaction to bestow life upon the child (that is paganism); *Christianly* it is anything but well pleasing to God, an act whereby one makes oneself thankworthy in his eyes, that one engages in begetting children (such a conception of God is paganism, even a lower form of paganism, or it is the sort of Judaism Christianity precisely would do away with); *Christianly* it is egoism in the highest degree that because a man and a woman cannot control their lust another being must therefore sigh, perhaps for seventy years, in this prisonhouse and vale of tears, and perhaps be lost eternally.

In the second place. That the world into which the parents introduce the child is a sinful, ungodly, wicked world, that lamentation, anguish, wretchedness, awaits everyone that is born, even if he is among the number of those that are saved, and if he is not of this number, eternal perdition awaits him—this the parents cannot say to the child. For one thing, the child cannot understand it, the child is in immediate *rapport* with nature, too happy to be able to understand such things. And secondly, the parents for their own sake cannot well say this to the child. Every child in its naïveté is more or less ingenious. Suppose now that this child in its naïveté were to say to its parents, "But if this is such a bad world, and if this is what awaits me, then indeed it is not well that I have come into this world." Bravo, my little friend, thou hast hit the mark! This is an exceedingly awkward situation for the parents! No, Christianity is not the place for bungling.

In the third place. The parents cannot give the child the true *Christian* conception of God, and they are egoistically interested in not doing it. That before God this world is a lost world, where he who is born is by being born lost, that what God wills (out of love) is that a man shall die from the world, and that if God is so gracious as to turn His love toward him, that what God then does (out of love) is to torment him with every anguish calculated to take his life; for this is what God wills (yet out of love), He would have the life out of everyone that is born, have him transformed into a deceased man, one who lives as though dead. This, even if it were said to him, the child cannot grasp, and the parents, for egoistic reasons, take good care not to say it. What then do they do? Under the name of the Christian education of children they jabber foolishly out of the stock of paganism along the lines above suggested: "It is an extraordinary beneficence that thou didst come into existence, this is a fine world into which thou hast come, and God is a fine man, only hold fast to Him, He will to be sure not fulfill all thy wishes, but He's a help all the same." Sheer lies.

And what then is the consequence of this much extolled Christian education of children? The consequence is, either that the child babbles foolishly the same twaddle throughout his life, as a man, a father, a grandparent, or that there may come an instant in this life when the child will be tried in the most dreadful pain by the query whether God is a mean man who lets a poor child imagine that He (God) is something quite different from what He really is, or whether his parents are liars!

And when this pain has been overcome, when the child understands that everything is all right so far as God is concerned, that He had no share in what it occurred to me to tell about Him, and that at all events his parents were well-meaning in human love towards him, he nevertheless will need perhaps a long, long time, the most painful cure, to get all that out of him which under the name of the Christian education of children has been poured into him.

Behold, this is the consequence of the much extolled Christian education of children, based upon a lie, a sheer lie. But the priests extol it. Well, that you can understand. One man is enough to give a whole town cholera, and 1000 perjurers are more than enough to infect a whole society, so that the life they live under the name of Christianity is, Christianly, a sheer lie.

The truth about the "priest's" importance to society

As a statistician who is familiar with such things, being informed of the population of a big city, must be able to indicate the number of public prostitutes such a city consumes; as a statistician expert in such matters, knowing the size of the army, must be able to determine the number of physicians an army of that size needs in order to be well supplied; so also a statistician engaged for such a purpose, upon being told the population of a country, must be able to determine the number of perjurers (priests) which such a country needs, if under the name of Christianity it were to be perfectly secured against Christianity, or under the appearance of having Christianity it were to be perfectly reassured of being able to live a life of paganism, a paganism which is moreover tranquillized and refined by the notion that it is Christianity.

From this point of view one can perceive the truth of the "priest's" importance to society, or how the case truly stands with regard to his importance.

Christianity rests upon the view of human existence which has as its presupposition that the human race is a lost race, that every individual who is born is by being born a lost individual. Christianity then would save every individual, but it makes no disguise of the fact that, when this is taken seriously, this life becomes the direct opposite of what is to man's taste and liking, being sheer suffering, anguish, misery.

This of course man is not willing to submit to; among millions there is perhaps not one man who is willing honestly to submit to it. So the problem for "man," for the "human race," for "society," is to protect itself with all its might against Christianity, which must be regarded as its mortal enemy.

But to break openly with Christianity, "No," says man, "that is not shrewd, it is even imprudent, and by no means gives promise of sufficient security. Such a prodigious power as Christianity is—when in the very face of it one is so honest, actually has to do with it to the extent that one flatly rejects it, one runs the risk that the game will end with this power getting a finger into one after all, as a punishment for the imprudence of having anything to do with it. For to reject it honestly is after all one way of having something to do with it."

No, entirely different measures are needed in this instance: "man," this clever pate, must here be thoroughly alert.

And now the comedy begins. For a population of such and such a size, says the statistician, there will be needed such and such a number of perjurers. They are engaged. The fact that what they preach and what their lives express is not the Christianity of the New Testament, they themselves see plainly enough; "But," say they, "this is our livelihood, so it behooves us not to yield, not to let anyone get the better of us."

This is what the perjurers said. Society has perhaps a sort of suspicion that there is something amiss about this oath upon the New Testament. "However," thinks society, "it naturally is our business not to yield, but to act as if everything were all right." "We," says society, "are only laymen, we can't meddle with religion in this way, we are tranquil in the confidence we repose in the priest, who is bound in fact by an oath upon the New Testament."

Now the comedy is complete: all are Christians, and everything is Christian, the priest included—and everything expresses the direct opposite of the Christianity of the New Testament. But it is almost impossible to get hold of the end of this cunningly tangled thread, it is almost impossible to get behind this specious appearance. How could it occur to anyone to doubt that Christianity exists? That is just as impossible as to get into one's head the notion that the priest is a tradesman, this man who is bound by an oath to renounce the world, so that this trade, this business, has therefore to be carried on under the corporate title: "Renunciation of This World," a thing just as confusing as if on arriving one were to say "Farewell." How could it occur to anyone on hearing the word "farewell" that a person is arriving? And how could it occur to anyone—indeed it never did occur to anyone, and if I myself had not said it, no one would have known what I am talking about when I speak of "perjurers," that I mean the "priest," precisely that man who is...a witness to the truth.

This is the "priest's" importance to society, which from generation to generation consumes a "necessary" number of perjurers, in order, under the name of Christianity, to be fully assured of being able to live a life of paganism, a paganism which is tranquillized and refined by the notion that it is Christianity.

Naturally in the whole clerical order there is not a single honest man. Yes, I know well enough that people who in other respects are even not disinclined to agree with me in what I say, think nevertheless that I ought to make exceptions, that there are some after all. No, I thank you kindly. To get into that would be to get into twaddle; for the result presumably would be that the whole clerical order and society as a whole would acknowledge that I am right in all that I say, for each one in particular would naturally think that he was the exception. But, quite literally, there is no exception; quite literally, there is not one honest priest. Only let the police look a little more sharply at this presumptively honest, this rare and extraordinarily honest man, and he who is willing to see will see at once that not even he is excepted, for, quite literally, there is not one honest priest.

In the first place, he surely cannot be so stupid as not to see that the way in which he is paid is, Christianly, entirely inadmissible, directly contrary to Christ's ordinance. *Item* that his whole existence as a combination of civil servant and disciple of Christ is entirely inadmissible, directly contrary to Christ's ordinance, is such an ambiguity that he might be required (though not for the reason that criminals wear stripes—for the "priest" will not run away, one need hardly be afraid of that) to wear a costume of two colors, to express: partly—partly, both-and. In the second place, by being a member of the order he partakes in the whole guilt of the order. When the whole order is depraved, honesty can only be expressed by ceasing to be a member of the order; otherwise all one accomplishes is (assuming for an instant the man's honesty) that by having him as a member of it, the order has one it can appeal to as honest, which it ought not to have. It is as when the police on the occasion of a riot have notified the people to get away—then no good citizen remains. To remain is precisely a sign that one is not a good citizen, for the fact of being a good citizen is expressed by not wanting to have fellowship with those who remain in spite of the prohibition of the police. But let us assume for an instant that this man who remains is a highly respectable man, a good citizen, let us overlook the fact that by remaining he invalidates this assumption. By remaining he does great harm in another way. The riot now gets one it can appeal to, and perhaps this has the effect that the police cannot go ahead as vigorously as is necessary, merely because this "good citizen" is in the party. In the third place, it is perhaps very far from being true that this presumptively honest man is an exception; it may be that, though in a more refined way, he is worse than the others. It is well known that among the blind the one-eyed man is king; and when one has a mind to succeed at a cheap price in counting for something extraordinary, it is a shrewd plan to enter the company of mediocrity, meanness and dishonesty. Here by the effect of contrast a man's bit of honesty will make a brilliant showing—aha, yes, if this shrewd employment of the art of illumination were not a deeper kind of dishonesty than the blunt dishonesty of the others.

No, there literally is not one single honest priest. On the other hand, by the existence of the priest, society as a whole is a baseness, a *Gemeinheit*, as it would not be if the priest were not a part of it.

From morning to evening these thousands or millions in society express the view of life which is the direct opposite of that of the New Testament, as opposite as are the conceptions of living and dying. One cannot call this base, it is human. But now comes the baseness, that with them there are 1000 perjurers who have taken an oath upon the New Testament, and who like all the rest of the community express that view of life which is directly opposite to that of Christianity, but *at the same time* reassure society that this is Christianity. Now society is thoroughly base.

In the New Testament sense, to be a Christian is, in an upward sense, as different from being a man as, in a downward sense, to be a man is different from being a beast. A Christian in the sense of the New Testament, although he stands suffering in the midst of life's reality, has yet become completely a stranger to this life; in the words of the Scripture and also of the Collects[59] (which still are read—O bloody satire!—by the sort of priests we now have, and in the ears of the sort of Christians that now live) he is a stranger and a pilgrim—just think for example of the late Bishop Mynster intoning, "We are strangers and pilgrims in this world"! A Christian in the New Testament sense is literally a stranger and a pilgrim, he feels himself a stranger, and everyone involuntarily feels that this man is a stranger to him.

Let me take an example. To live in such a way that one works more laboriously than any day laborer, and with that manages only to have to pay money out, to become nothing, to be jeered at, etc. This way of living must appear to the multitude a sort of madness, at all events it will feel itself strange to such a life, will look strangely upon it. The truth is nevertheless that such a life comports with the Christianity of the New Testament. Let then one who leads such a life live in a Christian community where there is a whole garrison of teachers bound by an oath upon the New Testament—then we have the baseness. These perjured teachers—indeed before them and their way of life the crowd does not feel itself strange, it is well acquainted with this, in fact it is its own: hail to profit, to activity in a business which promises both earthly and heavenly profit. But these teachers are priests, so as perjurers upon the New Testament they surely must know what Christianity is, and so can furnish a guarantee to the crowd that this profiteering is genuine Christianity. When the crowd thus instructed feels strange in the face of such a way of living as was described, and is inclined to regard it as madness, this is not base but human. But then the crowd thinks that *Christianly* it is justified in condemning such a mode of life as a sort of madness. This is base, and this baseness is due to...the existence of the "priest."

On one occasion I had the following conversation with the late Bishop Mynster. I said to him that the priests might just about as well give up preaching, that all their sermons produced no effect whatsoever, because in the back of their heads the congregation was thinking privately, "Yes, that's his business." To my surprise Bishop Mynster replied, "Yes, there's something in that." I had not really expected this answer; for though this was said, to be sure, under four eyes, yet on this point Bishop Mynster was usually prudence itself. For my part, in relation to that utterance of mine, I have altered my opinion only to this extent, that it has now become clear to me that in one sense the priest does in fact produce a prodigious effect, that his existence transforms society as a whole, Christianly speaking, into a *Gemeinheit*.

About the interest which is shown for my cause

In one way this interest is great enough; what I write has a large circulation, in a certain sense almost more than I could wish, although naturally I must in another sense desire the greatest possible circulation, but of course without being willing to employ in the very least the expedients which might in the remotest degree resemble the well-known tricks of politicians, quacks, and press gangs. People read what I write, many read it with interest, with great interest—that I know.

But with so many people this perhaps is all it comes to. The next Sunday they go to church as usual; they say, "What K. writes is substantially true, and it is exceedingly interesting to read how he shows that the whole official worship is making a fool of God, is blasphemy—but after all we are accustomed to do this, we are unable to emancipate ourselves from it, we lack the power to do so. But certain it is that what he writes we shall read with enjoyment; one can't help being impatient to get a new number and to learn something more about this prodigiously interesting criminal case, as it undeniably is."

This interest, however, is really not gratifying, rather it is distressing, one more dolorous proof that not only does Christianity not exist, but that men in our times are, as I would put it, not even so much as in a condition to have religion, but are strange to, unacquainted with, the sort of passion which every religion must require, without which one cannot have any religion, least of all Christianity.

Let me illustrate what I want to say by a parable. In one sense, I employ it very reluctantly, for I do not like to talk about such things; but I choose it and use it deliberately, yea, I think that I am not justified in not using it, for the seriousness of the case requires that every means be employed to make him who stands in need of it thoroughly disgusted with his situation, thoroughly disgusted with himself.

There is a man whose wife is unfaithful tc him, but he doesn't know it. There is one of his friends who (as a dubious proof of his friendship, perhaps many will say) informs him of it. The husband replies, "It is with lively interest I have listened to you talk, I admire the acumen with which you have been able to discover an infidelity so prudently concealed, and of which I really had no suspicion at all. But that for this cause, now that I know it to be true, I should get a divorce from her, no, that I cannot make up my mind to do. After all, I am now so accustomed to this domestic ease that I cannot do without it. Besides she has property, and I cannot do without that either. On the other hand, I do not deny that with the most lively interest I shall listen to what further information you can give me about this situation. For—not meaning to pay you a compliment—it is exceedingly interesting."

To have in that way a taste for the interesting is a frightful thing. And so also it is a frightful thing to know, under the form of interesting knowledge, that one's worship is blasphemy, and then to continue it, because after all one is used to it. Essentially this is not so much to despise God as to despise oneself. One finds it despicable to figure as a husband and yet not be one, though this may innocently befall a man through a wife's unfaithfulness. One regards it as pitiable to put up with such a relationship and remain in it. But to have religion in that way (which cannot possibly befall a man except by his own fault), that a man knows his worship is blasphemy, and yet is willing to figure as having that religion—this in the profoundest sense is to despise oneself.

Oh, there is something more deplorable than that which men are inclined to regard as the most deplorable fate that can befall a man, there is that which is more deplorable! There is an imbecility with respect to character, a drivel of characterlessness which is more dreadful than that of the understanding, perhaps also more incurable. And the most deplorable thing perhaps that can be said of a man is that he cannot be elevated, uplifted, his own knowledge cannot lift him up. Like the boy who lets his kite fly aloft, so does he let his knowledge mount on high; to follow it with his eye he finds interesting, prodigiously interesting, but...it does not lift him up, he remains in the mud, more and more crazy about the interesting.

Wherefore, whoever thou art, if such be the case with thee—shame upon thee, shame upon thee, shame upon thee!

THE UNCHANGEABLENESS OF GOD

A Discourse

By

S. Kierkegaard

Copenhagen
Published by C. A. Reitzel's Estate and Heirs
Bianco Luno's Press
1855
[The end of August]

This edifying discourse S.K. published in the midst of his fierce attack upon the Established Church, and immediately after the most outrageous articles which are to be found in the *Instant*. Inasmuch as I have already published Professor Swenson's translation of this discourse as the conclusion of the volume entitled *For Self-Examination* (Oxford, 1941), it does not seem necessary to print it here; but at least the title page must be inserted, to call attention to the fact that in the midst of this violent controversy S.K. did what he could to make his contemporaries understand that in attacking the Church he was speaking from within it, as a Christian.

He began this discourse, as he did all his sermons, with a prayer and a text from Holy Scripture; and he dedicated it, as he had dedicated each of the first *Eighteen Edifying Discourses*, "In memory of my deceased father, one time hosier in this city." He dated it as of August 1855; but in a brief preface (dated May 5, 1854, which was his birthday) he remarked: "This discourse was delivered in the Citadel Church on the 18th of May, 1851. The text is the first one I ever used. Subsequently it has often been employed. Now I return to it again." This favorite text was James 1:17-21, "Every good gift and every perfect boon is from above, coming down from the Father of lights, with whom can be no variation, neither shadow which is cast by turning," etc.

THE INSTANT

No. 8

CONTENTS

September 11, 1855. S. Kierkegaard.

Copenhagen

Published by C. A. Reitzel's Estate and Heirs

Bianco Luno's Press

From the Journal

A CHRISTIAN AUDITING

What money is in the world of finiteness, that the concepts are intellectually and spiritually. It is in them all transactions are conducted.

If things then go on from generation to generation in such a way that everyone takes the concepts as he gets them from the preceding generation —and then spends his time enjoying this life and laboring for finite ends, etc., it comes to pass only too easily that gradually the concepts are distorted, become quite different from what they originally were, come to mean something entirely different, become like false money—whereas quite tranquilly all transactions continue to be conducted by means of them, since the falsification does not affect the egoistic interests of men as does the dissemination of counterfeit money, especially when the counterfeiting of the concepts is precisely in the direction of human egoism, so that he who is hoaxed by it is (if I may use the expression) the other party in the business of Christianity: God in heaven.

XI^2 A 36

Contemporaneousness: what thou dost as a contemporary is the decisive thing*

"He that receiveth a prophet because he is a prophet shall have a prophet's reward; and he that receiveth a righteous man because he is a righteous man shall have a righteous man's reward. And whosoever shall give to drink unto one of these little ones a cup of cold water only, verily I say unto you, he shall in no wise lose his reward," says our Lord Jesus Christ in Matthew 10:41, 42.

MORE generous truly than royal or imperial generosity. Only the Deity is so generous!

Yet look a little closer. The question here is about what one does in relation to a contemporary, what one does as a contemporary to the prophet, the disciple. "Whosoever shall give to drink unto one of these little ones a cup of cold water only"—surely it is not on this the emphasis lies. No, the emphasis lies upon "because he is a disciple, a prophet." So then, if a contemporary were to say, "I am certainly very far from regarding the man as a prophet, a disciple; but on the other hand I am perfectly willing to offer him a cup of wine"; or if one who perhaps privately regarded this man as a disciple, a prophet, but because of cowardliness had not the courage to profess his conviction, or meanly took advantage of the consideration that the prophet, the disciple, does not enjoy recognition as such from his contemporaries, took advantage of this to make himself out better than the others by treating the disciple, the prophet, decently, but at a cheaper price—if he were to say, "I do not regard this man as a prophet, but after all he is an extraordinary man, and it gives me pleasure to offer him a cup of wine"—the answer in either case would be, "No, brother, you can keep your cup of wine; it is not about that the Scripture speaks."

It speaks about giving him a cup of water only—but *because* he is a disciple, a prophet, which means recognizing him fully and clearly for what he truly is. What Christ aims at is recognition for a disciple, a prophet, and that in the situation of contemporaneousness. Whether the recognition is expressed by giving him a cup of cold water, or by giving him a kingdom, is entirely indifferent; the point is contemporaneous

* This article dates from 1853, except that here and there I have inserted a few lines or altered a word; but the article as a whole dates from 1853. What my judgment is about the concluding paragraph, the reader will know from my article in the *Fatherland* entitled "With regard to the new edition of *Training in Christianity*" [pp. 54 f. in this volume].

recognition. So it is not as the mercenary priests with an eye to the church-rates make people believe, that since ten dollars is more than a cup of cold water, it makes him who gives ten dollars to a prophet, a disciple—but *not because* he is a prophet, a disciple—far more perfect than is he who gives him a cup of cold water *because* he is a prophet, a disciple. No, the point is that the gift is "*because*," being thus an expression of the fact that one recognizes the man for what he truly is.

And this is not easy in the contemporary situation. To this end it is not requisite of course to be oneself a prophet, a disciple; but what one must have is two-thirds the character of a disciple, a prophet—and do not forget that everyone who honestly will can have that. For in the contemporary situation this cup of cold water, or rather this "because," may cost one dear. For in the contemporary situation or in real life the prophet, the disciple, is scorned, derided, hated, cursed, abhorred, in every way persecuted; and thou canst be sure that at the very least the punishment imposed for handing him a cup of water "because he is a disciple" is that spoken of in the New Testament, of being put out of the synagogue, which was the punishment imposed in the contemporary situation for having anything to do with Christ, a fact which priestly mendacity of course "slurs over, conceals, suppresses, omits," whereas it yearns, expresses with hiccoughs, eructations and stifled sobs its inexpressible longing to have been contemporary with Christ...in order presumably to be put out of the synagogue—which naturally is the deepest yearning of salaried men and persons who enjoy official rank.

So then, he who gives a disciple a cup of cold water only, because he is a disciple, shall in no wise lose his reward, he shall have a prophet's reward—and on the other hand he who when the prophet, the disciple, is dead builds his tomb and says, "If we" etc., that man, according to Christ's judgment, is a hypocrite, his guilt is blood-guilt.

He is a hypocrite. It may be that contemporary with him who builds the tomb of the dead prophet there may again be living a prophet whom he in company with others is persecuting. Or if there be living no prophet, there is perhaps a righteous man who suffers for the truth—whom he who builds the tombs of the prophets persecutes as do the others. Or in case there should be no such contemporary living, thy way of avoiding hypocrisy is to make so vividly present the life of the glorious one departed that therewith thou wilt experience the same suffering thou must have experienced if in the contemporary situation thou hadst recognized a prophet as being a prophet.

And if in any way thou art eternally concerned about thy soul, art thinking with fear and trembling of the Judgment and eternity; or on the other hand if in any way thou art uplifted, and wouldst be more so, by the thought of what it is to be a man, and that thou too art a man, akin to the glorious ones, the genuine saints, whose worth therefore is not attested by the spurious marks of profit, stars and titles, but by the genuine marks of poverty, abasement, ill-treatment, persecution—then give good heed to this thought of contemporaneousness, that if in the contemporary situation there be living such a one who suffers for the truth, that thou then suffer what is involved in recognizing him for what he is; or, if there be no such contemporary, that thou make the life of the glorious departed so vividly present that thou wilt suffer like as thou must have suffered in contemporaneousness by recognizing him for what he is. Give good heed to this consideration of contemporaneousness; for the point is not what ado thou dost make over a deceased man; no, but it is what thou art doing in the contemporary situation, or that thou dost make the past so vividly present that thou dost experience the same suffering as if thou wert contemporary with it. This determines what man thou art. On the other hand, to make much ado over a deceased man—well, naturally that too determines what man thou art: that according to the judgment of Jesus thou art a hypocrite, yea, a murderer, more abhorrent to the deceased than those who slew him.

Take then good heed to this thought of contemporaneousness! And to that end do not fail to make thyself acquainted, if already thou hast not done so, with the book I published in 1850, *Training in Christianity*; for here precisely this thought is stressed. This book as it makes its appearance in the world is for all its militancy a peaceable book. I shall indicate to thee precisely how it stands related to the Established Church, to the official preaching of Christianity, or to the official representative of the official preaching of Christianity, i.e. to Bishop Mynster's preaching of Christianity. If Bishop Mynster says of it straightforwardly, "This truly is Christianity; so it is I myself understand Christianity privately in my heart"; then is the book a glorification of the Bishop Mynster's preaching of Christianity—a thought so infinitely dear to me! If on the other hand Bishop Mynster upon seeing the book so much as blinks at it, not to say violently fires up at it[60]—then read it, and thou shalt see that it illuminates the whole of Mynster's preaching of Christianity in such a way that it proves to be an extraordinary, extraordinary, extraordinary, most artful and masterly...optical illusion. That, however, the book cannot help. At all events it is not thine affair. On the other hand, if thou thyself art willing, the book can help thee to become attentive to the thought of contemporaneousness.

And this is the decisive thought! This thought is the central thought of my life. And I may say too with truth that I have had the honor of suffering for bringing this truth to light. Therefore I die gladly, with infinite gratitude to Governance that to me it was granted to be aware of this thought and to make others attentive to it. Not that I have discovered it. God forbid that I should be guilty of such presumption. No, the discovery is an old one, it is that of the New Testament. But nevertheless to me it was granted in suffering to bring this thought again to remembrance, this thought which, like ratsbane for rats, is poison for the "docents,"* this vermin which really is what has brought Christianity to ruin, these noble men who build the tombs of the prophets, objectively expound their doctrine in lectures, derive profit (presumably objectively, are proud presumably of their *objectivity*, for the subjective is morbid and affected) out of the suffering and death of these glorious ones, but themselves (naturally by the aid of this much lauded objectivity) keep aloof, far removed from everything which in the remotest way might resemble suffering in likeness with the glorious ones, or such suffering as one would have had to experience if in the contemporary situation one had recognized the glorious ones for what they were.

Contemporaneousness is the decisive thought. Imagine a witness to the truth, that is, one of the derivative patterns. For a long time he holds out, suffering all sorts of ill-treatment and persecution. Finally they take his life. Cruelly they determine the manner of his death, that he is to be burnt alive. With inventive cruelty they determine more precisely that over a slow fire he is to be broiled upon a grill.

Imagine this! Earnestness and Christianity require that thou make this so vivid to thyself that thou dost experience the suffering thou must have experienced if in the contemporary situation thou hadst recognized the man for what he is.

This is earnestness and Christianity. Rather different is the bestial practice to which the priests make no objection. Thus one bids good-bye to the witness to the truth and all his sufferings—and yet, no, this is

* Cf. *Fear and Trembling,* where for the first time I took aim at the docents, these base characters, of whom it is said [pp. 95 ff. in the American edition] that "No robber of temples condemned to hard labor behind iron bars is so base a criminal as the man who pillages holy things, and even Judas who sold his Master for thirty pieces of silver is not more despicable than the man who makes traffic of the great."

not yet the really bestial thing. No, one says, "We will not forget the glorious one; therefore we resolve that December 17,[61] which was the day of his death, shall be celebrated in his memory. And in order to keep well in mind the impression of his life, and in order that our life too may acquire 'some likeness' to his, as 'an effort' in that direction, be it solemnly ordained that every household shall eat a broiled fish, broiled, be it noted (do not miss the point), upon a grill; and the most delicious part the priest shall have." That is, the divine worship which consists in suffering for the truth, yea, suffering unto death, is exchanged for the worship of eating and drinking, with the priest getting the best piece—the genuine (official) Christianity, where the priest, like the broiled fish in its way, contributes his part in exalting the solemnity of the day, by a charming speech, it may be, thereby assuring himself of an increasing income in the course of years, perhaps of making a brilliant career, perhaps so brilliant that he goes clad in silk and velvet, bedecked with stars and ribbons.

This is only an example. I admit too that none of the derived patterns obliges every man absolutely—but neither does it oblige him to bestiality. And if the derived patterns do not absolutely oblige us, nor oblige absolutely every man; on the other hand, the Pattern, Jesus Christ, does oblige us absolutely, and obliges absolutely every man. If then in thy time there is no one living who suffers for the truth, so that thou wouldst encounter suffering if (as is indeed Christianly thy duty, is Christianly the requirement) thou wert to recognize him for what he truly is—then thou art to make the Pattern so vividly present that thou dost experience such suffering as if in contemporaneousness thou hadst recognized him for what he is. All ado made afterwards, all ado about building his tomb etc., etc., etc., etc., etc., etc., is, according to the judgment of Jesus Christ, hypocrisy and the same blood-guilt as that of those who put Him to death.

This is the Christian requirement. The mildest, mildest form for it after all is surely that which I have used in *Training in Christianity*: that thou must admit that this is the requirement, and then have recourse to grace. But not only not to be willing to comply with the requirement, but to want to have the requirement suppressed—and then on the other hand to want to spend money upon a monumental tomb, which is what the priest, for good reasons, calls being an earnest Christian—is what our Lord Jesus Christ certainly sought most of all to prevent.

One lives only once

This saying is so often heard in the world, "One lives only once; therefore I could wish to see Paris before I die, or to make a fortune as soon as possible, or in fine to become something great in the world—for one lives only once."

More rarely we encounter, but it may be encountered nevertheless, a man who has only one wish, quite definitely only one wish. "This," says he, "I could wish; Oh, that my wish might be fulfilled, for alas, one lives only once."

Imagine such a man upon his deathbed. The wish was not fulfilled, but his soul clings unalterably to this wish—and now, now it is no longer possible. Then he raises himself on his bed; with the passion of despair he utters once again his wish: Oh, despair, it is not fulfilled; despair, one lives only once!"

This seems terrible, and in truth it is, but not as he means it; for the terrible thing is not that the wish remained unfulfilled, the terrible thing is the passion with which he clings to it. His life is not wasted because his wish was not fulfilled, by no manner of means; if his life is wasted, it is because he would not give up his wish, would not learn from life anything higher than this consideration of his only wish, as though its fulfillment or non-fulfillment decided everything.

The truly terrible thing is therefore an entirely different thing, as for example if a man upon his deathbed were to discover, or upon his deathbed were to become clearly aware, of that which all his life long he had understood more obscurely but had never been willing to understand, that the fact of having suffered in the world for the truth is one of the requisites for becoming eternally blessed—and one lives only once, that once which now is for him already past! And he had it indeed in his power! And eternity cannot change, that eternity to which in dying he goes as to his future.

We men are prone by nature to regard life in this way: we consider suffering an evil which in every way we strive to avoid. And if we succeed in this, we think that when our last hour comes we have special reason for thanking God that we have been spared suffering. We think that everything depends upon slipping through life happily and well—and Christianity thinks that all that is terrible really comes from the other world, that the terrible things of this world are as child's play compared with the terrors of eternity, and that it distinctly does not depend upon slipping through this life happily and well, but upon relating oneself rightly by suffering to eternity.

One lives only once. If when death comes thy life is well spent, that is; spent so that it is related rightly to eternity—then God be praised eternally. If not, then it is irremediable—one lives only once.

One lives only once. So it is here upon earth. And while thou art living this once, the extension of which in time diminishes with every fleeting hour, the God of love is seated in heaven, fondly loving thee, too. Yes, loving. Hence He would so heartily that thou finally mightest will as He for the sake of eternity would that thou shouldst will, that thou mightest resolve to will to suffer, that is, that thou mightest resolve to will to love Him, for Him thou canst love only by suffering, or, if thou lovest Him as He would be loved, thou wilt have suffering. Remember, one lives only once. If that is let slip, if thou hast experienced no suffering, if thou hast shirked it—it is eternally irremediable. Compel thee—no, that the God of love will not do at any price, He would by that attain something altogether different from what He desires. How could it occur to love to wish to use compulsion to be loved? But Love He is, and it is out of love He wills that thou shouldst will as He wills; and in love He suffers as only infinite and almighty love can, as no man is capable of comprehending, so it is He suffers when thou dost not will as He wills.

God is love. Never was there born a man whom this thought does not overwhelm with indescribable bliss, especially when it comes close to him in the sense that "God is love" signifies "Thou art loved." The next instant, when the understanding comes, "This means to experience suffering"—frightful! "Yes, but it is out of love God wills this, it is because He would be loved; and that He would be loved by thee is the expression of His love to thee"—Well, well then! The next instant, so soon as the suffering becomes serious—frightful! "Yes, but it is out of love; thou hast no notion how He suffers, because He knows very well what pain suffering involves; yet He cannot change, for then He must become something else than love"—Well, well then! The next instant, so soon as the suffering becomes very serious—frightful!

Yet beware, beware lest time perhaps go by unprofitably in unprofitable suffering; remember, one lives only once. If this may help thee, view the case thus: be assured that God suffers more in love than thou dost suffer, though by this He cannot be changed. But above all remember, one lives only once. There is a loss which is eternally irremediable, so that—still more frightful—eternity, far from effacing the recollection of the loss, is an eternal recollection of it.

An eternity in which to repent

Let me tell a story. I did not read it in a devotional book but in what would be called entertaining literature. Yet I feel no hesitancy in making use of it, and I remark upon this only lest anyone might be disturbed by it, if by chance he knows the source of the story or should subsequently learn where I found it.[62] I would not have him think that I conceal this.

Somewhere in the Orient there lived a poor old couple, husband and wife. They possessed, as I have said, nothing but poverty; and naturally anxiety about the future increased with the prospect of old age. They did not assail heaven with their prayers, for they were too pious for that; but nevertheless they continually cried to heaven for help.

Then it chanced one morning that the wife, going out to the oven, found upon the hearth a precious stone of great size, which at once she made haste to show to her husband, who, having knowledge of such matters, saw at once that they were well provisioned for the rest of their life.

A bright future for this old couple—what joy! Yet, God-fearing as they were, and content with little, they resolved that, having enough to live upon for still another day, they would not sell the jewel that day. But on the morrow it should be sold, and on the morrow a new life would begin.

That night, the night before the morrow, the woman dreamed that she was transported into paradise. An angel conducted her around and showed her all the glories an oriental imagination could invent. Then the angel led her also into a hall where there were long rows of armchairs completely adorned with pearls and precious stones, which, as the angel explained, were for the pious. Finally he showed her also one which was intended for her. Looking more closely she saw that on the back of the seat there was lacking a very large jewel. She asked the angel how that had come about. He— — —

Now be alert, here comes the story! The angel answered, "That was the precious stone you found on the hearth. That you received in advance, and it cannot be inserted again."

In the morning the woman related the dream to her husband, and her opinion was that it would be better to hold out the few years longer they might have to live, rather than that the precious stone should be lacking throughout all eternity. And her pious husband was of the same opinion.

So that evening they laid the stone again upon the hearth and prayed God that evening that He would take it back. In the morning, sure enough, it was gone. Where it had gone the old couple knew: it was now in its right place.

Truly this man was happily married, his wife was a sensible woman. If it be true, as is often said, that there are wives who make their husbands forget the eternal, yet nevertheless, though all were unmarried, everyone has within himself something which more artfully and more urgently and more persistently than any woman is able to make a man forget the eternal and lead him to measure falsely, as if a few years, or ten years, or forty years, were a prodigiously long time, so that even eternity becomes something very short in comparison, whereas on the contrary these years are a very short time, and eternity prodigiously long.

Oh, remember this well! Thou canst perhaps by shrewdness avoid what it has pleased God once for all to unite with being a Christian, namely, suffering and adversity. Thou canst perhaps, by shrewdly evading this to thine own ruin, attain what God has eternally separated from being a Christian, namely, enjoyment and all earthly goods. Thou canst perhaps, befooled by thy shrewdness, be totally lost at last in the vain delusion that it is precisely the right path thou art on, because thou dost win the earthly—and then an eternity in which to repent! An eternity in which to repent, that is, to repent that thou didst not employ time upon that which can be eternally remembered: to love God in truth, with the consequence that in this life thou wilt suffer at the hands of men.

Therefore deceive not thyself, of all deceivers fear most thyself! Even if it were possible in relation to the eternal to take something in advance, thou wouldst yet be deceiving thyself by...something in advance—and then an eternity in which to repent.

What can be remembered eternally?

Only one thing: to have suffered for the truth. If thou wouldst have a care for thine eternal future, take heed to suffer for the truth.

And the opportunity, an opportunity to suffer for the truth, we have of course every second—how could it be otherwise in this world of lies and deceit and knavishness and mediocrity? But doubtless thou art not mad enough to make use of this opportunity, thou art far too shrewd—thou dost use thine acuteness to avoid a clash with this fine world, for fear of encountering suffering. At the same time thou art perhaps a bit hypocritical with thyself, and inclined to say that thou art willing enough to suffer if the opportunity were to present itself. O my friend, only thyself dost thou deceive, eternity never. The consequence is that eternally thou hast nothing to remember, and so wilt eternally be plagued by this emptiness and by the tormenting thought that thy life was wasted, filled up with what cannot be remembered eternally!

Perhaps thou art living contemporaneously with "a righteous man" who suffers for the truth. Here indeed is an opportunity. Recognize him for what he is, and thou shalt find suffering in likeness with him! But thou—thou thinkest that thou art behaving very shrewdly in not recognizing this man aloud and publicly for what he is, but shunning him in every way. Or perhaps thou dost think that thou art even behaving very nobly, that thou art not like the others, for thou dost recognize him for what he is, but in secret, so that no danger is connected with it, whereas thou dost not recognize him where danger is involved. O my friend, thou art deceiving thyself; foolishly thou didst not use the opportunity that was offered, whereby thou wouldst have experienced suffering for the truth—the only thing that can be remembered eternally.

Yea, the only thing. Take what thou wilt, it is true of everything else that it cannot be remembered eternally. Though thou hast loved the most beautiful girl, hast lived happily thy whole life long with her, the beloved wife—that is not a thing to be remembered, it is made of stuff more fragile than eternity. The greatest exploits in the external world, to have conquered kingdoms and lands; the most interesting and the most exciting developments, to have been the thought in them; the greatest discoveries in the natural world, to have been the discoverer, etc., are not things that can be remembered eternally. They will perhaps be preserved from generation to generation, throughout all subsequent ages, but thou thyself wilt not be able to remember them; neither are they the eternal truth, nor do they belong to thee eternally. Only one thing is left, only one thing is it possible to remember eternally: having suffered for the truth.

Here in the world truth walks in lowliness and humiliation, has not where to lay its head, must be thankful if one will give it a cup of water—but if one does this, recognizing it aloud and publicly for what it is, then this lowly figure, this lowly, despised, mocked, persecuted wretch, the Truth, has, if I may say so, in its hand a stylus and writes upon a little tablet "For eternity," which it hands to the man who conscientiously recognized it for what it is. His name is laid up in heaven, his life was employed in that which indeed a man is most reluctant to employ it, in doing the only thing which can be remembered eternally.

Whoever thou art, reflect upon this! Shun above all things the leadership of the priests. This surely thou also canst well comprehend, that from tradesmen thou wilt not learn anything true about the suffering truth, i.e. about Christianity. Shun them, they cheat thee out of the eternal by making thee believe that thou canst acquire the eternal upon any other terms than suffering. Watch thyself. For precisely this is the seriousness of existence, that thou art placed in a world where the voice which calls thee to the right path speaks very softly, whereas thousands of voices outside thee and within thee speak loudly enough about the very opposite—precisely this is the seriousness, that this voice speaks softly because it would test thee, whether thou wilt listen to even the slightest whisper. Reflect that it is not eternity which has need of thee, so that for its own sake it must raise its voice loudly when the other voices become loud; no, it is thou that hast need of eternity, and it would test thee—oh, the seriousness of it! Thine attention therefore becomes softer in proportion as the other voices become louder, as they cannot become except through thy fault. Nothing is easier than to drown out the voice of eternity which speaks about suffering for the truth and says that this is the only thing which can be remembered eternally. To this end the priests are not needed, but by their help this becomes of course the easiest thing in the world. Dreadful! To deceive oneself eternally! And again dreadful that this is so frightfully easy to do, that eternity is so serious that one may say that the easiest thing for a man to do is...to deceive himself eternally!

A picture of life
and
a picture from life

Take the pupils in a class—which is most admired by his comrades? Is it the laziest? No, that is out of the question. Is it the most industrious? Not that either. Is it then the one who has the greatest gifts of mind? Not that either. But if there is one who has the shrewdness to know how to deceive the teachers, and does it so adroitly that he always comes out of it well, always has good marks, always stands high in the class, always is praised and cited for distinction—he is the admired one. And why? Because his comrades understand very well that he has a double advantage. He has the advantage which the lazy boy also has, that he really does nothing, has constantly plenty of time to play and to amuse himself—an advantage which the lazy boy has too, but he suffers punishment for it. And then he has also the advantage which the diligent student has, he is the admired one. Of him his comrades say admiringly, "Ludvigsen, Ludvigsen, he's the very devil of a man."—"But Frederiksen is more industrious."—"Oh well, what good does that do him? Ludvigsen always has just as good marks, so Frederiksen has only one thing to the good—the trouble of studying."—"Yes, but Olsen after all has a much better head."—"Bah, a fig for that. That doesn't do him much good, it rather gives him more bother. No, Ludvigsen is the very devil of a man."

This was a picture of life. Now I go on to a picture from life.

In this world which is the most admired teacher of Christianity? Is it the shamelessly worldly man who *sans phrase* and without disguise admits that he seeks after the earthly, after money, power, etc., and succeeds in attaining it? No, that is out of the question. Is it then the truly pious man who takes Christianity seriously, therefore actually is without this world's goods and pleasures, so that his life is an exposition of the Apostle's saying, "If in this life only we have hope, we are of all men most pitiable"? No, not that either.

But if there is one who has the shrewdness to know how to deceive God, and in such a way that he always comes out of it well and wins (perhaps more surely than the shameless worldling) all worldly goods and pleasures, while constantly he is the pious man, the God-fearing man, the man of God, earnestness itself—he is the admired one. And why? Because he wins a double advantage: worldly goods—and at the same time the glory, the halo of the saint, and the corresponding respect and deference.

And if he is able to do this with such infinite adroitness that nobody, nobody at all can see through it, then the game is in his hands, this is the veritable *ne plus ultra*, peerless, unique—especially for womenfolks, but also for men, too. But especially for womenfolks; for it cannot be denied that woman was so made once for all that if she is to relish anything thoroughly, in particular if she is to be exalted in admiration, adoring admiration, there must be a shiver of dread (*Angst*) mixed with it. And of that in this situation there is a tiny bit. In the midst of the most blissful exaltation, in the midst of the most heavenly rapture prompted by the admired one, there is afar off, but yet it is there, a dread whether after all it might not be . . . But no, that is impossible! And this composition produces...adoring admiration.

There is nothing so objectionable to *God* as hypocrisy. According to God's appointment the precise task of life is to be converted, transformed, because by nature every man is a born hypocrite.

There is nothing the *world* so much admires as the finer and finest forms of hypocrisy.

The finer and the finest forms of hypocrisy! In this connection, however, one must observe that these forms may sometimes occur in such a way that they are not always the most guilty qualities in the person concerned. Given great talents, extraordinary shrewdness and weak character, this combination will yield one of the finest forms of hypocrisy, whereas the person in question is perhaps not so guilty, before God not so guilty. On the other hand it is quite certain that precisely this form is for other men the most dangerous of all, that is to say to other men who are related receptively, as learners, to such a teacher.[63]

The divine justice

If ever you have paid any attention to how things go in this world, you have probably like others before you turned away from the whole thing and said to yourself mournfully, "Is this a just rule? What has become of divine justice?" Encroachment upon the property of others, thievery, fraud, in short, everything that has to do with money (the god of this world), is punished, punished severely in this world. Even what hardly can be called felony, that a poor man, it may be only by a look, implores a passerby is punished severely—so severely are crimes punished in this...righteous world! But the most dreadful crimes, such as taking the holy in vain, taking the truth in vain, and in such a way that the man's life is every day a continuous lie—in this situation no retributive justice is seen to interfere with him. On the contrary, he has leave to expand without hindrance, to spread his toils about a larger or smaller circle of people, perhaps a whole community, which in its adoring, admiration rewards him with all earthly goods. Where then is divine justice?

To this the answer may be made: It is the divine justice precisely which in its frightful severity permits things to go on thus. It is present, all eyes, but it hides itself; precisely for the sake of being able to reveal itself wholly for what it is, it would not reveal itself prematurely; whereas when it reveals itself it is seen that it was at hand, present in even the least event. For in case the divine justice were to intervene swiftly, the really capital crimes could not wholly come into existence. The man who in weakness, infatuated by his lust, transported by his passions, but yet out of weakness, took the wrong path, the path of sin—upon him divine justice takes compassion and lets the punishment fall, the sooner the better. But the really capital criminal—remember now what it was you deplored, that justice was so mild, or did not exist at all!—him divine providence makes blind, so that to his eyes it seems delusively as if his life were pleasing to God, seems as if he had succeeded in making God blind. How frightful thou art, O divine justice!

Let no one be disturbed any more by this objection against divine justice. For precisely in order that it may be justice it must first allow the crime to develop its entire guilt. But the really capital crime needs—mark this well!—the whole of temporality to come into existence; it is the capital crime properly speaking by being continued through a whole life. But in fact no crime can be punished before it comes into existence. So this objection falls to the ground. The point of the objection really is that God ought to punish so quickly that He ought (for that's what it means) to punish the thief before he steals. But if the crime must exist before it is punished, and if the capital crime (precisely that at which you take offense) needs a whole lifetime to come into existence, then it cannot be punished in this life; to punish it in this life would not be to punish it but to prevent it, just as it would not be punishing theft if one were to punish the thief before he stole, but it would be preventing the theft, and preventing the man from becoming a thief.

Therefore never complain when you see the dreadful crime succeed which would stir up your mind against God; do not complain, rather tremble and say, "O just God! So this man then was one of the capital criminals whose crime requires a whole life in order to come into existence, and only in eternity can be punished."

So then it is precisely severity which accounts for the fact that the capital crime is not punished in this world. Also it is perhaps sometimes due to God's care for others. That is to say, there is a difference between man and man; one man may be in a high degree superior to another. But this too is an example of superiority, to be capable of being the capital criminal. So Governance leaves him unpunished, also because it would thoroughly confuse our conceptions if we should perceive that he was a criminal. You see that the case may be far worse than you conceived it when you complained that God did not punish what you can see was a crime. From time to time there has perhaps lived a criminal on such a scale that no one, no one at all, had a presentiment of it; yea, that it was as though God, if He had punished him, would not have been able to make Himself understood by the men amongst whom this criminal lived, that by wishing to punish him in time (apart from the fact that this would have prevented the crime) God must almost throw into confusion the men amongst whom this criminal lived; and *that* in His love and care for men He could not find it in His heart to do. So then the man remains unpunished in time. Frightful!

Yea, tremble at the thought that there are crimes which need a whole lifetime to come into existence, which sometimes perhaps, out of indulgence towards us others, cannot be punished in this life. Tremble, but do not impeach God's justice. No, tremble at the thought of this (how frightful it sounds when one expresses it thus!), this dreadful advantage of being able only to be punished in eternity. Only to be punished in eternity—O merciful God! Every criminal, every sinner, who can be punished in this world, can also be saved, saved for eternity!

But that criminal whose distinction was that he cannot be punished in this world, also cannot be saved, cannot by being punished in time be saved for eternity; no, he can (that indeed was his advantage!) only be punished in eternity. Does it seem to you that there is reason to complain of God's justice?

Tremble—for God is in one sense so infinitely easy to hoax!

The way people generally talk, if they talk about such things (but talk about such things as trembling is rapidly going out of fashion), is to give this turn to the matter: Tremble, for it is impossible to deceive God, He is the Omniscient, the Omnipotent. And that too is certainly true. Nevertheless I believe that by constantly stating the case thus one will not attain the desired end.

No: tremble—God is in one sense so infinitely easy to hoax! O my friend, He is something so infinitely exalted, and thou on the other hand art so infinitely nothing in comparison with Him, that thy sleepless effort in mortal dread throughout a whole life, aiming to please Him and to heed every hint of His, is yet infinitely too little to implore, deservedly, even for a single instant, His attention. And Him thou wouldst cheat! Therefore tremble, that is to say, watch, watch! He has a punishment which He Himself regards as the most frightful—He too is the only one who has a true conception of the infinite that He is. This punishment is: not to be willing to be conscious (as in one sense, in consequence of His exaltation, He is not) of the nothing which thou art. For an almighty being it must indeed (if one may speak thus) be the greatest exertion to have to look at a nothing, be conscious of a nothing, be concerned about a nothing. And then this nothing would hoax Him! O man, shudder, this is so infinitely easy to do!

Let me make this thought clear. Take a simple citizen—whom might one say it would be most difficult for this citizen to hoax? Would it not be precisely his equal? For this equal of his is concerned to watch out that he be not hoaxed, "I really cannot endure being hoaxed by him," etc. A superior man, a man of rank, the simple citizen will find it easier to hoax, for—after all the thing doesn't much concern the man of rank. The King still easier, for his Majesty does not concern himself at all about it. Do not misunderstand me. I evidently cannot mean that the superior man, or the King, if the thing should concern him, might not be able to see that this good citizen is hoaxing him; but he is not concerned at all about this simple citizen. Remember the tale of the fly and the stag. Thou wilt recall that the fly settled upon one of the antlers and said to the stag, "I hope I am not a burden to you." "I was not aware of your existence," was the reply.[64] The citizen's task might reasonably be, if it were possible, by his honesty, by his uprightness, to succeed in attracting his Majesty's attention. On the other hand, it is so infinitely stupid and lacking in spirit to wish to hoax the man who is too infinitely exalted to be able to concern himself about him—it is so infinitely easy to do!

And think how infinitely exalted is God, and think of the nothing which thou art—and tremble at the thought how infinitely easy it is to hoax God! Thou dost think perhaps because thou art accustomed to address Him as "Thou," because thou hast known Him very well from childhood up, because thou art accustomed lightmindedly to mingle His name with all sorts of talk, that God is thy comrade, that thou art related to Him as one barman to another, that therefore He will at once make an outcry when He notices that thou dost wish to hoax Him, to falsify His Word, to pretend that thou dost not understand it, etc., and that if He doesn't do this, it is a proof that thou hast succeeded in hoaxing Him. O man, shudder at thy success!

Yea, in His exaltation God Himself disposes the situation in such a way that it is as easy as possible for a man, if he will, to hoax God. That is, He disposes it in such a way that those whom He loves and who love Him must suffer dreadfully in this world, so that everyone can see that they are forsaken of God. The deceivers, on the other hand, make a brilliant career, so that everyone can see that God is with them, an opinion in which they themselves are more and more confirmed.

So superior is God; so far He is from making it difficult, so infinitely easy it is to deceive Him, that He Himself even offers a prize to him who does it, rewards him with everything earthly. Tremble, O man!

THE INSTANT

No. 9

CONTENTS

Sept. 24, 1855. S. Kierkegaard.

Copenhagen

Published by C. A. Reitzel's Estate and Heirs

Bianco Luno's Press

From the Journal

THE MODERN CLERGYMAN

When I think of what in my father's time was understood by a shop-clerk: an awkward Jewish bumpkin—and of what now is understood by it: a nimble, brisk fellow, a chevalier, etc.—this indeed is progress of a sort.

It is pretty much the same now with a modern clergyman: a nimble, adroit, lively man, who in pretty language, with the utmost ease, with graceful manners, etc., knows how to introduce a little Christianity, but as easily, as easily as possible. In the New Testament, Christianity is the profoundest wound that can be inflicted upon a man, calculated on the most dreadful scale to collide with everything—and now the clergyman has perfected himself in introducing Christianity in such a way that it signifies nothing, and when he is able to do this to perfection he is regarded as a paragon. But this is nauseating! Oh, if a barber has perfected himself in removing the beard so easily that one hardly notices it, that's well enough; but in relation to that which is precisely calculated to wound, to perfect oneself so as to introduce it in such a way that if possible it is not noticed at all—that is nauseating.

XI^1 A 69

Thus the case stands

May 31, 1855.

THE one party is a man who by his activity as an author through many years, and by his whole existence as a public personality, gives assurance (guarantees) of being, as not many are, perhaps as no other in this land is, justified in having a word to say about what Christianity is.

The other party is the clergy, which at first was voluble enough, so long as it was a question of this easy thing of taking advantage of the circumstance that there was a deceased man who had to be talked about in order to stir up womankind and children by funeral declamations; but thereupon, when the matter became serious, preserved in print the profoundest silence, but (with the courage of witnesses to the truth) is perhaps in secret all the more chatty.

The attack upon me—for the benefit of the "witnesses to the truth," whose silence is thereby made thoroughly manifest—is conducted by the *Copenhagen Post* and the *Flying Post*[65]; and the point, the deadly sting, of their attack is that I am called..."Søren."

Only one thing now is lacking, that as a witness to the truth Bishop Martensen too might (if there should be another rumpus, so that the Bishop, "like the boys on New Year's Eve, might think that he saw his chance"[66]) write an article against me, making the point that I am called "Søren." Then I must sink down, succumb before this power of the truth, which in vain I should strive to resist; for the truth is, my name is Søren.

Beloved Father of mine deceased, to think that thou shouldst become my misfortune! Viewed ideally, I have conquered; I deserved to—but my name is Søren.

But I shall put up with it—O my God, "gladly and thankfully"—put up with the bad temper of impotence. But it is another question whether the Danish people is well served by this labor to make it ridiculous, ridiculous in the eyes of every other nation which learns to know that this is a people among which the only argument used against mind and spirit is...that a man is called "Søren."

So I repeat: "This must be said: by ceasing to take part (if usually thou dost) in the public worship of God, as it now is, thou hast constantly one guilt the less, and that a great one." Whoever thou art, beware; thou surely wilt not come into eternity, if thou dost not take the matter of religion more seriously than by contenting thyself with an optical illusion as thy divine worship and taking part in treating God as a fool. Not for the sake of this life do we have religion, in order to get through this life happily and well, but it is for the sake of the other life. In this other life lies the seriousness of religion. And from the other world is addressed to thee as well as to me the Word of God: "Be not deceived, God will not suffer Himself to be mocked." No, He will not suffer Himself to be mocked, He will not endure eternally what He does not by His omnipotence prevent from occurring in time, that under the name of divine worship men get exactly the opposite from that which Christianity is in the New Testament. And the fact that this has come about slowly and sneakingly in the lapse of centuries may excuse but it will not help thee. Above all then, let not thyself be deluded by the priests. Believe me, or merely look an instant, impartially, at the New Testament, and thou wilt see that Christianity did not come into the world in order to assure the priests of a flourishing and agreeable business as their livelihood, and to tranquillize thee in thy natural state; but that, with the renunciation of all things, it came into the world in order by the terrors of eternity to tear thee out of the tranquillity in which thou naturally art.

In what has occurred up to this time there is only one thing which makes me shudder; and I shudder again when I reflect upon what I know, that even when I speak of this I shall not be understood.

What makes me shudder is this. While my life, though it is weak in comparison with the glorious ones who have lived, expresses nevertheless the thought of fighting for eternity with anxiety for the salvation of one's soul, I stand surrounded by contemporaries who at the very most are interested in this as "the public." In a fleeting way a man perhaps allows himself to be gripped by what I say, the next instant he judges it aesthetically, the next instant he reads what is written against me, then he is curious about the outcome, etc., etc.; in short, he is "the public." And not to any one of them does it occur that by being men they are subjected to the same conditions as I am, that they too must expect an accounting of eternity, and that one thing is certain, that eternity is closed to everything which in this life has no will to be more than "the public"—"just like the others." This makes me shudder, that these men are living in the notion that it is I who am in danger, whereas after all, eternally understood, I am much less in danger than they, inasmuch as I am fighting for eternity. And I shudder again when I reflect that this goes on in "Christendom," that these contemporaries therefore are a community of Christians which has 1000 teachers sworn upon the New Testament—and then the truth is that these teachers have no vaguest notion of what Christianity is. This is horrible. It is horrible for me to be in such a degree in the right in what I say, when I say that Christianity does not exist at all, and when I state how this fact hangs together with the preaching of Christianity by the "witnesses to the truth."

That the ideals must be proclaimed—otherwise Christianity is falsified in its deepest root

Take another situation. There is a proverb which says, "It's a poor soldier who does not hope to become a general."

So it should be; if there is to be life and enthusiasm in an army, this proverb ought to inspire all: a poor soldier who does not hope to become a general.

Rather different is that which experience teaches from generation to generation, that out of the prodigious mass of soldiers only a few even become noncommissioned officers, very few lieutenants, rarely several individuals become staff officers, very seldom by way of exception one becomes a general.

Now reverse the situation. One starts out with what experience teaches, what has been verified again and again from generation to generation—and thereupon one speaks thus: "It is foolishness for a soldier to cherish the notion of becoming a general. Be content with what you are, just as we are content, content with what experience teaches, that the thousands get no further." Is not this to demoralize the army?

So it is in the Christian sphere. Instead of proclaiming the ideals, they educe what experience teaches, what the experience of all the centuries has taught, that the millions get no further than mediocrity.

Thus they apply Christianity *tranquillizingly*; a base priestly lie, but one which pays, applying Christianity *tranquillizingly*, whereas instead it is in the deepest sense *arousing, disquieting*! They apply it tranquillizingly: "To strive after the ideals is folly, stupidity, madness, it is pride, conceit (things which are offensive to God); the *via media* is the true wisdom; be tranquil, you are completely like the millions; and the experience of all the centuries teaches that one gets no further! Be tranquil, you are like the others, will become blessed like all the others"—a euphemism for: You are going to hell like all the others. But this truth will not produce money, and the other teaching pays brilliantly.

If there lives an individual who is not content with, will not be tranquillized by that sort of blessedness, then the whole mass, commanded by the perjurers, turns against him, declares him an egoist, a dreadful egotist, for not wanting to be like the others.

The New Testament, however, is always in the right; for sure enough this individual encounters the genuine Christian collisions: of being hated by men because he is determined to be...a Christian. The only difference is that these men are costumed as Christians, are titularly Christians, and are led—how solemn!—by teachers who have taken an oath upon the New Testament.

In this way they have demoralized Christendom by doing exactly the opposite of proclaiming the ideals.

But what does it avail them? what does it avail that by the assistance of priestly lies they get this life made easy and comfortable? They do not fool eternity. And inflexibly as the human race stands up for its will to punish, to punish even by death, those who are not willing to be like the others, just so firmly does eternity stick to its purpose of punishing with eternal perdition those who are tranquillized by being like the others.

A dose of pessimism

Just as man—by nature—desires what is able to sustain and revive the lust of life, so does he who is to live for the eternal need constantly a dose of pessimism, in order not to dote upon this world, but rather learn to loathe and be weary of and disgusted with the foolishness and lies of this wretched world.

The God-Man is betrayed, mocked, deserted by all, all, all; not a single one, literally not a single one remains faithful to Him—and then afterwards, afterwards, afterwards there are millions who have made pilgrimage to the places where, many hundreds of years before, His foot perhaps has left a trace; afterwards, afterwards, afterwards millions have worshiped a splinter of the cross upon which He was crucified.

And so it is always, contemporaneously; but afterwards, afterwards, afterwards!

Must not one then be disgusted at being a man?

Again, must not one be disgusted at being a man! For those millions who upon their knees made the pilgrimage to His grave, the human crowd which no power was able to disperse: only one thing was needed, that Christ should come again—and all these millions would at once acquire feet and take to their heels, the whole crowd would be as if blown away; or perhaps as a mass would stand upright and fall upon Christ to put Him to death.

What Christ, what the Apostles, what every witness to the truth desires as the only thing...is imitation—the only thing humanity has no taste for, takes no pleasure in.

No, take away the danger...that we may play—then the battalions of the human race perform marvels of mimicry. Instead of the imitation of Christ we have (Oh, nausea!) the sacred apish tricks—under the leadership and command (Oh, nausea!) of perjured priests, who serve as sergeants, lieutenants, etc., ordained men, who therefore have for this serious business the special support of a Holy Spirit.

Be frivolous—and you will see, all difficulties disappear!

If by this advice I meant to teach the human race what it has to do in the future, it might well be said of me that I come too late, prodigiously late! For this has with striking good fortune and triumphant success been practiced for centuries.

Whereas every higher conception of life (even in paganism at its best, not to speak of Christianity) takes the view that the task for men is to strive after kinship with the Deity, and that this effort makes life difficult, all the more difficult in proportion as the effort is more earnest, more vigorous, more strenuous; the human race has in the course of time come to think differently about the significance of life and man's task in it. Shrewd as the human race is, it has ferreted out the secret of existence, has scented the fact that, if one would have life made easy (and that is just what men want), this is readily accomplished: one need only minimize more and more one's own significance, the significance of being a man—then life becomes easier and easier. Be frivolous—and you will see, all difficulties disappear!

There once was a time when "woman" was essentially determined [*forholt sig til sig selv*] by the conception of her emotion. One sorrow was enough to determine her way of life for a whole lifetime. The death of her beloved or his unfaithfulness was enough; she understood it as her task to be lost for this life, and that to carry this out consistently implies long, long inward struggles and temptations, occasions many a painful conflict with the surrounding world, in short, makes life difficult. And therefore to what purpose all these difficulties? Be frivolous—and you will see, all these difficulties disappear! The death or unfaithfulness of the beloved becomes at the most a little pause, pretty much like sitting out a dance at the ball. Half an hour later she is dancing with a new cavalier—it would be tiresome too to have to dance all night with one cavalier—and as for eternity, it is expedient to have more than one when one knows that there will be several waiting for her there. You see, all difficulties disappear, life becomes pleasant, cheerful, gay, easy, in short, it is a glorious world to live in, if only one knows how to adapt oneself rightly to it—by being frivolous.

There once was a time when "man" was essentially determined by a great conception of what it is to be a man of character. One had principles, principles which at no price one would abandon or let go, one would give up one's life, expose oneself throughout a whole lifetime to every ill-treatment, rather than give way in the least degree with respect to one's principles; for one knew that to give way in the least respect with relation to principles is to give them up, and to give up one's principles is to give up oneself. Thereby life of course became sheer difficulty. And therefore to what purpose all these difficulties? Be frivolous—and you will see, all these difficulties disappear! Be frivolous: have today one view, tomorrow another, then again the one you had yesterday, and again a new one on Friday. Be frivolous: turn yourself into several persons, parcel yourself out, have one view anonymously, another in your own name, one orally, another in writing, one as a professional view, another in private, one as the husband of your wife, another at the club—and you will see, all difficulties disappear, you will see that, whereas all men of character, and in the same measure as they are men of character, have found out and borne witness that this world is a mediocre world, a poor, wretched, depraved and evil world, you, however, will see, you will find, that this world is a glorious world, just as though it were contrived for you!

There once was a time when man was essentially determined by an infinite conception of what it is to be a Christian, when he took seriously the thing of "dying to the world," of hating oneself, of suffering for the doctrine, and then found life so difficult, yea, so agonizing, that even the most hardy almost sank down under the difficulties, shrank like worms, and even the most humble-minded were not far from despair. And therefore to what purpose all these difficulties? Be frivolous—and you will see, all these difficulties disappear! Be frivolous—and then be yourself a priest, a dean, a bishop, who (by virtue of a sacred oath upon the New Testament) once a week for three-quarters of an hour patters something very lofty, but for the rest bids adieu to everything high, or be yourself a layman who for three-quarters of an hour is uplifted by the lofty things the priest patters, but for the rest bids adieu to everything high—and you will see, all difficulties disappear! Falsify then in its deepest roots God's and Christianity's view of this life; let it be to you a sign that the way is the right one, that the way is well pleasing to God, when you note that (in precise contradiction to God's Word) it is easy—and you will see, all the difficulties disappear, this world becomes a glorious world, more glorious and more agreeable and more easy for every century we live in this way. And be quite unabashed; believe me, you have no need to be ashamed of yourself, the whole company is of the same quality, the eulogy therefore is ready for you, the eulogy upon your shrewdness, the eulogy of the others, who by pronouncing a eulogy upon you (how shrewdly calculated!) are eulogizing themselves, and who therefore would condemn you only if you were not...like the others.

The priests are cannibals, and that in the most odious way

Everyone understands what cannibals are, they are man-eaters. One shudders at hearing or reading about this frightful practice, that there are savages who kill their enemies in order to eat them. One shudders, one is inclined to disavow kinship with such beings, to deny that they are men.

I shall now show that the priests are cannibals, and in a far more odious way.

What is the Christianity of the New Testament? It is the suffering truth. In this mediocre, miserable, sinful, evil, ungodly world (this is the Christian doctrine) the truth must suffer, Christianity is the suffering truth because it is the truth and is in this world.

For this reason the Founder not only suffered death upon the cross, but His whole life was suffering from first to last. For this reason the Apostles suffered, for this reason the witness to the truth. And the Saviour required one thing, the Apostles after Him required the same thing, and the witness to the truth required only one thing: imitation.

But what does the "priest" do? This educated man is far from being crazy. "To imitate him! What a proposal to make to a shrewd man! First this shrewd man must have undergone a transformation, he must have become crazy, before it could occur to him to go in for such a thing. No, but might it not be feasible to describe the sufferings of these glorious ones, to preach their teaching as doctrine, and in such a way that it would yield so much profit that a man could live off of it, marry on it, beget children who are fed on it? That is to say, is it not feasible to turn the glorious ones into money, or to eat them, with wife and children to live by eating them?"

Here you have the cannibals, the proof that the priests are cannibals. O ye glorious ones, departed this life; in the animal world, which is called *a parte potiori*, the world of man, it is your fate in life and after death to be eaten: while you live you are eaten by the contemporary vermin, at last you are put to death, and when you are dead the real cannibals take hold, the priests who live by eating you! As in the farmhouses at the slaughtering season provision for the winter is salted away, so the "priest" keeps in brine tubs the glorious ones who were required to suffer for the truth. In vain the deceased man cries out, "Follow me, follow me!" "That was a good joke," replies the priest. "No, keep your mouth shut and stay where you are. What nonsense to require that I should follow you, I who have to live precisely by eating you, and not I alone, but my wife and my children! To suppose that I should follow you, perhaps myself become a sacrifice—instead of living off you, or eating you, so as to make the most brilliant career, to earn money like grass for me and my wife and children, who, if only you could see them, thrive in a way it is a pleasure to look at."

This is cannibalism, and it is the most odious form of it, as I shall now show.

1. The cannibal is a savage; the priest is an educated, a cultivated man, which makes the abomination far more revolting.

2. The cannibal eats his enemies. Quite differently the "priest." He makes a show of being devoted in the highest degree to the man whom he eats. The priest, precisely the priest, is the most devoted friend of these glorious ones. "Only hear him, hear how he is able to describe their sufferings and preach their doctrine. Does he not deserve a silver centerpiece, the cross of a knightly order, a whole stock of embroidered armchairs, a few thousand more a year, this grand man who, himself moved almost to tears, can so describe the sufferings of the glorious ones?" The cannibal is not like that; he admits openly that he is a man-eater, and he does not call the man he eats his friend; he calls him his enemy, and himself the enemy of this man. The priest on the contrary conceals with the greatest possible care that he is a cannibal (like the crocodile with its piteous tears), he conceals it by making a show of being most devoted precisely to the man he eats. The priest binds himself by an oath upon the New Testament, therefore binds himself to imitation, to the obligation of following the Saviour of the world—and then says good-bye to imitation, but with his family he lives by describing His sufferings (that is, by eating Him), by preaching His doctrine, by making a show of being a true, devoted disciple of the Crucified. "You should hear him on Sundays! That man is a true disciple of Christ, in such an affecting way he can describe Christ's sufferings and bear witness to Him. . . . Does he not deserve velvet stripes on the front of his gown, and stars, and thousands a year?"

3. The cannibal does it all in no time: savagely he springs up, overpowers his enemy, puts him to death, eats a bit of him. Then it's all over. Then he lives again off his customary food, until another time when savage hatred of his enemy comes over him.

It is different with the "priest" as a cannibal. His cannibalism is well thought out, cunningly planned, calculated on the basis of having nothing else to live on throughout his whole life, and that what one has to live on must suffice to feed a man with a family, in such a way that from year to year it yields more. The priest is snugly settled in his rural residence, with the prospect also of attractive promotion; his wife is plumpness itself, and his children no less. And all this is due to... the sufferings of the glorious ones, the Saviour, the Apostles, the witness to the truth, on this the priest lives, these men he eats, and with a joyful zest for life he feeds them to his wife and children. He keeps these glorious ones in brine tubs. Their cry, "Follow me, follow me!" is in vain. For a time he may perhaps defend himself against this cry, lest (in conjunction with the oath he has taken) it might make a disturbing impression upon his whole business venture. In the course of years he becomes so hardened against this cry that he hears it no more. At the beginning it is perhaps with a certain sense of shame he hears himself called a true disciple of Christ. In the course of years he has become so accustomed to hearing it that he himself believes he is that. Then he dies, as fundamentally depraved as it is possible for a man to be—and he is buried as a witness to the truth.

The priest not only proves the truth of Christianity, but he disproves it at the same time

There is only one relation to revealed truth: believing it.

The fact that one believes can only be proved in one way: by being willing to suffer for one's faith. And the degree of one's faith is proved only by the degree of one's willingness to suffer for one's faith.

In that way Christianity came into the world, being served by witnesses who were willing absolutely to suffer everything for their faith, and actually had to suffer, to sacrifice life and blood for the truth.

The courage of their faith makes an impression upon the human race, leading it to the following conclusion: What is able thus to inspire men to sacrifice everything, to venture life and blood, must be truth.

This is the proof which is adduced for the truth of Christianity.

Now on the contrary the priest is so kind as to wish to make it a livelihood. But a livelihood is exactly the opposite of suffering, of being sacrificed, in which the proof consists: it is the opposite of proving the truth of Christianity by the fact that there have lived men who have sacrificed everything, ventured life and blood for Christianity.

Here then is the proof and the disproof at the same time! The proof of the truth of Christianity from the fact that one has ventured everything for it, is disproved, or rendered suspect, by the fact that the priest who advances this proof does exactly the opposite. By seeing the glorious ones, the witnesses to the truth, venture everything for Christianity, one is led to the conclusion: Christianity must be truth. By considering the priest one is led to the conclusion: Christianity is hardly the truth, but profit is the truth.

No, the proof that something is truth from the willingness to suffer for it, can only be advanced by one who himself is willing to suffer for it. The priest's proof: proving the truth of Christianity by the fact that he takes money for it, profits by, lives off of, being steadily promoted, with a family, lives off of...the fact that others have suffered, is a self-contradiction, Christianly regarded, it is fraud.

And therefore, Christianly, the priest must be stopped—in the sense in which one speaks of stopping a thief. And as people cry, "Hip, ho!" after a Jew, so, until no priest is any more to be seen, they must cry, "Stop thief! Stop him, he is stealing what belongs to the glorious ones!" What they deserved by their noble disinterestedness, and what they did not get, being rewarded by unthankfulness, persecuted and put to death, that the priest steals by appropriating their lives, by describing their sufferings, proving the truth of Christianity by the willingness of these glorious ones to suffer for it. Thus it is the priest robs the glorious ones; and then he deceives the simpleminded human multitude, which has not the ability to see through the priest's traffic and perceive that he proves the truth of Christianity and at the same time disproves it.

What wonder then that Christianity simply does not exist, that the notion of "Christendom" is galimatias, when those who are Christians are such in reliance upon the priest's proof, assume that Christianity is truth in reliance upon the priest's proof: that something is truth because one is willing enough to make profit out of it, or perhaps even (by a greater refinement) to get the extra profit of protesting that he is willing to suffer. To assume the truth of Christianity in reliance upon this proof is just as nonsensical as to regard oneself as an opulent man because much money passes through one's hands which is not one's own, or because one possesses a lot of paper money issued by a bank which is insolvent.

THE INSTANT

No. 10

Contents

Note: The circumstance that at the foot of the title page there is no indication of the date, the authorship, the publisher, or the printer, is due to the fact that this last number of the *Instant* was not issued in S.K.'s lifetime. It was found upon his desk, complete in every other detail, when he died. It was finished therefore before he was carried to the hospital on October 2, 1855. It is interesting to note that the dates attached to the several articles are far anterior to this.

From the Journal

CHRISTIANITY

As an individual, quite literally as an individual, to relate oneself to God personally is the formula for being a Christian. . . . If once this occurs, then it is an event incomparably more important than a European war and a war which involves all the corners of the earth, it is a catastrophic event which moves the universe to its profoundest depths. . . . He whose life does not present relative catastrophes of this sort has never, not even in the remotest approximation, had recourse as an individual to God —that is just as impossible as to touch an electrical machine without receiving a shock.

My *Kierkegaard*, p. 525

What I call optical illusion

[Aug. 25.]

THIS consists in what looks as if it were serving a higher interest, the infinite, the idea, God; but upon closer inspection proves to be serving the finite, low things, profit. And it was this Bishop Mynster practiced with rare virtuosity.

As an example let me recall something which cannot by this time be quite forgotten, an incident which illustrates what I mean, and one in which the two bishops, the one who is deceased and the one now living, to wit, Mynster and Martensen, are the *dramatis personae.*

When Martensen had been a professor for several years,[67] there began to be talk in Copenhagen about the longing Professor Martensen felt to preach the Word to the people, in addition to his activity in the University.

Very pretty! Martensen is Professor, has, humanly speaking, made a success—well then, this longing to preach the Word also to the people, is something he would keep pure, remote from every qualification by the finite, by temporal rewards and the like; for in him this is a really religious longing. And in fact the thing is easily arranged: if he feels this longing, he has only to beg one of the priests of the city to grant him his pulpit. Every priest would do it with pleasure.

If Martensen had done this, as sure as my name is Søren Kierkegaard it would not have found favor in the eyes of Bishop Mynster. With his delicate nose he would at once have scented out: "A man who has a longing in this sense is not of my crew; and to me as a Church ruler this sort of longing is heartily repugnant. How far such a longing may lead a man, it is impossible to reckon." Mynster was like that; no one can know it better than I who know it from the experience that Bishop Mynster undoubtedly accounted it a great act of grace he showed me (his enemies were inclined to understand it as fear) by even so much as tolerating me, not to say (as something quite out of the usual!) showing a bit of liking for me. For my whole nature was repugnant to him in the highest degree; it was not in the least declined according to the Christian paradigm he virtually acknowledged on Mondays, the paradigm of perfected Christianity, according to which every striving after the infinite is measurable by finite advantage and reward, which a domineering man does well in recognizing as the only paradigm, for what is declined in accordance with that is easy, all-too-easy to manage and subdue.

But back to Professor Martensen. What if this longing might be satisfied by becoming...Court Preacher? That's another thing! That is four hundred Danish dollars for twelve sermons, and thereto also a prospect of the bishop's chair made more probable, which otherwise would be very doubtful. In this position moreover there can no longer be any question of gathering a congregation about him, as he might have done even as a professor by selecting one definite church, and (what would be infinitely easy to attain) if he were to occupy the pulpit every sixth Sunday.

So then: Court Preacher, four hundred dollars for twelve sermons, the possibility of the bishop's chair. Now that was to Bishop Mynster's taste, now he could in every way understand and approve and sympathize with this longing, could find it a pretty longing Martensen feels to preach the Word to the people. With a tranquil mind the domineering Church ruler played that evening his game of ombre and appeared to be the soul of cheerfulness; for from a sort of longing like this of Martensen one has no reason to fear any disturbing movement, on the contrary it is precisely the right thing for quenching the Spirit.

So then, in the text: a religious longing—and the note reads: Court Preacher, four hundred dollars, prospect of the bishop's chair. However, the good-natured populace notices nothing, is deeply touched by this religious longing: "How fine it is that Martensen feels such a religious longing; what confidence one must have in a man who feels such a deep longing to preach the Word." This is optical illusion.

And to optical illusion the whole of Bishop Mynster's Church rule was directed; his virtuosity in ambiguity had become his second nature. For a long series of years, with a virtuosity worthy of admiration, he led (Christianly speaking) his generation by the nose, a generation which then out of gratitude desired to erect a monument to him, presumably in the capacity to which Martensen had promoted him...as a witness to the truth, one of the genuine witnesses, a link in the holy chain—Martensen, who knows as well as I do that Bishop Mynster's secret was that of the Epicureans, of the Hedonists, of the self-indulgent: *après nous le déluge.* Yea, that he knows as well as I. If he should wish to deny it, I shall come to the aid of his memory.

"How can ye believe who receive honor from one another?" John 5:44

[July 15, '55.]

This again is a death-sentence to all official Christianity.

This prodigious castle in the air: Christian states, kingdoms, lands; this playing with millions of Christians who reciprocally recognize one another in their mediocrity, yet are all of them believers—this whole thing rests upon a foundation which, according to Christ's own word, makes it impossible to believe.

The Christianity of the New Testament is to love God in opposition to men, to *suffer* at the hands of men for one's faith, for the sake of the doctrine to suffer at the hands of men. Only that is to believe: to receive honor from men makes it impossible to believe.

As I say, Christianity simply does not exist. The sort of passion required in order that in the most complete separation, in a relation of opposition to men, one may deal only with God (only this Christ means by believing; and therefore in contrast to receiving honor from men, verse 41, or receiving honor from one another, He speaks of seeking the honor which cometh from the only God, verse 44)—that sort of passion is now no more met with. The sort of men who now live cannot stand anything so strong as the Christianity of the New Testament (they would die of it or lose their minds), just in the same sense that children cannot stand strong drink, for which reason we prepare for them a little lemonade—and official Christianity is lemonade-twaddle for the sort of beings that now are called men, it is the strongest thing they can stand, and this twaddle then in their language they call "Christianity," just as the children call their lemonade "wine."

In "Christendom" then, Christianity, the thing of being a Christian, follows the paradigm: "This or that man is a splendid man, a true man of faith, he ought to have a chivalric order"—"Ah, that is too little for such an eminent man of faith, he ought to have the title of commander," etc., etc. And the activity so rich in blessing of the Knight, the Commander, the Privy Counselor, etc., is based upon the New Testament, in which we read, "How can ye believe who receive honor from one another?" That is to say, from generation to generation, from century to century, "Christendom" performs the trick of declining *mensa* like *domus*.[68]

Therefore rather than take part in official Christianity with the thousandth part of my little-finger nail, I would rather engage in the following display of seriousness. A flag is purchased at a hardware store, it is unfurled, with great reverence I approach it, lift up three fingers and swear fidelity to the flag. Thereupon, rigged out in a cocked hat, a cartridge-belt and sword (all from the hardware store), I mount a hobbyhorse, proposing in union with others to make an attack upon the enemy, with contempt for the mortal danger into which I am evidently casting myself, with the seriousness of one who knows what it signifies to have sworn fidelity to the flag. Honestly, I have no disposition to engage in that sort of seriousness; but, if bad came to worse, I should infinitely prefer this to taking part in official Christianity, in the Sunday worship, the seriousness of the sworn teachers. After all, by the former one only makes a fool of oneself, by the latter one makes a fool of God.

What the echo answers

[July 9.]

Folios and folios have been written to show again and again how one is to recognize what true Christianity is.

This can be done in a far simpler way.

Nature is...acoustic. Only heed what the echo answers, and thou shalt know at once what is what.

So when in this world one preaches Christianity in such a way that the echo answers: "Glorious, profound, serious-minded Christian, thou shouldst be exalted to princely rank," etc., know then that this signifies his preaching of Christianity is, Christianly, a base lie. It is not absolutely certain that he who walks with fetters on his legs is a criminal, for there are instances when the civil magistrate has condemned an innocent man; but it is eternally certain that he who—by preaching Christianity!—wins all things earthly is a liar, a deceiver, who at one point or another has falsified the doctrine, which by God has been so designed, in such a militant relation to this world, that it is eternally impossible to preach what Christianity is in truth without having to suffer in this world, to be repudiated, hated, cursed.

When one preaches Christianity in such a way that the echo answers, "He is mad," know then that this signifies that there are considerable elements of truth in his preaching, without its being, however, the Christianity of the New Testament. He may have hit the mark; but presumably he does not press hard enough, either by his oral preaching or by the preaching of his life, so that, Christianly speaking, he glides over too easily, his preaching after all is not the Christianity of the New Testament.

But when one preaches Christianity in such a way that the echo answers, "Away with that man from the earth, he does not deserve to live," know then that this is the Christianity of the New Testament. Without change since the time of our Lord Jesus Christ, capital punishment is the penalty for preaching Christianity as it truly is: hating oneself to love God; hating oneself to hate everything in which one's life consists, everything to which one clings, for the sake of which one selfishly would desire to have God's aid to get it, or to console one that one did not get it, console one for the loss of it—without any change capital punishment is the penalty for preaching this in character. Preaching this in character; for if the preacher (doing what our age regards as the far greater thing) plays at being objective, so that his life expresses precisely the opposite of this, then we get forms of the interesting, and the interesting never arouses persecution; on the contrary, all characterlessness is pleasing to this world.

But the merit of "Christendom" is, that by the aid of the doctrine that Christianity is perfectible it has transformed Christianity into worldliness. This was the first lie: to transform Christianity into worldliness. The second lie then is: that the world has now become tolerant, has made progress, for the fact that persecution no longer takes place—the fact is that there is nothing to persecute.

Oh, yes, Christianity is perfectible! and it is steadily going forward! Christianity came into the world and found it lost in earthly desire and endeavor. Christianity then taught...renunciation. But, said "Christendom," Christianity is perfectible; we cannot stop here, renunciation is a moment of transition, we must go further, must go on...Hurrah for profit! What a refinement! Paganism was worldliness prior to renunciation; the worldliness of Christendom claims to be higher than renunciation, which it regards as one-sidedness.

That the crime of Christendom is comparable to that of wishing to obtain stealthily an inheritance to which one is not entitled

[Aug. 24.]

A man dies and leaves his whole fortune to an heir—but there is a condition, something which is required of the heir; and this the heir does not like. What then does he do? He takes possession of the property bequeathed to him (for he is indeed the heir, says he) and says good-day to the obligation.

This, as everybody knows, is dishonesty; it is a lie, that without more ado he is heir to the whole fortune; he is heir only upon the condition of assuming the obligation, otherwise he is no more heir than any other man whatsoever.

So it is with "Christendom." If you will, it is devised to mankind by the Testament of the Saviour of the world; but in the case of Christianity the situation is this: the gift and the obligation correspond to one another in an exact proportion. In the same degree that Christianity is a gift it is also an obligation.

The knavish trick of "Christendom" is to take the gift and say good-day to the obligation, to want to be heir to the gift, but without assuming the obligation, to want to make it appear that mankind is indeed the heir, whereas the truth is that only by performing the obligation is mankind, or rather (for precisely because it is an obligation, such an abstraction as mankind can only in an extremely figurative sense be called the heir) I would say that every single individual of mankind is the heir.

However, hypocritical as everything is with "Christendom," they have made it appear as if Christendom too did maintain that Christianity is an obligation—one has to be baptized. Ah! That is making confoundedly short work of obligation! A drop of water on the head of an infant, in the name of the Trinity—that is obligation!

No, the obligation is: the imitation of Jesus Christ.

However, if this has to be included, if the gift and the obligation are to be in an equal proportion to one another, then "mankind" declines Christianity with thanks, then there is nothing for it but to resort to falsification...and so you have "Christendom," the crime of which is: wishing to obtain underhand an inheritance to which it is not entitled.

When is "the Instant"?

[May 29, '55.]

The Instant is when *the* man is there, the right man, the man of the Instant.

This is a secret which eternally will remain hidden from all worldly shrewdness, from everything which is only to a certain degree.

Worldly shrewdness stares and stares at events, at circumstances, it reckons and reckons, thinking that it might be able to distill the Instant out of the circumstances, and so become itself a power by the aid of the Instant, this breaking through of the eternal, hoping that itself might be rejuvenated, as it so greatly needs to be, by means of the new.

But in vain. Shrewdness does not succeed and never will to all eternity succeed by means of this surrogate—any more than all the arts of cosmetics succeed in producing natural beauty.

No, only when *the* man is there, and when he ventures as one must venture (which is precisely what worldly shrewdness and mediocrity want to avoid), then is the Instant—and the circumstances then obey the man of the Instant. In case nothing is brought into play but worldly shrewdness and mediocrity, the Instant never comes. Things may go on for hundreds of thousands and millions of years constantly the same—it looks perhaps as if it might now soon come; but so long as there is only worldly shrewdness and mediocrity, etc., the Instant comes not, no more than does an unfruitful man beget children.

But when the right man comes, yea, then the Instant is there. For the Instant is precisely that which does not lie in the circumstances, it is the new thing, the woof of eternity—but that same second it masters the circumstances to such a degree that (adroitly calculated to fool worldly shrewdness and mediocrity) it looks as if the Instant proceeded from the circumstances.

There is nothing worldly shrewdness so broods over and so hankers after as the Instant. What would it not give to be able to calculate rightly! Yet no one is more surely excluded from ever grasping the Instant than worldly shrewdness. For the Instant is heaven's gift to—a pagan would say, to the fortunate and the enterprising, but a Christian says, to the believer. Yea, this thing which by worldly shrewdness is so deeply despised, or at the most dressed up with borrowed phrases of Sunday solemnity, this thing of *believing*, that and that only is related as possibility to the Instant. Worldly shrewdness is eternally excluded, despised and abhorred, as things are in heaven, more than all vices and crimes, because in its nature it of all things most belongs to this wretched world, and most of all is remote from having anything to do with heaven and the eternal.

My task

[Sept. 1, '55.]

"I do not call myself a Christian, do not say myself that I am a Christian." It is this I must constantly reiterate, and which everyone who would understand my quite peculiar task must train himself to be able to understand.

Yes, I know it well enough, it sounds almost like a sort of madness, in this Christian world where all and everybody is Christian, where to be a Christian is something therefore which everyone is as a matter of course—that there, in this Christian world, one says of oneself, "I do not call myself a Christian," and especially one whom Christianity concerns to the degree that it concerns me.

But it cannot be otherwise; in the world's twaddle the truer view must always seem like a sort of madness. And that it is a world of twaddle in which we live, that incidentally it is precisely by reason of this twaddle that everybody is a Christian in a sense, is certain enough.

Nevertheless I neither can alter my statement nor do I dare to—otherwise there would come about also perhaps another alteration, that the Power, it is an omnipotent Power, which in a singular way makes use of my impotence, might take its hand off me and let me sail on my own sea. No, I am neither willing to alter my statement, nor do I dare to; I cannot be of service to the legions of knavish tradesmen, I mean the priests, who by falsifying the definition of Christianity for the sake of business profits have acquired millions and millions of Christians: I am not a Christian—and unfortunately I am able to make it evident that the others are not either, yea, even less than I. For they imagine that they are Christians, or they claim it mendaciously, or (like the priests) they make others believe it, so that thereby the priests' business becomes flourishing.

The point of view which I have to indicate again and again is of such a singular sort that in the eighteen hundred years of "Christendom" I have nothing to hold on to, nothing that is analogous, nothing that corresponds to it. So also in this respect, with regard to the eighteen hundred years, I stand literally alone.*

* Note. Inasmuch as I have made a critical comment[69] upon "the Apostle," the following is to be noted. (1). I am entirely within my rights, for the Apostle is only a man. And my task requires that it must be followed out to the extreme. If in the teaching of the Apostle there is found even in the least degree anything that can be related to what in the course of the centuries has become the sophistic which consumes all true Christianity, I must raise an outcry, lest the Sophists at once appeal to the Apostle. (2). It is of great importance, especially for Protestantism, to straighten out the prodigious confusion Luther

The only analogy I have before me is Socrates. My task is a Socratic task, to revise the definition of what it is to be a Christian. For my part I do not call myself a "Christian" (thus keeping the ideal free), but I am able to make it evident that the others are that still less than I.

Thou noble simpleton of olden times, thou, the only *man* I admiringly recognize as teacher; there is but little concerning thee that has been preserved, thou amongst men the only true martyr to intellectuality, just as great *qua* character as *qua* thinker; but this little, how infinitely much it is! How I long, afar from these battalions of thinkers which "Christendom" puts into the field under the name of Christian thinkers (for after all, apart from them, there have in the course of the centuries lived in "Christendom" several quite individual teachers of real significance)—how I long, if only for half an hour, to be able to talk with thee!

It is in an abyss of sophistry Christianity is lying—far, far worse than when the Sophists flourished in Greece. These legions of priests and Christian docents are all Sophists, living (as was said of the Sophists of old)[70] by making those who understand nothing believe something, then treating this human-numerical factor as the criterion of what truth, what Christianity is.

But I do not call myself a "Christian." That this is highly embarrassing to the Sophists, I understand very well, I understand very well that they would much prefer that with kettledrums and trumpets I should proclaim myself the only true Christian, I understand very well too that they seek, untruly, to represent my course of action in this way. But one does not dupe me! In a certain sense I am very easily duped; I have been duped in almost every relationship into which I have entered—but then that was because I myself willed it. When I do not will it, there is in my generation no one who dupes me—a consummate detective talent such as I.

So then they do not dupe me: I do not call myself a "Christian." In a certain sense then it seems easy enough to get rid of me; for in fact the others are all of them men of a very different kidney, they are all true Christians. Yes, yes, so it seems; but it is not so. For just because

has brought about by inverting the relationship, and in effect criticizing Christ by Paul, the Master by the disciple. I on the other hand have not criticized the Apostle, as though I were something, I who am not even a Christian. What I have done is to hold up Christ's preaching alongside of the preaching of the Apostle. (3). One thing it is to be able intellectually to make a true observation, it is something else to want to belittle, to weaken, the Apostle, from which certainly I am as remote as anybody.

I do not call myself a Christian it is impossible to get rid of me, possessing as I do the confounded quality of being able, precisely by the aid of not calling myself a "Christian," to make it evident that the others are still less Christians.

O Socrates, if with kettledrums and trumpets thou hadst proclaimed thyself the most knowing man, the Sophists would soon have had the better of thee. No, thou wast the ignorant man; but thou didst possess at the same time the confounded quality of being able, precisely by the aid of the fact that thou thyself wast ignorant, to make it evident that the others knew still less than thou, did not even know that they were ignorant.

But as it befell thee (according to what thou sayest in thy "Defense,"[71] as ironically enough thou hast called the cruelest satire upon any generation), that thou didst bring down upon thee many enemies by making it evident that they were ignorant; and as they imputed to thee the inference that thou thyself must be what thou wert able to show the others were not, they therefore out of envy conceived a grudge against thee; so it has also befallen me. It has exasperated men against me that I am able to make it evident that the others are Christians still less than I am, who yet am so very diffident about my relation to Christianity that I truly see and admit that I am not a Christian. And they would impute to me the inference that this affirmation that I am not a Christian is only a hidden form of pride, that I surely must be what I am able to prove the others are not. But this is a misunderstanding: it is entirely true that I am not a Christian; and it is an overhasty conclusion that because I can show that the others are not Christians, therefore I myself must be one—just as overhasty as it would be to conclude, for example, from the fact that a man is a foot higher than another, *ergo* he must be six yards high.

My task is to revise the definition of a Christian. There is only one man living who is competent to furnish a real criticism of my work—that is I myself. There was some truth in what was said to me a good many years ago by Dean Hoefod-Hansen, as he now is, apropos of the intention he had had of writing a review of the *Concluding Postscript*. He said that on reading the review that book contained of the earlier literary work, he gave up the thought of writing a review in an instance where the author was the only person capable of furnishing a real criticism of my work. The only man who occasionally has said a fairly true word about my significance is Professor R. Nielsen; but it is true perception he got from private conversation with me.

When now such competent judges as, for example, Messrs. Israel Levine,[72] Davidsen, Siesby, or such unbefuddled thinkers as Grüne, or such frank and open characters as the anonymous writers and the like, before so illegitimate a tribunal also as the public, pass judgment upon a work so singular, it naturally will come to—well, just what it has come to, a thing which pains me for the sake of this little nation, which by such a sight is made ridiculous *qua* nation.

But even if one man or another somewhat more competent undertakes to say something about my taste, it comes to nothing more than that after a fleeting glance at my situation the author finds in a trice some earlier instance or another which corresponds to it, as he declares. In that way it comes to nothing just the same. That upon which a man with my leisure, my diligence, my talents, my culture (for which Bishop Mynster in fact has given me a certificate in print[73]) has spent not merely fourteen years but essentially his whole life—that then some priest or another, at the most a professor, should not need more than a fleeting glance in order to be able to appraise it, is of course a piece of foolishness. And that what is singular to such a degree that at once it was branded, "The individual—I am not a Christian," a thing which quite certainly has not occurred in the eighteen hundred years of Christendom, where everything is branded, "Congregation, society—I am a true Christian"—that then some priest or another, at the most a professor, should at once find an analogy to it, is also a piece of foolishness. Upon more careful inspection one would find that it is precisely an impossibility. But this one does not think worth while; one prefers a fleeting glance at my situation, and then an equally fleeting glance at the earlier one, and with that one has immediately analogies enough for mine...as the public is well able to understand.

Nevertheless it is as I say: in the eighteen hundred years of "Christendom" there is absolutely nothing corresponding to my task, nothing analogous to it; it is the first time in "Christendom."

That I know, and I know too what it has cost, what I have suffered, which can be expressed however in a single word: I was never like others. Oh, in the days of youth it is of all torments the most frightful, the most intense, not to be like others, never to live a single day without being painfully reminded that one is not like others, never to be able to run with the herd, which is the delight and the joy of youth, never to be able to give oneself out expansively, always, so soon as one would make the venture, to be reminded of the fetters, the isolating peculiarity which, isolatingly to the border of despair, separates one from everything which is called human life and merriment and joy. True, one can by a frightful effort strive to hide what at that age one understands as one's dishonor, that one is not like the others; to a certain degree this may succeed, but all the same the agony is still in the heart, and after all it succeeds only to a certain degree, so that a single incautious movement may revenge itself frightfully.

With the years, it is true, this pain diminishes more and more; for as more and more one becomes spirit, it causes no pain that one is not like others. Spirit precisely is this: not to be like others.

And so at last there comes the instant when the Power which once did thus—yea, so it seems sometimes—ill-treat one, transfigures itself and says, "Hast thou anything to complain of? Does it seem to thee that in comparison with what is done for other men I have been partial and unjust? Though—out of love—I have embittered for thee thy childhood and both thine earlier and later youth, does it seem to thee that I have duped thee by what thou didst get instead?" And to this there can only remain the answer, "No, no, Thou infinite Love"—though nevertheless the human crowd doubtless would emphatically decline with thanks to be what I have become in such an agonizing way.

For by such torture as mine a man is trained to endure to be a sacrifice; and the infinite grace which was shown and is shown to me is that I should be selected to be a sacrifice, selected to this end, and then one thing more, that I should be developed under the combined influence of omnipotence and love to be able to hold fast the truth that this is the highest degree of grace the God of love can show towards anyone, and therefore shows only to His loved ones.

My dear reader, thou dost see that this does not promptly lead to profit. That will be the case only after my death, when the sworn teachers or tradesmen will appropriate my life too for salting down in the brine tubs.

Christianity is situated so high that what it understands by grace is what the profane (*Procul, o procul este profani*[74]) would of all things most heartily decline with thanks. False priests, or priests pure and simple, manage to transform grace into indulgence. According to them, grace consists in the fact that man, quite bluntly, has profit out of God, and the priests have profit out of men whom they make to believe this, inviting them with Christ's own words, "Come hither all"—the true significance of which words is, that the invitation is undeniably for all, but that this, when it comes to the pinch and it has to be determined to what it is Christ invites men (by imitation to become a sacrifice), and when this is not turned into something agreeable to all, then it will result, as in the age of Christ, that all most heartily decline with thanks, and that only quite exceptionally a single individual follows the invitation, and of these individuals in turn only a very singular individual follows the invitation in such a way that he holds fast to the truth that this is an infinite, an indescribable grace which is shown him...to be sacrificed. An indescribable grace; for it is the only way in which God can love a man and be loved by a man; but indeed it is an infinite grace that God wills to do this and wills to permit it. So a fig for the fact that, for prudential reasons, in order to put at a distance every profane consideration, an intermediate qualification is introduced, that of being sacrificed. And then too it would be almost loathsome, stifling, nauseating, suffocating, if this thing of being loved by God and loving Him were to be stupidly, bestially, encumbered by the thought that one had profit out of it.

Thou plain man! The Christianity of the New Testament is infinitely high; but observe that it is not high in such a sense that it has to do with the difference between man and man with respect to intellectual capacity, etc. No, it is for all. Everyone, absolutely everyone, if he absolutely wills it, if he will absolutely hate himself, will absolutely put up with everything, suffer everything (and this every man can if he will)—then is this infinite height attainable to him.

Thou plain man! I have not separated my life from thine; thou knowest it, I have lived in the street, am known to all; moreover I have not attained to any importance, do not belong to any class egoism, so if I belong anywhere, I must belong to thee, thou plain man, thou who once (when one profiting by thy money pretended to wish thee well[75]), thou who once wast too willing to find me and my existence ludicrous, thou who least of all hast reason to be impatient or ungrateful for the fact that I am of your company, for which the superior people rather have reason, seeing that I have never definitely united with them but merely maintained a looser relationship.

Thou plain man! I do not conceal from thee the fact that, according to my notion, the thing of being a Christian is infinitely high, that at no time are there more than a few who attain it, as Christ's own life attests, if one considers the generation in which He lived, and as also His preaching indicates, if one takes it literally. Yet nevertheless it is possible for all. But one thing I adjure thee, for the sake of God in heaven and all that is holy, shun the priests, shun them, those abominable men whose livelihood it is to prevent thee from so much as becoming aware of what Christianity is, and who thereby would transform thee, befuddled by galimatias and optical illusion, into what they understand by a true Christian, a paid member of the State Church, or the National Church,[76] or whatever they prefer to call it. Shun them. But take heed to pay them willingly and promptly what money they should have. With those whom one despises, one on no account should have money differences, lest it might perhaps be said that it was to get out of paying them one avoided them. No, pay them double, in order that thy disagreement with them may be thoroughly clear: that what concerns them does not concern thee at all, namely, money; and on the contrary, that what does not concern them concerns thee infinitely, namely, Christianity.

Little observations

[Aug. 2.]

1. *Little observations.*

Take a perfectly arbitrary example, in order the better to see the truth.

Let us assume that God's will was that we men must not go out to the Deer Park.[77]

This of course "man" could not put up with. What then would be the upshot? The upshot would be that the "priest" would make out that if, for example, one blessed the four-seated Holstein carriage and made the sign of the cross over the horses, then taking a drive to the Deer Park would be well pleasing to God.

The consequence therefore would be that people would go out to the Deer Park just as much as they do now, without any change, except that it had become dearer, cost perhaps five dollars for persons of rank, five dollars for the priests, and four cents for poor people. But then the excursion to the Deer Park would also have the enchantment of being at the same time...divine worship.

Perhaps the priests would have hit upon the thought of taking in hand themselves the business of hiring out horses and carriages, so that if it were to be thoroughly pleasing to God that one went out to the Deer Park, the carriage must be hired from the priests, perhaps a priest would go along, perhaps even (so that it might be singularly well pleasing to God) a priest would be the coachman, perhaps even (so that it might be well pleasing to God in the highest degree) a bishop would be the coachman. But to attain this, the absolute maximum of well-pleasingness to God, would be so costly that divine worship of this sort could only be enjoyed by those who, according to perfected Christianity (for the New Testament, it is well known, has another view) are also the only ones who have the means to please God perfectly...the millionaires.

2. *The priests—the actors.*

The actor is an honest man who says plainly, "I am an actor."

One never gets a priest to say that, at any price.

No, the "priest" thinks he is the very opposite of an actor. Entirely without prejudice (because he knows that it does not apply to him) he will raise and answer the question whether an actor may be buried in Christian ground. It never occurs to him (a masterpiece of scenic art, if it is not stupidity) that he is cointerested in the decision of this question, yes, that even if it is decided in favor of the actor, it nevertheless might be doubtful whether it is justifiable for the priest to be buried in Christian ground.

3. *The priest as a screen.*

As in the business world, one has a partner, something close to a fictitious entity,[78] a mere formality—but when there is a question of acting a bit disinterestedly, a bit leniently, not being too egoistic, yea, then the word is: "My good man, I would serve you with pleasure, I am soft-hearted; but my partner—there can be no thought of moving him." The whole thing of course is a knavish trick, calculated for the sake of living as hard-heartedly, as commercially minded as possible, and yet at the same time assuming the appearance of being something different...if only one did not have that partner.

As in everyday life, one has a wife—and when there comes an occasion when it would be seemly for one to act a bit courageously, a bit stout-heartedly, one says then, "Yes, my friend, be assured that for my part I have my heart in the right place; but my wife—it doesn't help me a bit to think of such a thing." Of course the whole thing is a knavish trick, whereby one would manage at one and the same time to be a coward and enjoy the advantage of it in life, and also to be a stout-hearted fellow...if only one were not so unlucky as to have that wife.

So the existence of the "priest" has the significance of making society feel secure in its hypocrisy. "We have no responsibility, we are privates, we abide by the priest, who has taken an oath." Or, "We dare not criticize the priest, we abide by what he says, he is a man of God who has taken an oath upon the New Testament." Or, "We should be willing enough to renounce everything, if that is required, but whether that is required we dare not assume to decide, we are only laymen, the priest is the authority, we do not dare to withdraw, he says that it is an exaggeration," etc.

All the shrewdness of "man" seeks one thing: to be able to live without responsibility. The priest's significance for society ought to be to do everything to make every man eternally responsible for every hour he lives, even for the least thing he undertakes, for this is Christianity. But his significance for society is: to make hypocrisy feel secure, while society shoves responsibility away from itself upon the priest.

4. *Paganism—the Christianity of "Christendom."*

The difference is that between the dram a drinking man drinks as a matter of course, and the dram which a man drinks as a reward for his temperance. The latter is infinitely worse than the former, for it is a refinement; the former is honest intemperance, the latter is refined intemperance, being at the same time temperance.

5. *A frightful situation.*

The situation is not this, that for every man who truly has willed the truth (the consequence of which would be that he became a sacrifice) there are one hundred thousand sensual, worldly-minded, mediocre men. No, the situation is this: for every one man who truly has willed the truth there are—shudder!—one thousand priests who, with their families, live by preventing the sensual, the light-minded, the worldly-minded men, the prodigious multitude of the mediocre, from getting a truer impression of that one who truly would will the truth.

6. *Heartiness—heartlessness.*

People who themselves have their heart in the throat, upon the lips, in the trousers, in short, everywhere except in the right place, quite naturally blame for heartlessness precisely that man who has his heart in the right place.

That is to say, after they have vainly looked for his heart in every place they know of, they are convinced that he has no heart; for he has it in the right place, and it does not occur to them to look there.

7. The refined meanness

is in a certain sense not seen in this world: precisely that is its crowning glory, that it looks like exactly the opposite.

What one sees in this world, and sees branded as odious and mean, may be frightful enough, but it is a small thing in comparison with the refined sort, which, when refined, counts for exactly the opposite of meanness. We speak of the "heaven-crying" sin; but the most "heaven-crying" sin is that which—refined—knows how to give itself the appearance of holiness, so that least of all sins can it be said to cry to heaven, which nevertheless it does, precisely because with the soundlessness of hypocrisy it is more "heaven-crying" than the so-called "heaven-crying" sin.

Let me devise an example.

In a town there lives a stranger; he possesses only one thing, but that is a bank note for a very large amount. However, no one in the town recognizes this note, so that for them it is = 0, and of course no one will give him anything for it.

Then a man, a stranger it may be, who recognizes the value of the note very well, comes to him and says, "I am your friend, as is becoming in a friend I will help you out of your embarrassment, I offer you"—and then he offers him the half of its value. This, you see, is refined! It is calculated to look like friendship and devotion, which must be admired and extolled by the inhabitants of that town, and at the same time it is cheating him out of 50 per cent. But that is not seen; the inhabitants of that town could in fact not see it, they see on the contrary the very unusual magnanimity, etc.

As it is in a commercial relation, so it is with relation to intellect.

A man may be so situated in his generation that no one of the many has any conception of who he is, of his value, of his significance. In this of course there is nothing to be indignant about, that the many regard him and all that is his as null and naught.

Then there comes to him a man who knows his real value and says to him, "I am your friend, I wish to bear witness to you"—and thereupon he gives him publicly one half the recognition he knows is due him. This is refined, it is calculated to count in the eyes of the contemporaries as a rare, rare example of disinterested devotion, a rare courage and enthusiasm which does justice to an unappreciated man; and yet, by putting himself to the least possible pains, he does the unappreciated man the greatest possible injury, for the fact that he procures for him a new and still greater difficulty than that of remaining unappreciated, namely, a half appreciation. That is not seen; the contemporaries could not in fact see anything else but the refined man's noble, disinterested, courageous enthusiasm.

[July 7, '55, on the rough draft of Nos. 8-10.]

8. *"It is for the sake of the successor."*

After all, perhaps I do the priests injustice. True enough, when one sees how stoutly they stand up for their rights, require every shilling that is due them, and like the lawyers hardly take a step without being paid—then one is tempted to take with a grain of salt their protestations that the worldly does not concern them at all.

But perhaps it is I that am at fault, I who am so impractical that I have entirely overlooked something which alters the case entirely. So when Bishop Martensen makes application for 600 tons of barley instead of 300,[79] it is perhaps I who have overlooked something, namely, that it is not by any means because earthly things of this sort concern such a holy man, but His Holiness does this for the sake of his successor, because it is the duty of His Holiness towards his successor, who then in his turn does the same thing...for the sake of His Holiness who will be his successor. Yes, that's something different. So this is even a noble act...for the sake of the successor!

Now I understand Bishop Martensen, I find his application in harmony with what I know from his own mouth—so it certainly is true—into which I do not hesitate to initiate the others, since it conduces to his glorification. He said that it was a sense of duty, that and that alone, which moved him to be willing to accept the election as Bishop. Truly, just such a man as that it was we needed for the episcopal see of Seeland—that is certain.

So then it was for the sake of the successor, for that and for that alone, out of a sense of duty towards the successor—so that if, for example, Bishop Martensen were to encounter this change of affairs, that there would not any more be a successor, he would at once withdraw his application; or, if it had already been granted, he would at once relinquish the 300 tons—for indeed it was not for his own sake he made the application, by no means, it was for the sake of the successor. Or if there was a Cultus-Minister who, in consideration of the fact that it was simply and solely for the sake of the successor, resolved that the 600 tons of barley should be granted, but in such a form that the 300 were regularly put aside for the successor (for this indeed was only for the sake of the successor), or that the extra grant (300 tons) should commence only with the coming of the successor—then Bishop Martensen would thank the Cultus-Minister who helped to remove from the Bishop every possible suspicion that after all it might perhaps be also, perhaps "at the same time," for his own sake, yea, that he might be very much delighted if only he were sure that he would get the 600 tons, whatever happened to the successor.

9. *Convent beer.*

This was one of the points where I was happy—my fond recollection!—to be in complete agreement with the late Bishop Mynster. He too regarded the Convent performances[80] as thin beer.

It was therefore with a certain satisfaction that I happened a short while ago to see in a book what I had not known before, that thin beer is called "convent beer." In case Bishop Mynster was unacquainted with that term, he would have been delighted to know it.

10. *The higher wisdom in the consideration that there is a predecessor and a successor.*

Everything bad is ascribed to the predecessor:
that we strive for earthly goods is for the sake of
the successor.

In that way, by the help of having a predecessor and a successor, we go pleasantly through life, and are at the same time witnesses to the truth. God help him who has no predecessor and no successor! For him truly life becomes what according to the will of Christianity it should be: an examination in which one cannot cheat.

NOTES

Articles in the *Fatherland*, etc.

1 Bishop Mynster died on Jan. 30, 1854, and was buried eight days later, on the Thursday following Prof. Martensen's eulogy, which he pronounced on a Sunday in the Castle Church of Christiansborg, where he functioned as Court Preacher. He chose as his text Hebrews 13:7 f. and took occasion to say of the late Bishop, "From the man whose precious memory fills your hearts, your thought is led to the whole line of witnesses to the truth which like a holy chain stretches," etc.

2 It should be remembered that in his Works as well as in his Journal S. K. had emphasized this concept strongly and defined it sharply. Nothing could have offended him more deeply than Martensen's use of the word in this connection, and the fact that he deferred publishing his protest for so long a time is evidence of extraordinary self-control.

3 On April 15, 1854, Martensen was appointed by the Crown to the vacant episcopal see. But he attained this appointment with some difficulty, seeing that H. N. Clausen was a strong competitor, supported by the National Liberal Party, with which S. K., as he says subsequently, was loath to ally himself.

4 While Mynster was still alive S. K. had written out in full several drafts of a projected attack upon him, which now can be read in his *Papers*, X^6 B 162-170, pp. 255-396.

5 This was Martensen's reply to S. K., which he published in the *Berlinske Tidende* (a Copenhagen daily) on Dec. 28, 1854.

6 In a brochure which Prof. Martensen published in 1850 he said of S. K.'s writings, "My acquaintance with this prolix literature is only very slight and fragmentary."

7 This is told in the Journal, X^3 A 563 f., which may be read in my *Kierkegaard*, pp. 514 f. Cf. Article XX in the *Fatherland*.

8 *Marriage of Figaro*, Danish trans. by Ponte, act iii, scene 10.

9 The theological candidate W. Hjort, in the *Berlinske Tidende* for Jan. 6, 1855: "In the strictest sense of the word Mynster is not a preacher of repentance but a messenger of peace."

10 Taken not directly from Epicurus but (with some change) from Cicero, *De natura deorum*, 1, 20, 52.

11 Cf. Journal, EP '54-'55, p. 514.

12 Prof. Nielsen, writing in the *Fatherland* (No. 8, 1855) in praise of S. K.'s deed, used an unlucky expression when he said, "a case which unfortunately has raised so much scandal."

13 Martensen was consecrated the day after Christmas 1854, and rather truculently took as his text Acts 1:8—"But ye shall receive the power of the Holy Ghost which shall come upon you, and ye shall be my witnesses," etc. He repeated the word "witnesses" many times.

14 Quoted from a jingle which every Danish child knew.

15 This was naturally the claim of men like Martensen who were bent upon interpreting Christianity in a Hegelian sense, and of course S. K. denounces it again and again.

16 Vigilius Haufniensis in *The Concept of Dread*, chapter 2, §2.

17 See Mark 9:47-50.

18 Cf. the Journal, XI^2 A 54, 55, 130, 133.

19 The world wishes to be deceived, *ergo* the priests—a proverbial saying.

20 Referring to Prof. Nielsen's defense of him which was noticed in Article IV.

21 To explain once for all S. K.'s satirical references to the claim that one was "endeavoring" to be a Christian, I point to the passage about a North Pole expedition which may be read in my *Kierkegaard*, p. 546.

22 S. K. was a candidate in theology, and naturally he was several times on the point

of taking the next step of seeking a cure, which would have led to his ordination as a priest.

[23] The Danish editors quote a good part of the anonymous proposal, which not only demanded a complete exposition of New Testament doctrine, but affirmed that it was time to stop ringing the fire alarm—to which S. K. responded in the following article.

[24] It was issued about a month later, on May 8, and was announced on May 16 in S. K.'s twentieth article in the *Fatherland*.

[25] The fact that S. K. was about to issue a magazine entitled the *Instant* suggests that this was for him an important category. How it is related to Greek thought is explained in the long footnote at the beginning of chapter III of *The Concept of Dread*. In the *Fragments* he had already connected it with the "leap," he says in another place that "the instant is not an atom of time but of eternity," and in one of the articles in the *Instant* he speaks of it as "the breaking through of eternity." On the other hand, he said of the mere "instant of time" that "it is filled with emptiness." This was the decisive instant for Christianity.

[26] He quotes a Danish version of Usteri's drinking song, "*Freut euch des Lebens*."

[27] Shakespeare's Henry IV, 1, act iv, scene 2.

[28] Scene 2. Heiberg's figure was 1,400 feet, but S. K.'s favorite expression for an immense depth was 70,000 fathoms.

[29] The name of the pseudonym who appeared as the editor of *Either/Or*.

[30] Block was Dean of the Cathedral at Aarhus.

[31] It was the case of Rabbi A. A. Wolff. That he should be wearing a *cross*, the insignium of the Order of Dannebrog, was absurd enough, even if the statutes of the order had not required that none but Evangelical Christians be admitted to it.

[32] Referring to Holberg's play, *The Eleventh of June*.

[33] The pseudonym to whom was attributed both the *Fragments* and the *Postscript*. The reference is to the latter.

[34] The Danish editors quote the relevant passages in Dr. Zeuthen's series of articles in the *Ugeskrift*, which deal only incidentally with S. K.

[35] In the original draft S. K. wrote: "As one says petulantly that where a fool goes he takes one with him, so there is One with me."

[36] Another reference to the individuals alluded to in Article III. Cf. note 8 above.

[37] Cf. note 7 above.

[38] Recalling a phrase in the Preface to *Training in Christianity*.

[39] It is said that the Prime Minister made it known that if S. K. were arrested he would at once liberate a man who had shed so much luster upon Denmark.

[40] By Prof. Nielsen in the *Fatherland*, which is quoted fully enough in a note by the Danish editors.

[41] In *Don Juan* (Kruse's trans.), act ii, scene 8.

[42] Johannes Climacus in the *Concluding Postscript*, pp. 504 ff.

[43] Lessing's *Emilia Galotti*, act iv, scene 5.

[44] In Norway, where the *Christiania Post* published several articles defending S. K. and criticizing Bishop Martensen.

[45] S. K.'s polemic in the *Fragments* and the *Postscript* against "speculation" was directed principally at Martensen, though without mentioning his name; and in return Martensen, in the Preface to his *Dogmatic*, but again without mentioning names, spoke disparagingly of S. K.'s philosophical works. Cf. the Journal, X^1 A 553 ff.

[46] "The System" always means the Hegelian philosophy, which Martensen was one of the first to introduce into Denmark.

[47] *Gospel Faith and the Modern Consciousness*, a book in which Prof. Nielsen, who, hitherto had been close to Martensen, appeared for the first time as an adherent of S. K., though without mentioning either man by name.

[48] "On the imagined reconciliation of faith and knowledge, with special reference to

Prof. Martensen's *Dogmatic*," Copenhagen, 1850. Prof. Stilling mentions Johannes Climacus only incidentally, but evidently he was deeply influenced by S. K., and (as he remarks in the Preface) he too had long been in friendly relations with Martensen.

49 Again by Prof. Nielsen, in two books (published in 1849 and 1850) in which he expressly compared Martensen's *Christian Dogmatic* with S. K.'s works.

50 Quoted from *Training in Christianity*, p. 52. Alas, in my translation I said, "not ally," when I should have said, "have nothing to do with."

51 In the above-mentioned article in the *Fatherland*, urging Martensen to withdraw the term "witnesses to the truth," he assumed, perhaps too politely, that the Bishop "had already put himself in the position of Christian resignation."

52 He was forty-six years of age when he was consecrated.

53 This, it will be remembered, is S. K.'s definition of purity of heart.

54 The anonymous writer of this letter may have been a pastor, but he said he was not a theologian and claimed a right to speak only on the ground that he is a daily reader of the Scriptures. He says of S. K., "While the priests see in him almost a personal enemy, plain, sensible people call his talk twaddle."

The *Instant*, Nos. I to X

1 Book I, cap. 19, and Book VII, cap. 5.

2 Frater Taciturnus in the *Stages*, p. 200.

3 Oelenschläger's *Palmatoke*, act v, scene 2.

4 At that time a special distinction was worn (not only in gala uniform) by officers who served as adjutants to the King.

5 This served at that time to frank a letter.

6 Recalling the Preface to all the Edifying Discourses.

7 Referring to the permission given hotel keepers since 1826 to sell beer and brandy outside the house.

8 This is said more effectively in the parable of the cabman, in the Journal. See my *Kierkegaard*, pp. 532 f.

9 Since this charge is constantly reiterated in the *Instant*, it is important to know that the second part of the oath at that time required of priests before their ordination was as follows (translated from the Latin): "In the second place I promise that I will labor with great diligence in order that the heavenly instruction contained in the Prophetic and Apostolic books may be faithfully imparted to the hearers."

10 From Ovid, "A Remedy against Love," where one is advised to "put a stop to it at the beginning."

11 This simple parable, to which S. K. often refers, meant to him that, if anything is to be accomplished (if the sewing is not to come undone because there was no knot made in the thread), someone has to die for it. Cf. the Journal, XI^2 A 281.

12 He has in view radical Hegelians, like David Strauss and L. Feuerbach.

13 This is what Bishop Martensen complained of in his reply.

14 The mother tongue gradually replaced Latin for examinations during the first half of the nineteenth century.

15 *Pedars Paars*, 2nd song, verse 48.

16 This was implied in the anonymous proposal mentioned in Article XIII.

17 The proposal for a new hymnal came from the party of Grundtvig, who wanted *his* hymns included, which in fact have become the most popular in Denmark. The Bishop was opposed to it, and S. K. was never tired of making fun of it.

18 An ordinance of 1845.

19 Cf. the Journal, XI^2 A 50, 300, 303.

20 The first line of a popular song by Søeborg.

[21] J. L. Heiberg's *King Solomon and Jørgen the Hatter*, scene 23; "For the ditty lasts an eternity."

[22] *April Fools*, scene 29—but S. K. was here inexact: it was "Madam" who thought it unseemly that Miss Trummeir was shut in a closet with Herr Zierlich's coat.

[23] Holberg, *Ulisses von Ithacia*, act ii, scene 1.

[24] Act i, scene 9 (Kruse's trans.).

[25] Quoted from Bishop Martensen's Pastoral Letter of June 6.

[26] As Bishop Martensen promised in his Pastoral Letter.

[27] Acts 2:40. "Three thousand souls in one day."

[28] As suggested by the Fourth Gospel.

[29] You drive out nature with a fork, etc. A familiar proverb derived from Horace's *Letters*, I, 10, 24.

[30] Who wrote an article in the *Berlinske Tidende* criticizing Prof. Nielsen's defense of S. K. No special reason is evident for calling him a veterinary, but "veterinary science" was often mentioned by S. K. by way of reminding "scientists" that not every science is sublime.

[31] In the Journal (EP '54-'55, p. 25) S. K. refers scathingly to the fact that the Danish law prohibited anyone but a Christian from keeping a whorehouse.

[32] I remark tardily that a velvet facing on the gown was a distinction of bishops and deans—also of doctors of theology.

[33] It might have been remarked earlier that, in contrast to the *objectivity* which was (and is) so highly extolled by scientific men and philosophers, S. K. insisted upon the necessity of *subjectivity* in religion and theology, in a sense which is made clear in the *Postscript*.

[34] Cf. Psalm 56:8. In the Journal for 1852 (X^4 A 566. See my *Kierkegaard*, p. 518) S. K. remarks upon the fact that Mynster in one of his *Meditations* dwells pathetically upon the futility of the tears people have shed when listening to him: "whereas they do not act accordingly. And with these tears I shall step forth at the Day of Judgment and say, I have done my part." "Strangely enough," says S. K., "I had just been thinking of gathering up all the tears Mynster has shed upon the pulpit, whereas it has been made clear that he does not act accordingly."

[35] In the fifteenth century this story was told of a friar at Naples, who on Good Friday had harrowed the congregation by his description of the Lord's Passion, and seeing them in tears had tried to comfort them by the reflection that "all this was a long time ago, so let us hope it is not true."

[36] Cicero (*De divinatione*, ii, 24, 51) recalls a saying of Cato the Elder, that he could not understand how the haruspes (priests who followed the Etruscan tradition of divining the future by inspecting the entrails of slain beasts) could look at one another without smiling.

[37] This is what he affirmed in criticizing Hans Christian Andersen's book for representing that genius was a delicate thing which must be coddled.

[38] Has in view an article in the *Flyve-Post* which spoke of Grundtvig as "a man with a certain Apostolic authority." Cf. the Journal, EP '54-'55, p. 535.

[39] This promise was cited against S. K. in an article in the *Fatherland* of April 3, 1855.

[40] Cf. the Journal, EP '54-'55, p. 390. Evidently S. K. was embarrassed by his would-be defenders.

[41] The anonymous article, mentioned above, in the *Copenhagen Post* of April 3, 1854, says of S. K.: "Such intolerable pride as he has shown in a series of aphoristic articles in the *Fatherland* one surely has never seen matched in the Danish press."

[42] The motto of Caesar Borgia. *Aut/aut* is Latin for either/or.

[43] *Hamlet*, act iv, scene 3.

[44] As there is no evidence that the Apostles were baptized, S. K. uses the general term "disciples."

[45] The five-dollar bills were blue.

[46] Cf. the Journal, XI² A 211.

[47] The Seminary was founded in 1809, with the expectation that the course would last a whole year, but by this time it had been shortened to one half.

[48] As everywhere else on the Continent, all official documents bore a stamp equivalent in cost to the tax imposed.

[49] Holberg, *Den Stundesløse*, act i, scene 2.

[50] This is pretty much what happened to S. K.'s elder brother Peter. The living he had applied for and obtained proved not to his liking, and the King, with a reprimand, allowed him to withdraw his application.

[51] Like Martensen, who was a good Hegelian.

[52] Horace's *Letters*, I, 1, 54.

[53] There is hardly any phrase S. K. so often uses with reprobation. He has in mind Martensen's boast of "going further" than Hegel, but also further than the naïve phase of Christianity registered in the New Testament. This hangs together with the claim that Christianity is "perfectible."

[54] A reference to Wessel's *Stella*, vii.

[55] John 20:19-31, which was the Gospel for the First Sunday after Easter, the day which in S. K.'s time was appointed for Confirmation in Copenhagen.

[56] A Latin saying, dwelling upon the comfort of common shipwreck.

[57] By Diogenes Laertius (i, 86) this story is ascribed to Bias.

[58] Carstensen founded in 1812 the Tivoli, which was (and is) the great place of refection and recreation in Copenhagen. At this time he had just returned from a tour in America and was much acclaimed by the press.

[59] Collect for the First Sunday after New Year's Day, which takes this phrase from 1 Peter 2:11.

[60] As Mynster in fact did. I refer again to the Journal, or rather to the quotation from it in my *Kierkegaard*, p. 514.

[61] Not the festival of St. Lawrence, which is Aug. 10. S. K. seems to have chosen deliberately almost the only day which in the Roman Calendar is dedicated to no saint. He also seems to have invented the peculiar celebration of this festival—perhaps in ridicule of certain well-known customs, like hot cross buns on Good Friday.

[62] In the *Thousand and One Nights*.

[63] The reader hardly needs to be told that S. K. had Mynster in mind.

[64] One of Aesop's Fables.

[65] Referring to an article in the first of these journals, on the date of May 30, which exclaims, "Poor, wretched Søren, that thou shouldst come to such an end!" and to the letter of May 31, which compares the boy Søren to the grown man.

[66] See the last Article in the *Fatherland*.

[67] He became Professor *Extraordinarius* in 1840, Court Preacher in 1845.

[68] In Latin grammars these were the usual paradigms for two different declensions.

[69] Cf. The *Instant*, No. V, Article 2; and No. VII, Article 5. S. K. has been charged by his adversaries with inconsistency in thus belittling the Apostle. It was a shrewd criticism, and this long note is not an adequate answer to it. For no one had ever exalted more highly than he the idea of what it was to be an Apostle of Jesus Christ. "I always keep," says he, "a separate account for the Apostle." Reproaching Luther for discarding the word of the Apostle James, "Faith without works is dead," he exclaimed, "and think what a high conception he had of an Apostle!" This could now be retorted upon him. In the heat of controversy he had been tempted to sacrifice the Apostle to "the witness to the truth." And this points to a fundamental flaw in his contention. But, all appearances to the contrary notwithstanding, it never was S. K.'s intention to affirm that only martyrs (i.e. witnesses to the truth) can be saved, or that the true Church is composed solely of martyrs. The martyrs were held in singular honor because there

were few of them. And it was not the Apostles only who believed that men might be saved without being dead sacrifices, or even "living sacrifices." Christ himself, as in the case of the rich young man, was comforted by the thought that "with God all things are possible." The Apostle was the only objective authority S. K. recognized, his only objective link with Catholicism, indeed with the Church as a community of faith. This note shows how loath he was to reject this saving link—but also how much he was tempted to reject it, though with that he would have been left to unbridled subjectivity.

[70] By Plato in *Gorgias*, cap. 19; and Aristotle, *On the Sophists' Proofs*, cap. 1.

[71] Plato's *Apology*.

[72] Aaron Levin, who for some years was S. K.'s secretary, gained notoriety by publishing revelations of S. K.'s private life, which were neither sensational nor reliable. S. K. needed a secretary to transcribe his pseudonymous works, for so scrupulous was he in preserving his anonymity that he would not send to the printer a manuscript in his own handwriting. Davidsen and Siesby were editors of the *Flyve-Post*, in which S. K. was violently attacked. Grüne was editor of the *Copenhagen Post*, and was equally zealous in his opposition. He was notorious for his talent for holding two apparently opposite points of view at the same time.

[73] In Heiberg's *Intelligensblade*, Nos. 41-42, he spoke of his "rich culture."

[74] A Virgilian line: "Hence! keep far away, ye uninitiated!" *Aeneid*, vi, 258.

[75] Aaron Goldschmidt, when he ridiculed him in the *Corsair*. S. K. was not fortunate with his Jewish friends—but it was not them only he thought of when he said, "I have been hoaxed in every relationship I entered into."

[76] "National Church" is what Grundtvig preferred to call it.

[77] *Dyrehaven*, an immense park rather remote from Copenhagen, and the favorite excursion.

[78] He seems to have had in mind the relation between Spenlow and Jorkins in *David Copperfield*.

[79] By Royal Resolution of June 29, 1854, there was accorded to the Bishop of Seeland, besides his ordinary income, 600 tons of barley, to be paid to him in money. The Danish editors remark that Mynster's income was much greater than that of Martensen.

[80] The party of Grundtvig held regularly a convention of ministers which they called "the Convent." S. K. and the Bishop agreed perfectly in their dislike of this party and its Convent, in which Peter Kierkegaard had a prominent place.

Index

Note that in this diatribe the key words are to be found on almost every page, because the weakest points are incessantly attacked, and therefore it is not necessary—indeed it would be hardly possible—to include in the index such words as New Testament, God's Word, Christianity, Christendom, and priest, except to indicate passages where one or another of them is the principal theme. For a similar reason I have not tried to indicate the many passages where Christianity is represented as essentially suffering.